Evert Gummesson

Qualitative Methods in Management Research

Second Edition

Foreword by John Van Maanen

Sage Publications, Inc.
International Educational and Professional Publisher
Thousand Oaks ■ London ■ New Delhi

For information:

Sage Publications, Inc.
2455 Teller Road
Thousand Oaks, California 91320
E-mail: order@sagepub.com

Sage Publications Ltd.
6 Bonhill Street
London EC2A 4PU
United Kingdom

Sage Publications India Pvt. Ltd.
M-32 Market
Greater Kailash I
New Delhi 110 048 India

Printed in the United States of America

Library of Congress Cataloging-in-Publication Data

Gummesson, Evert, 1936–
    Qualitative methods in management research / by Evert
Gummesson. — 2nd ed.
        p.   cm.
    Includes bibliographical references and index.
    ISBN 0-7619-2013-7 (cloth: acid-free paper)
    ISBN 0-7619-2014-5 (pbk. : acid-free paper)
    1. Industrial management—Research. 2. Participant observation.
3. Action research. 4. Management—Research. I. Title.
    HD30.4 .G85 2000
    658'.007'2—dc21   99-6640

This book is printed on acid-free paper.

00   01   02   03   04   05   06   7   6   5   4   3   2   1

Illustrations by:	Bengt Mellberg
Acquiring Editor:	Harry Briggs
Editorial Assistant:	MaryAnn Vail
Production Editor:	Denise Santoyo
EditorialAssistant:	Nevair Kavakian
Copy Editor:	Linda Gray
Typesetter/Designer:	Christina Hill
Indexer:	Juniee Oneida
Cover Designer:	Candice Harman

Contents

Figures and Tables

Foreword

Qualitative research methods in general and case studies in particular have a long and certainly distinguished history in the social sciences and beyond. Yet, given the much discussed prominence if not dominance of quantitative research currently, it is helpful to recall that qualitative analysis was the primary means by which virtually all social research was conducted up to about mid-century. This is certainly true for management research which until the early 1960s was tightly linked to a case study approach. From the descriptive and prescriptive writings of Frederick Taylor, to the anthropological studies of shop floor behavior at Western Electric's Hawthorne plant near Chicago, management research rested largely on sustained, explicit, methodical observation of work situations in their naturally occurring contexts. From such studies has come a good deal of empirical and theoretical advancement as well as critical and useful interventions into organizational functioning. Statistical analysis is, in fact, a scholarly latecomer.

As the new century begins, a rather widespread resurgence of qualitative work is occurring across disciplines as well as across applied domains. Qualitative research is back and back with a vengeance as many of the promises associated with quantitative study have come up empty. Counting and classifying can take one only so far. Meaning and interpretation are required to attach significance to counts and classifications and these are fundamentally qualitative matters. The two approaches are then bound together, neither capturing truth alone nor trumping the other. But, while quantitative skills are broadly identifiable and widely taught, qualitative skills are not. This will not last long for interest is keen and growing. Indeed, for evidence of this one need only consider that Evert Gummeson's first edition of this book sold so well that a second edition was soon required.

And a good second edition it is—full of new material offering a wide range of practical tips, useful examples and wise words for neophyte and veteran researchers, management consultants, and practicing managers with an interest in organizational change through thoughtful experimentation. Informed by a most practical aim—to improve organizational life and performance—Evert Gummeson approaches qualitative work as akin to a clinical process moving from diagnosis to treatment and assessment. It is a participative process as well for those who presumably are to gain from management research must play active roles as it is designed, carried out and eventually put to use in organizational settings. The benefits, ease, comfort, relatively low cost and timeliness of a good deal of qualitative research is highlighted in this edition. So much so that I suspect few readers will be able to read the work from beginning to end without imagining a number of modest yet important research adventures they would like to begin (perhaps tomorrow) in those organizations near and dear to them. This is then not only a good read but a most practical field-guide for getting started and carrying through on the kinds of management studies we now need.

—John Van Maanen

Preface

In this second edition, examples and literature have been up-dated, and the basic concepts of the book have been further developed, notably in the chapters on action science and quality of research. Throughout, I have attempted to express myself more clearly.

This book is a very personal document. That may be perceived as irregular and self-centered for a book on methodology, but it is intentional. When I mean "I" I write "I," and I do not take cover behind "we" or "the author." A true scientific approach is intimately personal; it is an approach to life, a search for truth and meaning. We do not find truth and meaning in social life by watching the world from a distance and detaching ourselves from its turmoil, isolating ourselves in ivory towers, just reading what the well-known philosophers and authorities have said, and elevating science to divine status. The search—and re-search and research . . .—goes on all around us in every little activity and event of private and professional life. We need to fine-tune ourselves as research instruments; we need to take science personally. We have to trust our own experience and reflection, simultaneously keeping up a dialogue with others through books, conferences, late-night conversations at bars, and since the mid-1990s, through e-mail and the Internet.

My ideas in this book have evolved over two decades. They are not new; they are in accord with ideas that have evolved in the philosophy of science and human practice during millenniums. They are inspired by contemporary sociology and anthropology and by my own experience of business. During the spring of 1980, I worked on a consulting assignment that involved strategic and organizational change in a large corporation. In the course of the strategic process, I documented what happened and related it to literature on corporate strategy and organization theory. I had become intrigued by the connection between the role of consultant and the role of academic researcher and with the opportunities for access to change processes that this combination created. I began to structure my experiences, at the same time studying the literature on theory of science, on methodology in social and natural sciences, and on management consultancy. The combined role of academic researcher and management consultant turned out to be unclear despite the fact that it is customary for business school professors to work as management consultants.

The book gradually broadened beyond the mere academic researcher versus consultant topic into treating qualitative research issues in management disciplines and the use of case studies for research purposes.

The text unfolded through a series of working papers, drafts, and published editions that have been discussed in research seminars and Ph.D. courses at several universities for the past fifteen years. I am grateful to numerous professors, doctoral candidates, students, and management consultants who have contributed with advice and stimulation; in fact, they are so many that I dare not even attempt to list their names.

—Evert Gummesson

One

Qualitative Research in Management

Qualitative methodology and case studies provide powerful tools for research in management and business subjects, including general management, leadership, marketing, organization, corporate strategy, accounting, and more. However, qualitative methods are used only to a limited degree. Universities and business schools often oppose their use and classify them as second-rate. Case studies are extensively used as tools in education, but they are usually considered as not good enough for research purposes.

Through my traveling and correspondence, I know that the problems dealt with in this book occupy the minds of business school students and scholars around the world. Many who want to do more qualitative research and case studies—for example, for Ph.D. work or master's theses—are discouraged from doing so. They complain, "My professor does not understand me. What shall I do?" A minority of business schools accept and promote the use of qualitative methods and case study research, but opportunities to do so need to be expanded, and the methods need to be properly taught.

The reason for the conflict is that most business schools are preoccupied with the mechanics of statistical techniques, believing that these techniques in themselves offer a highway to the advancement of knowledge and science. Faculty members are often unfamiliar with the opportunities offered by qualitative methodology and case study research. This ignorance concerns the underpinning theory of science as well as the choice and application of research methods and techniques.

This book is targeted toward *students at business schools and universities, academic researchers,* and *management consultants.* Although its focus is on *business,* the text is largely applicable to other types of organizations and therefore is also of interest to researchers in *government and voluntary not-for-profit organizations.*

The book can provide guidance in the writing of papers, articles, and theses at different levels of business education and academic careers. The focus is on *case study research* and the use of *qualitative methods for data collection and analysis.* It aims to make the researcher more aware of research opportunities inherent in the application of a qualitative approach. It provides answers and commentary to the question, "How do researchers relate to their object of study in order to make a useful contribution?" As a consequence, the text also deals with the research *paradigms*—the underpinning values, procedures, and rules—that govern the thinking and behavior of researchers.

In using qualitative methods, the borderline between the *academic researcher* and the *management consultant* becomes blurred, particularly as the role of the consultant provides opportunities for intensified inquiry into the behavior of business firms and other organizations. These opportunities receive inadequate attention in the literature on methodology as well as in actual academic research.

A greater awareness of the possibilities and limitations of carrying out research by means of qualitative methods—and also through the role of management consultant—ought to lead to improvements in the quality and usefulness of academic research in business administration. In some instances, professional management consultants are intimately associated with academic research, whereas in others, there is no connection at all.

It is hoped that practicing management consultants who read the book will gain insights into their profession. The book also addresses itself to those companies and organizations that purchase the services of academic researchers and management consultants. It may facilitate their evaluation of the quality of their providers.

Case study research is becoming increasingly accepted as a scientific tool in management research. If you want an in-depth understanding of the mechanisms of change, you need not study a large number of cases. Management consultants are involved with a limited number of cases. *Action research,* or *action science*[1] as it has been recently called, is one particularly exciting method that can be adopted when working with case research. Here, the researchers take on the role of active consultants and influence a process under study.

Particular attention will be paid to the study of *decision making, implementation,* and *change processes* within companies and other organizations.

Although both *quantitative* and *qualitative* methods are used for data collection in case studies, the latter will normally predominate in the study of processes in which data collection, analysis, and action often take place concurrently. At research seminars where the manuscript for this book has been under discussion, I have been asked whether I support the quantitative, allegedly more "scientific" methods, or whether I reject them in favor of a qualitative approach. Because this book is primarily concerned with the latter, it is often concluded that I am against the use of quantitative methods. However, I am neither a priori for nor against any methods. They should be used where they are appropriate. If they are not suitable, it is hardly scientific to provide one-sided support for one or another method, although one-sidedness is not unusual in research circles. The same applies to management consultants, who can be subject to the dictates of fashion as well as to traditional but obsolete ways of working.

The book will present conclusions from an inquiry based on literature on scientific theory, research methodology, management consultancy, and various management subjects, together with biographies, memoirs, and other publications written about life in business and other organizations. It is also based on my previously published study on the marketing and management of consulting services.[2] Finally, my own personal experience as a management consultant and practicing manager has had a positive impact on my approach to research. My special interest in challenging established procedures in management research began in 1980. It has proceeded ever since and is turning into a lifelong journey. There are numerous intermediate stops, however. This second edition of the book is the latest stop. But it's not the last stop.

I have taken the liberty of writing the book in a personal manner. This is well in line with the tradition of qualitative research, in which *the personality of the scientist is a key research instrument.* The book is written in such a manner that it can be read by those who are not closely acquainted with scientific theory or management research. This is not to say that the book can be read without effort; neither academic research nor management consultancy are suitable fields for those who wish to lead an easy life. It is not just a matter of intellectual "understanding," however; it is as much a matter of personal maturity, judgment, common sense, and emotional balance.

The remainder of this chapter will introduce phenomena and concepts that constitute the focal point of analysis for this book.

Qualitative Methods Applied to the Study of Businesses and Other Organizations

Books on qualitative methodology stem from sociology, psychology, education, or anthropology/ethnography.[3] They provide examples and cases from the study of society in general and the government sector rather than businesses. Such research may be inspiring to a manager as a concerned citizen, but not in the role of businessman. To enhance your understanding of research methodology in business administration, you are not looking for studies of witchcraft, oracles, and magic among African tribes[4] or the case of a lingering, dying trajectory[5] or life in the classroom[6] or how school districts use evaluative information about students' performance.[7] Although most methods used there and in management are in essence the same, *their application, emphasis, and significance can vary considerably;* they are dealing with human life in different types of settings, with different purposes, and from different perspectives.

Key business phenomena such as profit, competitiveness, corporate strategy, productivity, total quality management, operations management, relationship marketing, virtual organizations, balanced scorecard, and so forth are rarely, if ever, mentioned in textbooks on qualitative methods. But you need this knowledge to select scientific approaches. You could not, for example, have understood life in big American corporations during the 1980s without knowledge of the impact of corporate raiders, hostile takeovers, junk bonds, and leveraged buyouts. Currently, we must follow closely the developments of information technology, above all the impact of the Internet and electronic commerce, as well as new megaconditions for business set by NAFTA (North American Free Trade Agreement), the EU (European Union), and the aftermath of the fall of the Soviet empire.

Although there is an abundance of textbooks on market research reviewing quantitative methods, I have found only one textbook focusing on qualitative methods applied to the study of consumers and other buyers of goods and services from a commercial perspective.[8] And I have only found one book on research in management subjects in which quantitative and qualitative methods are treated as equals.[9]

Studies in management are concerned with understanding and improving the performance of a business. They can be done to give recommendations for solutions to the specific problems of a specific company or industry. We are then dealing with *applied research,* which is close to consultancy. In contrast, *basic research* is concerned with theoretical and philosophical relevance and the long-term and general advancement of management disciplines.

The cases and illustrations referred to in this book concern issues in organizations and their economic environment. Even if the management issues are primarily associated with private businesses, they should be of significance to the government and voluntary-action sectors. The government sector—central, regional, and local—has become increasingly interested in learning from private industry, mainly from service companies, as the government sector was once intended to be of service to its "investors," the citizens. The methods dealt with therefore apply to both sectors, although institutional differences—finance through taxes, the dual management by politicians and administrators, frequent monopolies, and so forth—partially create a different mode for application.

The connection between the private and the government sector is clearly visible in the *perestroika* ("openness") and *glasnost* ("information") introduced by Soviet Premier Gorbachev in the 1980s. It was not only an issue for the communist and ex-communist planned economies; Gorbachev was a "turnaround CEO" on the largest scale ever heard of.[10] Even the largest global companies have fewer than a million employees, and very few exceed 500,000; "Soviet Union, Inc." had 250 million plus another 150 million in "subsidiaries." In quality management, there is talk of "the hidden firm," existing within every company and specializing in producing nonquality.[11] Although we may hate to admit it, nonproductive or even counterproductive islands of the former East German character are hidden in Western businesses and governments as well.

Deregulation is a Western *perestroika* strategy for improving the performance of organizations and whole industries. "The most drastic discontinuity in the history of any major U.S. industry"[12] is the breakup of AT&T—the American Telephone and Telegraph Company, "Ma Bell"—into several companies with different ownership. In a similar vein, British Prime Minister Margaret Thatcher's advocacy for *privatization* has taken the form of a sellout of organizations such as British Telecom, the gas and electricity utilities, and the British Airport Authority that runs London's Heathrow and other airports.

Academic Researchers and Management Consultants:
Both Are "Knowledge Workers"

We have long heard that agriculture and manufacturing will employ fewer and fewer people while services, the "third wave"[13] in the development of society, are gaining. In most Western nations today, two thirds or more of the workforce is employed in services.[14] Both academic researchers and management consultants are in professional services; they are "intellectuals," "knowledge workers," or even "gold-collar workers"; they belong to "knowledge-based organizations," a subset of the service economy.[15]

Knowledge, along with information, is a particularly nebulous word, and yet we use it every day. There is a special branch of the philosophy of science, *epistemology*, that poses the question: Can knowledge exist? Three schools of thought give the answers "yes" (dogmatism), "no" (agnosticism), and "maybe" (skepticism). Although Chapter 4 will question the existence of the ever-so-popular "fact," I will have to take the existence of a fuzzy phenomenon called knowledge for granted. Even if this fuzziness is somewhat frustrating, we will probably keep working whether we are academic researchers or consultants—not in the least to pay telephone bills and mortgages; those are certainly for real.

The knowledge-based organization is characterized by the following:[16]

- A significant portion of its activities consists of problem solving and nonstandardized production, but routine handicraft is also necessary
- Production of interesting and novel ideas, approaches, solutions, and recommendations
- Strong reliance on the individual and a high degree of independence and integrity
- Creativity, both individually and in the organizational setting
- Ability to communicate the results to selected audiences

This is general to all types of knowledge-based organizations, so in this respect, researchers and consultants are similar. It is, however, a description on a fairly high level of abstraction. Climbing down the ladder toward more concrete behavior, differences begin to occur. The similarities and the differences as well as the symbiosis between academic research and management consultancy will be treated in this book.

Knowledge workers populate all organizations in greater or fewer numbers. They are found in business school research programs, on management teams, in pharmaceutical laboratories, and in other R&D (research and development) departments; they could be computer systems analysts, chefs at gourmet restaurants, or specialists at the New York Stock Exchange. There are many types of consultants apart from management consultants: advertising agencies, accountants, lawyers, consulting engineers, and so forth.[17] In the present context, we will be dealing with *management consultants,* sometimes called business consultants—that is, consultants who have been brought into a company to work on problems that concern the management of the whole company or its different functions. But the text is also relevant to related professions. For the sake of brevity, the term *consultant* will be used here to refer to a management consultant, and *researcher* will be used as an abbreviation for academic researcher.

"Practitioners"—that is, consultants and their clients, "the no-nonsense men of action"—are prone to characterize discussions on theory and methodology as "academic," which for them is synonymous with impractical and of little use in business life. I would like to illustrate the practitioner-scientist relationship by quoting from the memoirs of Sune Carlson, ex-member of the Nobel Prize Committee for the Economic Sciences, former U.N. chief economist, and professor of management:

In the early 1960s—a quarter of a century after I had completed my university studies—I joined the board of AGA [a major international corporation specializing in gases] and participated in decision-making on foreign investment and different types of international financial operations. For a number of years, I did not really understand what we were doing, nor, I felt, did anyone else. There was certainly no shortage of facts; there was an abundance of available data. However, I lacked a theoretical system that would have permitted me to arrange and structure these data. I was forced to sit down and work out for myself a purely mathematical theory for decisions on international investments. It was in this way that I came to write my book on *International Financial Decisions* and to understand what we were doing at AGA. As Eli Heckscher often said: "There is nothing as practical as good theory."[18]

Academic researchers in management frequently work with companies and governmental organizations to help them improve their operations. Thus, they become management consultants. Professors are often allowed, even urged, to spend a day per week as consultants. They are frequently engaged on surveys and in-house seminars, sometimes also as advisers to management. A major rationale for such engagements is that the scientists get continuous insights into the "real" world as opposed to the academic ivory tower. The consulting experience not only provides input for research but also stimulating and "live" cases to be used in the classroom.

There are both similarities and differences between academic research and management consultancy. Those similarities and differences should be laid bare and understood by academic researchers as well as by consultants. If they are not, professors and other researchers risk providing consultancy of low quality, even if what they do is approved by academic standards.

When an early draft of this book was discussed at a research seminar, one of my professors passed me a sketch, drawn at the spur of the moment (Figure 1.1). With artistic simplicity, it shows a difference and similarity between consultants and academic researchers: Backed by bits and pieces of theory, the consultant contributes to practice, whereas the scholar contributes to theory supported by fragments of practice.

Although many academic researchers lack experience of consultancy or consultant strategy, they still like to be known as consultants. They live in the belief that knowledge of academic research can be directly applied to consultancy. As one university professor said to me, "Consultancy is just a simpler form of scien-

The consultant: Pecks at theory and contributes to practice

The researcher: Pecks at practice (empirical data) and contributes to theory

but there is a lot in common

Figure 1.1. The Management Consultant Versus the Academic Researcher
SOURCE: Drawing by Paulsson Frenckner, Professor Emeritus of Business Administration, University of Stockholm, Sweden. Used by permission.

tific research." Businessmen and managers who enter a consulting career often assume that a combination of business experience and some management model or philosophy is a satisfactory and efficient basis on which to operate as a consultant. It is sometimes assumed that consultancy experience can be quite simply converted into research by dressing it up in academic guise.

The roles of researcher and consultant and their interface are not very actively discussed. Two thirds of all consultants in the United States work on their own or with a partner and a secretary,[19] the result being that professional contacts with colleagues are limited. Arthur D. Little, McKinsey & Co., Arthur Anderson, Boston Consulting Group, Bain, and other large management consultancies provide an environment for active interchange of knowledge. Those who work in large consulting firms, however, usually associate with only a narrow group of fellow consultants. Among academic researchers, scientific and methodological issues are naturally the subject of discussion. Unfortunately, this dialogue frequently suffers from inadequate input of real-world data, lack of practical business experience, and not least, lack of time.

Processes of Decision Making, Implementation, and Change

I have talked about processes of decision making, implementation, and change and stated that this book will concentrate on the work of researchers and consultants in projects related to such processes. We are, however, bombarded with messages that society keeps changing and technology keeps developing faster and faster, making extant professional knowledge obsolete at the speed of lightning. During the 1990s, TQM (total quality management) has become an accelerator of change in all types of organizations. The ISO 9000 standard and the now-ubiquitous quality awards provide systematic approaches pressing for continuous improvements. In conclusion, change is ongoing, and every issue in a company is exposed to change or the threat of change in the near future. Therefore, everything in a company includes elements of change processes, and the approach of this book becomes a general approach to investigating management disciplines. The processes could encompass complex turnarounds of a whole company or might concern limited problems.

I will now briefly describe the type of consulting or research projects in question.

A company finds itself in a given situation that may be characterized in a number of different ways: the goods and services that it produces; the markets for these products; its resources, structure, profitability, financing; and so forth. As long as the company is doing well, it will have a reasonably harmonious relationship with its environment and stakeholders. But as "times are a-changing" the requirements of society, investors, personnel, and markets have to be assessed, influenced, and adjusted continuously. A company will also have more or less explicit perceptions of the future together with objectives that it hopes to achieve. This is partially a product of experience and intuition and partially achieved by more systematic approaches, such as statistical forecasts, scenario writing, environmental studies, and market research. A company must accept the consequences of its decisions and ensure that they are implemented or changed as new conditions emerge.

These processes of change may be characterized as teleological processes—that is, processes that lead the company toward certain objectives, the most basic and primitive ones being survival and eternal youth. In its efforts to do so, the management has to ask the following question:

* What should the company's business mission be, and how should the company be organized and managed?

This question has given rise to a number of methods and approaches that may be characterized by concepts such as corporate strategy, marketing strategy, organizational structure, TQM, business process reengineering, mergers and acquisitions, financial management, downsizing, outsourcing, relationship marketing, alliances, globalization, and "green" policies.

A company may change direction by means of a process of continuous adjustments within an existing framework of operations. Other types of changes may be more dramatic—for example, in relation to a company merger, a takeover, a changeover to new areas of production, a change of management philosophy (e.g., from mass marketing to one-to-one marketing), or a change in the scale of operations. Successful changes in strategy require the capacity to take a fresh look at company operations in the light of new circumstances. These changes occur within processes that raise numerous analytical problems as well as personal and emotional conflicts. They may lead to new work tasks, recruitment of new chief executives, new power constellations in networks and virtual (or imaginary) organizations, and so on.

Although the purpose of these changes is usually to secure the survival of the company through expansion, contraction, and improved profitability, it is sometimes necessary to find the most favorable means of closing down operations.

Two examples of change projects are given below.

Example 1[20]

The company belonged to an industry undergoing a severe structural crisis. Profitability was unsatisfactory. An attempt was made structurally to regroup the company's operations. During this process of restructuring, I acted as a consultant for 18 months, working closely with employees at many levels. This process can be roughly divided into the following "steps" (*step* refers to areas of work that received greater emphasis than others at a certain stage in the process; the steps should be viewed as parts of an iterative and concurrent process rather than a sequential process):

- Definition of business concepts, objectives, and strategies together with decisions on these issues (February-September, Year 1)
- Proposal on new organizational structure (September-October, Year 1)
- Appointment of senior executives (October-November, Year 1)
- Detailed specification of business concepts, organization, planning, and so forth (November, Year 1-March, Year 2)
- Development of new systems of financial control (November, Year 1-November, Year 2)
- Company functioning within the framework of its new, restructured operations (March, Year 2 onward)

Example 2

This company was profitable and expanding but confronted with the need to adjust to dramatic future technological changes.

These changes were associated with the rapid development in electronics and the expansion of the computer industry. Strategic and organizational changes were considered essential to the company's survival in the future market. I worked together with about two hundred of the company's employees for two years to establish a new strategic and organizational base for the company. The steps mentioned in Example 1 are roughly applicable to this case, also. Substantial internal marketing[21] efforts had also to be made, however. These were highly complex due to the size and wide geographical distribution of the company.

I have attempted in these brief accounts to describe the types of processes that I have in mind. Such processes are going on continuously in the business world. In the two examples above, the scope was wide, but other assignments could concern a limited task of less dramatic and shorter-term changes. The descriptions also reveal some of the value judgments that have governed my actions. I have not said anything about my working methods, however, nor have I made any appraisal of the various approaches that have been adopted by academic researchers and management consultants. These will be dealt with throughout the rest of the book.

The Researcher's Number 1 Challenge: Access to Reality

In my view, the traditional research methods used in business research do not provide satisfactory *access*. Access refers to the opportunities available to find empirical data (real-world data) and information. A researcher's or consultant's ability to carry out work on a project is intimately tied up with the availability of data and information that can provide a basis for analysis and conclusions. The use of technically advanced and computerized quantitative techniques to process data will be in vain if the real-world input is flawed. Even if the methods of collecting and processing data are sophisticated, the well-known adage "garbage in, garbage out" cannot be discounted.

Access is a question of vital importance for both scientists and consultants. It will be specifically treated in Chapter 2 and will be referred to throughout this book.

The Researcher's Number 2 Challenge: Preunderstanding and Understanding

The concept of *preunderstanding* refers to people's insights into a specific problem and social environment before they start a research program or consulting assignment; it is an input. *Understanding* refers to the insights gained during a program or assignment; it is an output. This output in turn acts as preunderstanding before the next task.

Traditionally, academic researchers' preunderstanding takes the form of theories, models, and techniques; generally, they lack institutional knowledge, such as knowledge of conditions in a specific company, industry, or market. They have seldom had the opportunity to apply their skills in an actual corporate setting. Most academic researchers in business schools have never held a position in a company where leadership, risk taking, and responsibility for results are demanded (there are exceptions, however). Management consultants frequently have extensive experience of a particular function within a company or from general management. In this way, they also acquire specific institutional knowledge of one or several industries.

The problems of access and preunderstanding are significant. I am frequently dissatisfied with either the information available on a specific project or the extent to which other academic researchers or consultants have been able to penetrate below the surface of a certain sequence of events. It is my experience that when starting to work with a company, it is often difficult to understand the business culture in which the company or industry operates: things such as values held by employees, business terminology, general rules of procedure, and informal organization. Hence, the contribution that I am able to make to the project will increase with the extent of my preunderstanding of the problem area and the project environment.

The dark side of preunderstanding is that it can serve as a blockage to new information and innovation. This is a common cause for concern in deductive, hypotheses-testing research and will be discussed later in the book.

The Researcher's Number 3 Challenge: Quality

The choice of criteria used to assess the quality of research and consultancy work is governed by different values. Consequently, there is a wide range of possible criteria. To some extent, the criteria used to evaluate research findings are different from those used to assess the work of consultants. Researchers must be able to substantiate their findings and produce a report in which it is possible for the reader to follow a certain line of reasoning and the resultant conclusions. The methods used are considered to be of critical importance. On the other hand, questions of methodology and report writing are often of secondary consideration in the evaluation of consultancy where greater weight is placed on the ability of the consultant to make implementable recommendations and initiate change.

Lists of quality criteria for research and consultancy—reliability, validity, objectivity, relevance, and so on—are ambiguous. Not only is the selection of criteria arbitrary, but it is also difficult to apportion weights to the criteria and then add them up to produce a final assessment. With the passage of time, I have become increasingly cautious when reading statements of university professors, journal reviewers, and promotion committees regarding what is and is not good research. As an academic judge, you can easily become the victim of some particular methodological approach or current fashionable concern that curbs your view of reality.

The history of business and management abounds with examples of trendy methods and management techniques. During the past decades, various schools of thought have asserted that quantitative, statistical studies constituted the only true scientific approach; that operations research (even called "management science") was a godsend to company decision making; that the methods of psychiatry and social psychology, packaged as "sensitivity training," "T-groups," and so forth could be used to solve relational problems within organizations; that management information systems (MIS) would turn management into a computerized exercise; that formalized long-range planning systems would provide a risk-free highway into the future; that everything should be viewed in terms of processes; and also the reverse—that everything should be viewed in terms of structures.

Even recent experience bears this out. Currently, relationships and networks, as well as knowledge-based, virtual or imaginary organizations represent some of the buzzwords. The same fashionable concerns appear in packages provided by management consultants.

All of these methods deal with facets and perspectives of reality that may be highly important in relation to a specific situation. Provided that they are correctly applied, they may yield valuable insights and results. When people claim, however, that their method has universal validity or that its quality is superior to all other forms of research or consultancy, they have mistaken rigorous research for intellectual rigor mortis and the dictates of fashion.

The combination of research and management consultancy that involves intervention into processes of decision making, implementation, and change is known as *action research* or *action science*. But it is difficult to establish criteria for good research and good consultancy respectively that would allow the same individual to take on both roles to the satisfaction of both the academic and the business community.

Quality will be treated at length in Chapter 5.

Personal and Scientific Values: The Paradigm Platform

This book stresses the interplay between the basic vantage points for the researchers' work—the "absolute"—and the selection of methods. It is claimed that there exists an "absolute absolute" constituting the foundation of the universe, expressed in terms such as *God* and *pure consciousness*.[22] I will not dispute the existence of this, but unfortunately, very few researchers have yet reached such a state of enlightenment. Therefore, in the practice of today's research, the "absolute platform" is subjectively chosen; on that platform research can be conducted with varying degrees of "objectivity." Mainstream scientists who just apply "approved" methods without being aware of the subjective foundation of their activities are not scientists; they are technicians. In my experience, most "workers" within the university world never get beyond the stage of technician.

Lacking an "absolute truth" from which to approach the world, we create via social consensus an absolute reference point, our *paradigm*.

The concept of paradigm was brought to the fore by Thomas Kuhn[23] in the early 1960s. It will be used here to represent people's value judgments, norms, standards, frames of reference, perspectives, ideologies, myths, theories, and approved procedures that govern their thinking and action. In a similar sense, Fleck,[24] twenty-five years before Kuhn, used the concept of *thought style* to define shared values and ideas that scientists, often unknowingly, came to consider "the absolute truth." We can even go back to the years around 250 BC and hear Greek mathematician and physicist Archimedes exclaim, "Give me somewhere to stand and I will move the Earth."

In science, a paradigm consists of the researcher's perception of what one should be doing and how one should be doing it. In other words, what are the interesting research problems and which methodological approach can be used to tackle them? For example, astronomy is considered a science by today's scientific community, whereas astrology and horoscopes are considered frauds or at least nonscientific.

The basic premises, value judgments and modes of operation that characterize the academic researcher and the consultant will be referred to as the *scientific paradigm* and the *consultant paradigm*, respectively. The scientific and consultant paradigms are different, but they could also overlap as Figure 1.1 suggests.

The subject of paradigms is often discussed in terms of an antithesis between two schools of philosophy: the *positivistic*, traditional natural science school and the *humanistic* school. Both have many facets and names, particularly so the humanistic school. To avoid too much detail and confusion, it will subsequently be referred to as *hermeneutics* (from Greek *hermeneuien*, to interpret). In business administration, both schools of thought are influential, although the academic community favors the positivistic paradigm at the expense of the hermeneutic paradigm.

To some extent, researchers and consultants are governed more by personal considerations than by a particular scientific approach or the problems confronting clients. For example, a consultant may wish to sell more assignments to buy a fancier car, and the researcher may adopt an opportunistic approach to get tenure at a prestigious university. Such driving forces are also part of the paradigm and affect the behavior of researchers and consultants.

Kuhn's use of the term *paradigm* has been interpreted in twenty-two different senses,[25] although he himself attributes this to linguistic inconsistencies.[26] Nevertheless, paradigm will be used here as a word with a distinctive meaning that cannot be readily confused with words from everyday conversation.

Paradigm is associated with the existing foundation of science as well as with revolutionary discoveries and changes in the sciences. Periods of *normal science* are superseded by *paradigm shifts* when the established scientific norms are challenged. When our personal paradigm is attacked, we may feel threatened or excited—our "somewhere to stand" is being snatched away—and react by raising our defenses or by a frank appraisal of a new position. The breakdown of the communist concept of the centrally planned economy is such a dramatic paradigm shift that will have far-reaching effects on business globally. The story of a personal paradigm shift is well told by Capra in his philosophical biography, *Uncommon Wisdom*.[27] Capra started out with a Ph.D. in physics but discovered the shortcomings of the traditional natural science paradigm as it is applied to society.

By analogy with this thinking, Argyris and Schon apply two concepts to learning in corporations:

> *Single-loop learning* is like the thermostat that learns when it is too hot or too cold and turns the heat on or off. The thermostat can perform this task because it can receive information (the temperature of the room) and take corrective action. *Double-loop learning* occurs when error is detected and corrected in ways that involve the modification of an organization's underlying norms, policies and objectives.[28]

In other words, single-loop learning takes place within the existing paradigm, whereas double-loop learning requires a new paradigm. During normal periods, companies work like thermostats; during periods of major changes in the financial, technological, and competitive conditions, more fundamental revisions are required. These have to start with an audit of the company's business mission, goals, and strategies, often followed by a restructuring of the whole company, new leadership, and new control systems. Both fine-tuning within the existing paradigm and major changes caused by a paradigm shift are of concern to researchers and consultants.

It is desirable that academic researchers account for their personal values, at least to themselves. It is equally desirable that consultants share their values with clients. Tornebohm points out that the "greater the researcher's awareness of his own paradigm, the better the research that he can carry out."[29] The authors of another book refer to the feeling of being invisibly taken over: "Quite unnoticed, we have inherited a way of seeing that prevents us from discovering our own points of departure . . . that we are quite willing to question the details of a process of thought but not the actual process itself."[30]

In practice, the paradigm that governs individuals and organizations often resists identification; it becomes an invisible backseat driver. *Tacit knowing*, a term ascribed to Polanyi,[31] implies that we know and do things without actually being able to explain how. A sentence in my French textbook that had a slightly frustrating effect read as follows: "In France even small children speak French fluently." They certainly do, but they will not be able to articulate the structure of the French language, its grammar; it is a tacit cognitive map.

There is also the risk that we can actually deceive ourselves and others into believing that we have identified our paradigm.[32] Argyris and Schon[33] have introduced a *theory of action* in which they use two fundamental concepts. The first one is *espoused theory*, the way we claim that we think and operate; the second is *theory-in-use*, the way that we actually think and act. A consulting firm may, for example, state in its advertising and promotional material that senior consultants with long experience supervise the assignments (espoused theory), while in practice, young, inexperienced consultants are left very much on their own (theory-in-use). This may be deliberate deception, but it could also be that the management of the consulting firm is not aware of the actual theory-in-use. They may live in a myth—that is, "a way of thinking so deeply imbedded in our consciousness that it is invisible . . . a way of understanding the world that is not problematic, that we are not fully conscious of, that seems, in a word, natural."[34] In a similar spirit, Habermas[35] says that the most important task for the social scientist is that of emancipator: freeing ourselves from conditions and dependencies that we may so far have considered as given or fixed. He also relates this process to Freudian psychoanalysis, which seeks to lay bare individuals' subconscious motives and thereby allow them to gain control over their actions.

If academic researchers are aware of their paradigm, it is naturally desirable that they discuss it at the outset of their work.[36] This assumes, however, that the paradigm is static and does not change during the course of the research project. It's quite apparent to me that I was only partially aware of my scientific paradigm when I started work on this book. It certainly has changed during the course of my studies. Consequently, and within the humanistic tradition, I will present aspects of my own paradigm as frankly as possible as the book unfolds. This may take the form of personal views expressed on different subjects. At times, this may be interpreted as "chatty," not to say egocentric. I have decided to run this risk in order to put forward certain ideas, arguments, and examples that could undoubtedly be abbreviated and presented in a more structured fashion. In their less structured form, however, they provide the reader with a more complete picture of the research process and my own conclusions.

Science Is a Journey, Not a Destination

What science is, is far from clear. There are those who claim they know. In my view, "scientists" who claim they know what science is are not scientists. They have stopped developing. Their search is over. They do not do "re-search," which literally means "search again."

Science is a continuing search; it is a continuing generation of theories, models, concepts, and categories. It is realistic to view research as a journey on which each program represents a temporary stop on the way and each report is a point of departure for further inquiry. This may sound trivial, but all the same, it is constantly misunderstood. A few lines from a Sherlock Holmes story—which one I can't recall any more—at one point in time represented for me a research ideal. On completing his work on the behavior of bees, Holmes states that this would be the final work on the subject and that there was nothing more to be added.

Working on the subject of scientific theory and methodology in business and management research, I have felt vastly inferior to Holmes. I have rather been reminded of the Chinese boxes; one opens a box only to find another box inside. A sufficient display of stubbornness can perhaps reduce the size of the boxes to a point where they can be ignored. I have felt, however, that I am approaching the world from the very smallest box, which I then open only to find myself in a larger box. The subject keeps expanding. At the same time, this process of discovery is genuinely exciting; many books in the field of scientific theory and methodology represent real challenges.

I get some consolation from reading a book on science by Finnish philosopher George Henrik von Wright and a review of the book.[37] In his mid-seventies, von Wright summed up the collected wisdom of his philosophy and triggered an intense debate on the role of science. Despite his lifelong devotion to the philosophy of science and the acquisition of international fame, von Wright was criticized for having grasped only limited aspects of his subject and being ignorant of others.

Structure of the Book

This chapter has introduced concepts and thoughts that will be used and further developed in subsequent chapters. Chapter 2 deals with access through different roles and Chapter 3 with pre-understanding and understanding. In Chapter 4, arguments for and against case study research are presented, with special emphasis on action science. Chapter 5 examines the scientific paradigm and the consultant paradigm, and the quality criteria used to assess academic research and management consultancy. A management action science paradigm is proposed in Chapter 6, together with a summary of the contributions of the book.

The text contains references to notes, which are listed at the end of each chapter. A reference list and an index of subjects and names are presented at the end of the book.

Notes

1. Argyris et al., 1985.
2. Gummesson, 1977, 1979.
3. See overviews in Burell and Morgan, 1985; Patton, 1990; Tesch, 1990; Bernard, 1995; and Silverman, 1997.
4. Evans-Pritchard, 1937.
5. Strauss and Glaser, 1970.
6. Jackson, 1968.
7. Alkin et al., 1979.
8. Seymour, 1988.
9. Easterby-Smith et al., 1991.

10. Goldman, 1988.

11. Crosby, 1984.

12. Toffler, 1985, p. 6.

13. According to Toffler, 1981, the agricultural society constituted the first wave, industrial manufacturing the second, and service/information the third.

14. For an account of this transition and its impact on business, see Gronroos, 1990.

15. See Drucker, 1989; Quinn, 1992; Sveiby, 1994, 1997; "gold-collar worker" is a designation used by Kelley, 1985.

16. Gummesson, 1990; the characterization is also influenced by Sveiby and Risling, 1986.

17. Gummesson, 1977, pp. 43-72.

18. Carlson, 1983, p. 60.

19. Liles, 1989, p. 8B.

20. Part of this project is described in Gummesson, 1982.

21. Internal marketing is a relatively new concept that suggests that the use of know-how developed in marketing to customers (the external market) be used in approaching personnel (the internal market) with new ideas, changed modes of operation, and so on. See Gronroos, 1990, pp. 221-39.

22. See Orme-Johnson, 1988; for an application to organizations, see Gustavsson, 1992.

23. See Kuhn, 1962, and his comments to his critics in a later edition, 1970, pp. 143-69. See also Lindholm, 1980, pp. 21-64; Tornebohm, 1983, pp. 349-50; Arndt, 1985, pp. 14-16. The significance of personal values for research is discussed in relation to objectivity by Myrdal, 1970.

24. Fleck, [1935] 1979.

25. Masterman, 1970.

26. Kuhn, 1970, "Postscript—1969," p. 181.

27. Capra, 1988. The conflicting paradigms of natural and social sciences and efforts to integrate the two are also treated by Zukav, 1979; Bohm, 1977, 1980; Capra, 1982, 1984; and Davies, 1984, 1987.

28. Argyris and Schon, 1978, p. 3.

29. Tornebohm, 1976, p. 37.

30. Arbnor et al., 1981, p. 91.

31. Polanyi, 1962.

32. Myrdal, 1970, p. 52; Lindholm, 1980, p. 51; Molander, 1983, p. 198.

33. Argyris and Schon, 1974, pp. 6-7.

34. Postman, 1985, p. 79.

35. From a discussion on Habermas in Kalleberg, 1972, pp. 121-31.

36. Myrdal, 1970, pp. 52 and 58.

37. von Wright, 1986.

Two

Achieving Access to Management Reality

Access has already been defined as the researcher's Number 1 problem. Access refers to the ability to get close to the object of study, to really be able to find out what is happening. Although access is an important issue, the hurdles associated with it are neglected in the study of management. Our concern here will be with the opportunities available to the academic researcher and management consultant to gain access to data and information on particular areas of inquiry.

The first part of the chapter presents my reasons for discussing access. Next, access is discussed in relation to different roles.

Why Discuss Access?

This chapter will examine the following questions:

* How do researchers/consultants gain access to processes within companies?

* How satisfactory is their access?

Two episodes will be used to illustrate these questions.

Over lunch, the following conversation took place between myself and a senior marketing executive from a major multinational corporation based in Europe (E = executive; A = author).

E: Some type of professor is over here again from the USA wanting to interview us about strategy. He had a long questionnaire with him containing about fifty different factors. He wants to find out which factors are important when we decide to enter a new market.

A: What are these factors?

E: Just the usual sort of thing—market potential, competition, political stability, et cetera.

A: What did you reply?

E: Well, you know, you go through the list and tick off a few factors, show him some marketing plans, and then send him off to meet a few other people. I have no idea what he gets out of it all.

A: You don't seem too enthusiastic about his research.

E: No, it doesn't really work like that in practice, does it? Let me tell you what happened when we decided to enter a country in Latin America. Four of us got together over dinner in New York: a divisional director, the vice president of R&D, a department head, and myself. We sat and chatted around the problem but just couldn't agree. In the end we had to take a vote: two in favor, one against, and one undecided. Well, that was it; in we went. Two men flew down on the following Thursday to check the lay of the land.

A: Did you tell the professor about all this?

E: Of course not! He might have thought that we're not serious.

This episode illustrates the difficulties of gaining access; the method adopted by the researcher did not succeed in getting the company to describe how it arrived at its decision.

The next episode consists of a conversation I had, in my capacity as a consultant, with a board director of a company that was in the midst of a crisis. The board director not only represented ownership and power but also had a consulting role by giving advice to management as well as to the government that owned this particular company. Many academic researchers and professional consultants also take on positions as members of the board of directors (D = director; A = author).

A: How do you find out about what is going on in the company?
D: I keep in touch with them and visit them from time to time.
A: When was the last time that you visited them?
D: Well, I just haven't had the time recently. It must be a few months ago.
A: How long do your visits usually last?
D: About half a day.
A: Well, then you will only have time to meet the chief executive and possibly some other senior manager?
D: Oh no, I get in touch with people at many different levels, including trade unionists.
A: Do you consider that you find out what is going on in the company?
D: Oh yes, all the important things. I feel that I have established good contacts with both the chief executive and trade union representatives. They speak very frankly to me.

Although I was involved with this company on more or less a full-time basis, it took me several months to create a reasonably open working relationship with the staff and to gain sufficient insight into the company's situation. This contrasts with the experience of the board director, who considered that the occasional brief visit was sufficient to establish an open and informed relationship with the company. The director's access to the company was highly limited, and his level of understanding of the company must be characterized as inadequate.

The possibilities of access for external board directors received considerable attention in Northern Europe during the late 1980s when the Fermenta scandal was revealed. Fermenta was an international producer of base penicillin, a mature product that the company allegedly handled more cost-effectively than the competition. The company expanded rapidly and became the favorite of the press and the stock market. The price of the stock rose to fantastic heights until, first, an environmentalist and, later, an accountant revealed that the assets and operations of Fermenta were suspect. The president of Fermenta had been able to conceal this for several years from the board of directors—all reputable and experienced business executives from large companies. The board did not have access to the actual decision processes, nor did financial reporters manage to reveal the actual state of affairs.[1]

I doubt that the director's/consultant's superficial understanding is unique. As the first episode illustrated, academic researchers are also highly susceptible to these shortcomings.

The difficulties of access are exemplified by Harold Geneen, former CEO of the international conglomerate ITT. A question that kept bewildering the business world was, "How did the Japanese do it when they conquered the world market for TV sets, radios, cars, and other products during the 1970s and 1980s?" Geneen is critical of the way Japanese management has been interpreted in the West: "American observers in Japan could have Japanese customs explained to them and could witness the group discussions, the singing, cheering and smiling faces in the factories. However I wonder whether they saw where the management decisions were made."[2] A Japanese[3] businessman told me that Western visitors to Japan ask questions such as, "How do you make decisions?" He claimed that the Japanese find it difficult to put the subtle decision-making procedures into words, although they have "lived" them and understand how they work. Their answers may therefore not be very illuminating, although at face value they may appear revealing. Visitors cannot get proper access to the knowledge by asking straightforward questions.

It is often claimed that academic research in management is directed toward practical application, making it shortsighted, a victim of fads and current topics directed to particular situations and thus of little general interest, that it has less autonomy because of its dependence on business executives. In two separate articles, Whitley and Warneryd discuss the scientific status of academic research in management. Whitley lists a number of alleged problems of academic research in management:

> The practical constraint that research access is often controlled by gatekeepers who have a direct interest in the outcome, results in practically oriented management research having rather less social and intellectual autonomy. . . . Practitioners' goals, perceptions and beliefs enter into the formulation of research goals and evaluation criteria more directly than in other areas and the availability of alternative audiences than scientific colleagues reduces the collegiate control over research practices. Research here tends to be more related to current topics of concern among practitioners and focused on particular situations rather than following collegiate goals and looking for general social processes that underlie a range of phenomena.[4]

Warneryd, in a similar spirit, states that science should have "wider aims than just providing one particular company with decision material for one particular situation. In other words, it deals with the generation of knowledge that is generalizable to some extent at least."[5]

In my interpretation, the authors are actually discussing the two different roles of academic researcher and management consultant: the academic researcher who tends to become more of a consultant but still poses as a scholar. But I find it equally problematic that because of too superficial access to business life, researchers may not even notice topics that have been current for five, ten, or more years and that have momentum to last for several decades! Such an example is research in the service sector—service management, services marketing, service quality—that started on a big scale in the 1980s, although because of the impact of services on our economies, it should have started twenty, or even thirty, years earlier. Another example is quality management, in which the Western world was left behind by the Japanese; the quality revolution in Western industry started during the 1970s but was noticed by the majority of business schools only in the 1990s. Bruce Henderson, founder of the Boston Consulting Group, claims that "consultants have greater opportunities for creativity than either their clients or academics. Clients are bound by their own history, culture, and beliefs." He proceeds to emphasize the significance of close access to the object under study: "Academics can collect data, but they are not exposed enough to the reality of real problems to visualize them as system effects and generalize conceptual insights from them."[6]

My own view can be summarized by the following statements:

* It is imperative to lay bare the distinguishing characteristics between research and consultancy.

* Researchers/consultants are frequently unable to gain sufficient access to the processes of change they wish to examine or influence. They seem to be insufficiently aware of the problems created by restricted access.

* Therefore, there is a need to investigate whether consultancy can *contribute* to academic research and vice versa rather than to isolate academic research from consultancy.[7]

Naturally, there wouldn't be much to discuss if access was simply a matter of doing personal interviews or distributing questionnaires. In that case, the access curve might be depicted as in Figure 2.1. The curve illustrates that a reasonable input of research resources would give access to a large portion of data. It would then be straightforward and economical to be *pareto optimal*—that is, to follow the 80/20 rule: 80% of the information would be obtained through a limited input of effort, whereas the remaining 20% would require huge resources. It is my contention, however, that access develops by leaps as a function of the degree of sophistication of the methods of research and the amount of time involved (see Figure 2.2). Hence, the actual choice of research method and the competence of the researcher/consultant will be of decisive importance.

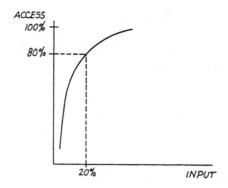

Figure 2.1. Continuous Development of Access

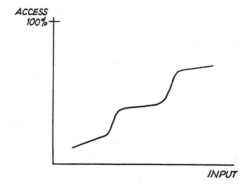

Figure 2.2. Access Developed in Stages

The literature on scientific research and consultancy seldom deals with the concept of access per se. I have found only one book that explores the concept of access.[8] It consists of some thirty descriptive case studies on the basis of which readers may draw their own conclusions. At the outset, the authors discuss a number of systematic approaches to the question of access.[9] They say that access can be viewed from the point of view of three interested parties: the researcher, the subject of research, and the consumer of the research.[10] To evaluate the research, the consumer must be able to establish how access took place and be in a position to assess the respective strengths and weaknesses of the method adopted. The authors maintain that the problem of access is often left unresolved in research reports.[11]

The authors discuss three types of access: access to money to finance a project, access to the system (i.e., the organization to be studied), and access to individuals in the system.[12] I would also include the converse to this final point—namely, the access of the system and its individuals to the researcher/consultant. People might want to give information but are not selected by the researcher/consultant to do so.

Taylor and Bogdan mention three types of access: to organizations, to public and quasi-public settings, and to private settings.[13] They are primarily concerned with an *overt* approach to physical access: how to be allowed to visit or stay in a setting. There is also a *covert*[14] research approach that raises several ethical problems. How do you sneak into a setting where you are not wanted? Would it be OK to bug somebody's apartment in the name of science? Or as has been done, to study consumption patterns by investigating people's garbage cans?

Physical access is usually a basic condition for research and consultancy, particularly when decision, implementation, and change processes are studied. This includes not only initial access but also the problem of ensuring *continued* access.[15] The next step is *mental access:* how to understand what is actually happening in the setting, how to get people to describe it, how to observe it, or how to experience it through the researcher's own involvement.

In the researcher's/consultant's efforts to gain access, two types of figures are essential: *gatekeepers* and *informants*.[16]

Gatekeepers are those who can open or close the gate for the researcher/consultant; informants, those who can provide valuable information and smooth the way to others. Barnes states that a "social scientist may well find that gaining access to the people that he wants to study may be as difficult and lengthy a process as gaining financial support for his work."[17] Investigative reporter Ake Ortmark[18] vividly describes how he tried to get access to the

industrialist and investor David Rockefeller after having interviewed all other significant members of the Rockefeller family. He
made use of introductions from influential people, made several
personal visits to David Rockefeller's office, and frequently tried
to contact him by phone. This went on for several years. The gatekeepers consisted of an army of assistants, public relations offi-
cers, and secretaries who protected Rockefeller. Ortmark was finally granted a thirty-minute interview with the man, who
unfortunately said nothing worth relating. Frequently, however,
physical access does not pose any problem at all, and sometimes
people even drag you into the setting.

You need to interview people, and they are usually referred to
as interviewees, respondents, or informants. But you also need informants to help you locate people to interview and observe.
Without at least one efficient and benevolent informant, you are
lost in an unfamiliar setting.

In the rest of this chapter, I will examine access from the point of
view of the different roles that can be adopted by researchers and
consultants. These roles are closely related to the research methodology.

Roles

Different roles are adopted to gain access to companies and their
employees. There are three possible avenues of approach: via the
researcher role, the consultant role, or *the role of employee* (including
board director and owner). Research may occur in all three roles:
traditional academic researcher, researcher/consultant, and re-
searcher/employee.

The term *traditional academic researcher* refers to researchers
who belong to a university or similar institution and who are engaged in scientific research and usually also in teaching. Their
principal frame of reference is academic literature, recognized
authorities in the discipline, professors and other research colleagues, students, and the experience they have gained from their
own research.

As stated in Chapter 1, the term *consultant* refers to management consultants who are concerned with the problems of running a business. Usually, they have attended a business school and/or studied the social or technical sciences. They sometimes have several years of practical business experience prior to taking on the role of consultant; sometimes they are hired by a consulting firm fresh out of college. Colleagues from the world of consultancy and the employees of client firms represent the consultant's normal frame of reference.

University professors in business subjects are also frequently involved in management consultancy. This is one means of increasing their income and of financing research, but it also allows the researcher to get firsthand experience of companies. In addition, the consultant role creates opportunities for research that are not normally available to the traditional researcher.

The roles of academic researcher, educator, and management consultant are unclear. For example, Kenneth Blanchard, co-author of the best-selling *The One Minute Manager*, was presented in three different positions in the book:[19]

> He presently serves as professor of leadership and organizational behavior at the University of Massachusetts, Amherst.
>
> He has advised distinguished corporations and agencies such as Chevron, Lockheed, AT&T, Holiday Inns, Young President's Association (YPA), the United States Armed Forces, and UNESCO (United Nations Educational, Scientific and Cultural Organization).
>
> In his role as management consultant, he teaches seminars across the country.

I have personally used most of the roles and methods evaluated below—just reading about them is not adequate. If researchers/consultants do not proceed beyond the stage of secondhand understanding (see Chapter 3), their knowledge will be restricted to a consideration of principles and will remain at a superficial level. The increased personal insight gained by researchers/consultants from having applied a method to a number of particular cases will allow them to form a more balanced judgment.

The methods recommended to the traditional academic researcher in business schools embrace *desk research* of existing written material together with *field studies* in which *survey techniques* are deployed to acquire *empirical data.* The surveys use *questionnaires* and *interviews* and *statistical, quantitative processing* of data. Preferably, the researcher should start out with a set of *hypotheses,* which are tested by means of the empirical data.

It is my belief that these methods can be used only to *complement* the analysis of processes within a company. If each method is used on its own, processes of decision making, implementation, and change will tend to be examined in a far too fragmented and mechanistic manner, which will scarcely inform the reader and indeed may only lead to misunderstandings. These methods may be used to analyze well-structured fragments of problems—but strategic changes or reorganizations do not fall into this category. Among the methods available to the traditional researcher, *qualitative (informal) interviews* and *observation* provide the best opportunities for the study of processes. They have been only partially accepted as scientific methods in management, although they are meeting with increasing sympathy. A step that will take the researcher/consultant still farther is the application of *participant observation,* the major access method used by anthropologists. The most advanced step is *action research/action science.* These qualitative methods will be discussed later on.

Let me now examine more closely the various roles that may be adopted by researchers and consultants and start by using the iceberg metaphor (Figure 2.3). An iceberg is known to show only 10% to 15% of its mass above the water's surface. Are researchers/consultants comfortable with a look at that percentage of the company that shows when watched from above (the helicopter view of economists)? Or are they satisfied with the access gained through questionnaires and personal interviews with employees—the most common survey techniques used in the social sciences—where they at least set foot on the iceberg, if only on its top? Or should they aim at a close-up of the remaining 85% to 90%

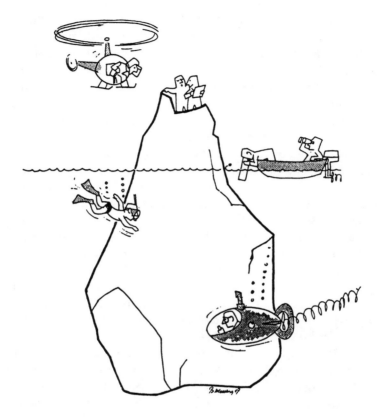

Figure 2.3. The Iceberg Metaphor

by getting under the surface, mobilizing more resources, and getting more involved? The answer is easy, but the traditions and methods of access go for the superficial part, leaving the rest as "not amenable for research."

The *combined researcher/consultant* may adopt several different roles and methods of approach. One essential distinction is between the expert consultant and the process consultant.[20] The *expert consultant* is often described by means of the old doctor-patient model[21] according to which the doctor, the almighty expert, tells the ignorant patient which pill to take. In the same spirit, the expert researcher/consultant diagnoses what is wrong and prescribes a therapy. Schein says that "this model is fraught with difficulties."[22] One difficulty is the reluctance of people to give access to the information that the researcher/consultant needs. Moreover, the information tends to be distorted. Finally, clients sometimes do not believe the researcher's/consultant's diagnosis and refuse to accept the prescription, or it may be the other way around: They do whatever the expert says without actively involving themselves and contributing to the process. It is a linear, *one-way relationship.*

This contrasts with *process consultation* in which the client enters an *interactive relationship* with the researcher/consultant. The latter becomes the midwife, helping the client to deliver a baby. The process consultant attempts to release the client's own resources through self-diagnosis and self-intervention. The researcher/consultant is referred to as an interventionist or facilitator. This approach is based on the assumption that the resources to take action and implement change exist within the client's organization.[23] It is even questioned whether the researcher's/consultant's expertise in one or several management functions may be at all desirable. Schein expresses as his opinion that

> the process consultant may or may not be expert in solving the particular problem . . . such expertise is less relevant than are the skills of involving the client in self-diagnosis. . . . If I permitted myself to become interested in a particular management problem in sales, marketing, or production, I would be switching roles from that of process consultant to that of expert resource. Once I have become an expert resource, I find I lose my effectiveness as a process consultant.[24]

In my view these roles are not necessarily contradictory;[25] rather, one of them may carry more weight than the other in a specific situation. Consequently, my analysis of the role of the researcher/consultant chooses a different point of departure. After several attempts, I have chosen to define seven different roles that cover the essential aspects of research and consultancy. Each role has a discriminating core, but the boundaries between the roles are by no means clear, and there is no universal agreement on their content.[26] The roles will be examined in relation to the methods used by the academic researcher and management consultant (see Table 2.1).

The role of *analyst* is the traditional research role. Researchers/consultants do not usually have particularly good access to a strategic or organizational process, although they may have access to essential documents, both official and classified information.

During *project* work*, the researcher/consultant will come into contact with one or several groups: those who work with the task and those who act in reference or steering committees. In this way, he or she will get to know many of the company's employees and will, to a certain extent, be able to see them interact. The researcher/consultant gets closer access both to the issue at hand and to the social setting. Work on the project will sometimes be formalized, and it may be difficult to get beneath the surface. The researcher/consultant runs the risk of adopting a tactical, pliable approach—for example, avoiding sensitive questions.

Work as a *catalyst or therapist* attempts to fulfill the role of adviser and listener—the "wise men and women"—whose mere presence may have a magic effect. They may be able to establish a close and influential relationship with one or several employees. Catalyst is a chemical term that denotes a substance that influences a process without being affected by it. The use of the term to describe the role played by the researcher/consultant in a process of change is therefore somewhat misleading in the sense that the latter also wish to develop their own abilities and thereby change.

The *organizational development (OD)* approach[27] uses scientific methods and results, primarily from the behavioral sciences, to promote development processes in organizations. Operating within the framework of psychology, psychiatry, sociology, and

---

*In this chapter, the term *project* will also be used in a general sense to denote all types of research or consultant projects.

TABLE 2.1 Characterization of Researcher/Consultant Roles

Roles	Characteristics
Analyst	Intellectual work; performed by one or a small group of individuals; duration could range from very brief to several years; occasional visits to the company; tends to make frequent visits to other groups—e.g., customers and suppliers; considerable desk work involved; written report essential.
Project participant	Intellectual work; group work; formalized list of participants and times of meeting; duration of project ranges from a couple of months to several years; occasional or frequent visits to the company; frequent presentations at meetings; written memos; presentation of final written report occasionally important.
Catalyst/ Therapist	Intellectual work but with considerable emphasis on human relationships and emotional states; based on experience and judgment; discussions with one or a few individuals; may comprise anything from a few hours to a long-term assignment carried out at the company.
OD Consultant/ Interventionist/ Clinician	Behavioral science approach in which knowledge of human relationships and emotional states is combined with intellectual analyses; avoidance of expert advice; assignments often spread over time; occasional or frequent visits to the company; time often spent on training and development sessions.
Change agent	Assignments may comprise all or only some of the above roles; in addition, provision of expert recommendations that in practice may be interpreted as mandatory; strongly action oriented; assumes active participation for a period of several months up to a couple of years; regular periods of residence at the company.
External board director	Position of defined legal status and responsibility; works on behalf of both shareholders and company management; acts as a combined catalyst and decision maker; often holds the position for many years but is active on only a few occasions per annum.
Management-for-hire	Holds line management or staff position in a company; usually for a period of six months to two years; may comprise all of the above roles; risk of becoming tied down by routine work; resident at the company.

social psychology, a large part of the work will be concerned with individual or group exercises involving human relationships and emotions that are of central importance to the processes under investigation. It involves conflict resolution and training to improve cooperation and personality development. Although the application of behavioral science methodology to business processes represents the point of departure for OD studies, they may also contain elements of expert advice. Sometimes researchers/consultants may be expected to adhere strictly to the role of process consultant. Researchers/consultants may be considered to have fallen into "a major trap" if they use their position to provide expert advice.[28] The role of the behavioral researcher and the process consultant together with the possibility of integrating these roles has been analyzed at length by the *interventionist school*.[29]

In OD approaches, I also include *clinical research* and *clinical consultancy*, which are based on behavioral sciences and medicine, primarily clinical psychology.[30] Only an experienced researcher/consultant can use this approach because clinical judgment is needed that, according to Calder, is "an analytic skill of somewhat nebulous dimensions."[31] He further states that the clinical approach "is basically an art. As is the medical model in general, it is widely held to be scientific because clinical judgement is supposed to take scientifically valid theory as a starting point and as a problem-solving framework." One application of the clinical model is *motivational research*, which at one time was heavily in vogue—and deeply controversial—among market researchers.[32] It was unabashedly speculative and creative and, consequently, deeply controversial.

To learn the OD approach, it is necessary for researchers/consultants actually to participate in the process themselves. This type of insight cannot be gained from a written report or from its presentation at a meeting. Consequently, it is also vital that the real decision makers participate in the process. What actually appears to take place is the following:

* A limited number of people in a company understand what needs to be done. It is generally recognized in qual-

ity management that those who are closest to a problem are also those who are best suited to identify the problem and suggest solutions.[33] Those who are close to a problem can be found everywhere in an organization, on the plant floor as well as in top management. Frequently, those who have the insight lack the power to make decisions (e.g., the members of a development team or call center employees), whereas those who have the authority lack the insight (e.g., members of the board who are not close enough to "where the action is").

* The company's senior management must ensure that new institutional arrangements necessary for the actual implementation of change have been introduced; it may be a new business concept, a new organization, or a new system of financial control. Employees then have to decide whether to adjust to the changes or to leave the company.

* The expert advice of external researchers/consultants who are accustomed to dealing with processes may be required to assist those with the executive responsibility for both the decisions to be made and the implementation of change.

It is quite obvious that the behavioral science approaches described above are quite different from the original expert research and expert consultancy approaches in management. The expert was inspired by F. W. Taylor and others to introduce "scientific management"[34] to clients where, for example, the focus was on work study that aimed to enhance productivity in the factory. Work study is a highly structured, quantitative method based on detailed analysis and measurement of manufacturing procedures to discover the single best way for the worker to carry out an operation. Modern applications of the same thinking are the highly successful franchise operations found in fast-food restaurants and retailing, such as McDonald's and 7-Eleven. These operations are designed in detail around well-tested success formulas that must be strictly adhered to by each outlet; no drifting allowed. In this way, it is possible to open restaurants and stores in new locations at a fast pace; growth is based on the multiplication of the exact same concept over and over again.

Whereas the scientific management approach stems from engineering, another expert tradition originates in accounting. The latter type of experts master the balance sheet; the profit and loss statement; the procedures and systems of finance, accounting, and bookkeeping; and the techniques for product cost calculations. In their view, either one or several of the concepts of cost, revenue, capital, and profits is central to business and management. Today, this expert knowledge is challenged by a broader approach—*the balanced scorecard*—which also includes the precursors of future financial success. Among these are the value of customers, employees, internal procedures, and the potential to improve and innovate; these are increasingly referred to as *intellectual capital*.[35] Behavioral scientists are usually innocents in the realm of these experts.

In 1970, Argyris[36] claimed that very little was known about the effectiveness of management consultants and researchers. He talked about the "dry rot" that spread throughout organizations in the shape of defensive actions, apathy, indifference, noninvolvement, and mistrust, largely stimulated by the expert approach and the lack of compassion for human response. Ten years later, we were hit by Japanese management[37] and the "excellence wave" where the concerted, dynamic forces of finance, engineering, computers, and human resources are in focus. In this spirit, Peters and Waterman[38] introduced the McKinsey 7-S framework of management, the "happy atom," where strategy, structure, systems, skills, leadership style, staff, and shared values together created excellence. This framework is an effort to integrate the humanistic and technocratic dimensions of corporate life, and leads us to the role of *change agent*.[39]

A change agent may be involved in all of the above roles: analyst, project participant, catalyst, and interventionist. But the actual emphasis given to the various roles will vary from project to project. The change agent is a *contingent consultant*.[40]

The change agent is evaluated by the results caused by change, not by methods. To bring about change, it is essential that researchers/consultants actually take part in the decisions and the implementation of change and do not limit their participation to the preparation of analytical material. It is my impression that the analytical work may well be the simpler task. The tough problems actually start once decisions have been made and the company organization is slow to carry the process forward; decisions are watered down and delays occur. If the entire process of change is viewed as three more or less parallel subprocesses—analysis, decision, implementation—it can be seen that no significant change will actually take place until the final stage is completed. Hence, the change agent ought to be able to participate in all of the constituent parts of this process.

The categorization of the different researcher/consultant roles is somewhat lacking in precision because the roles sometimes overlap. This may be illustrated by the following example from public administration:

> An analyst is also able to be more actively engaged in creating events. . . . Carrying out an interview, sending out a questionnaire, arranging a meeting, etc. are examples of such intervention. Thus there is a moving scale along which the degree of intervention becomes increasingly marked; for example, the arrangement of a seminar to be attended by individuals from different departments within an organization is subject to some degree of internal conflict. Many of the research methods used by so-called process consultants are of this type. Participation in the normal processes of work is also an important element in process consultancy. For example, at meetings during which certain decisions will be made, the consultant may decide to make occasional contributions to the discussion rather than merely observe what is taking place.[41]

Researchers and consultants are often involved in *training and education* in the form of management courses and conferences. Many of those who describe themselves as consultants are to all intents and purposes educators and course administrators, some providing a completely standardized educational package. A special variant are conference speakers who offer a unique competence or experience. They are often captivating presenters, sometimes with celebrity status, thus adding to the prestige and symbolic value of an event. In these roles, researchers and consultants may help in laying a foundation for a change process.

Academic researchers and management consultants sometimes become *external board directors.* This position may act as a platform from which to maintain a close working relationship with the chief executive, the top management team, and the owners as well as providing access to essential information. The main function of the board is to engage in changes in the firm's direction, its scale of operations, and the appointment of competent senior executives; it is concerned with strategic and organization issues.[42] As exemplified at the outset of this chapter, membership on the board is sometimes a disadvantage when it comes to access to information; employees are likely to watch their step when talking to a board director. In addition, an external board director is not normally paid to take on a major role in the company. Sometimes they play a more active part in the company. They may work on either a part-time or full-time basis at the company and are sometimes a former chief executive concerned with long-term, strategic issues. This type of role is almost equivalent to that of an employee who is part adviser/consultant, part operative.

A closely associated category is that of *owner* and *investor.* Today, it is common that ownership of public corporations is dominated by large institutional investors such as pension funds, who may have a seat on the board.

Throughout this gray area where it is often difficult to distinguish between the roles of employee and researcher/consultant, the opportunities for access are greater than those normally available to the academic researcher. Conditions do vary markedly between companies, however.

Management-for-hire is a consultant role that involves a limited period of engagement in a managerial position, usually ranging from six months to two years. The consultant remains employed in the consulting firm, but his or her position in the client company resembles that of an employee. The position of company employee bestows certain advantages: access to information, participation within the system, and the opportunity for close contact with individual employees. Senior company management—chief executive, division heads, and so forth—are right at the center of events when it comes to strategic and organizational issues. Line management farther down the hierarchy is often able to obtain only a worm's eye view of strategy and consequently devotes a proportionately greater amount of time to everyday, operative issues. On the other hand, one might get a much more realistic picture of strategic and organizational changes at this level than is available to top management. Personnel belonging to *specialist units* such as personnel or market research departments are often not directly involved in the major decision-making processes, although they can occasionally play a key role in processes of change.

Large companies may have *in-house consultants* on their staff. Their methods of operation are the same as external consultants, although working with only one company does allow them to gain a better insight into the company's operations, its culture, and so forth. The boundary between in-house and external consultancy may well overlap. Long-term assignments would place the external consultant in a similar position to that of the in-house consultant. I have personally worked with major assignments in one large company for 10 years, and I am acquainted with a consultant who has worked about half-time for more than 30 years with the same client. Some in-house consultants also take on external assignments. I have come across consultants from SAS (Scandinavian Airlines) and General Electric in this role. In-house consultants may also work with companies that have been taken over and are therefore completely new to them.

There are substantial problems involved in combining the roles of academic researcher and company employee. The most common are insufficient time for scientific research and the development of a rather shortsighted perspective as a result of becoming too much a part of the system. The appointment of executives and specialists from industry as part-time professors is an effort to bring company employees into research and teaching. It requires, however, that these professors have a research background and also can make themselves available.

One question that sometimes creates conflicts concerns the actual identity of the researcher's/consultant's client. To whom do they primarily owe their loyalty? There are a number of possible candidates, including, among others, the board of directors, senior managers, the company's employees, an investor, a research grant foundation, or a research institute. Researchers/consultants may also see themselves as independent professional workers whose first loyalty is to their profession. This may be illustrated by reference to an example drawn from my own experience:

> An assignment had resulted in a large number of proposals for change. In the view of the consultant, several of these proposals that had received the backing of middle management could be implemented. The problem was to get the projects off the ground. In each and every case, the participation of the consultant proved to be essential because no one within the company had either the necessary competence or time to run the projects. At the middle-management level, the agreement on this was almost complete. The consultant had received his directives from the chief executive who had forced the consultant's presence on a divisional director who happened to be an elderly, conservative, authoritarian figure. About the same time, the chief executive had decided to give his divisional heads greater freedom and informed the consultant that he ought to discuss his future involvement in the company with the divisional director. Due to the strong support that the consultant received from the divisional director's management team, he was able to continue with his work. However, the actual implementation of the proposals for change were subject to considerable delay due to a general lack of commitment on the part of the divisional director. Although it was possible to get round the canceled meetings, the evasions, and the vague directives, this obstructiveness nevertheless led to inevitable delays and a watering down of the projects. The whole process was very cumbersome, and it became quite apparent that the implementation was going to take far too long.

Where should the loyalty lie in such a situation? It is up to researchers/consultants to use their own judgment and ethics to determine this from case to case. As a preventive measure, it is wise for them to have a "contract" with their client. I'm not referring to an elaborate legal document (even if that is likely to be increasingly essential, particularly in the United States) but to a "gentlemen's agreement." A successful consultant specializing in company turnarounds has stated that he will accept assignments only directly from a board of directors in order not to be dependent on the decisions taken by a chief executive or senior managers.[43]

Usually the consultant is hired by the board or by management. Some countries in Europe have *wage earner consultants*. Wage earner consultants are, through personnel and trade unions, assigned to look into the company and help the personnel to understand and become influential in a change process. The company is obliged to pay their fees.

As both a researcher and a consultant, I have gone through many different stages in my work on strategic and organizational projects. I have become increasingly dissatisfied with the role of analyst because it gives inadequate access. The idea underlying the project group approach is that analysts should not be working on their own but in tandem with the client staff who will subsequently take on responsibility for the project's implementation. It is an attractive idea, and it can work very well if there is management commitment and the projects are given enough status and priority. I have nevertheless experienced a number of disappointments when company employees consider the project a burden that adds to their daily workload, something for which there just isn't time.

OD approaches offered new opportunities to advance beyond the application of intellectual methods. The considerable promise that these approaches seemed to provide has been fulfilled to a limited degree. Access to information and individuals has been improved, and certain new insights have been obtained. The central thrust of these approaches—that the employees of the client company should gain insight into their own situation and take over responsibility for it—is often not achieved. The work involves exercises in interpersonal relationships that are designed to create a frank atmosphere in which individuals are encouraged to give vent to feelings and aggression. From my own experience, these exercises may either be of considerable value or lead absolutely nowhere. It has also proved particularly difficult to persuade senior executives to participate. A true management commitment—lip service is not enough—is required to create long- lasting effects.

The establishment of a close working relationship with senior executives, profit center managers, and other company staff is an essential part of a change agent's role. This requirement has, however, created problems that I have not always been able to deal with in a satisfactory manner. Close cooperation has proved to be particularly difficult in large companies. Heads of departments and other managers are short of time and frequently away on business trips; meetings are often too short, sometimes interrupted by the telephone or postponed. The contacts made are often too brief to allow the establishment of a personal relationship, particularly in the area in which such relationships are most valuable—namely, with the chief executive and the other senior executives. There is an obvious risk that the tentative relationship established will not be sufficiently robust to withstand the consideration of controversial issues.

To build up a close working relationship, researchers/consultants may find that they will have to be resident in the company, preferably working in the immediate vicinity of senior management, spending time together over lunch or coffee, staying on after 5 p.m. when the telephones have stopped ringing, arriving early, traveling together, meeting socially in the evening or on weekends in a restaurant or at someone's home. All of these various opportunities for contact increase access. It is essential that the researcher/consultant make use of these informal opportunities because the establishment of a close working relationship by purely formal contact gives inadequate access.

On one occasion, I received a vague directive from a chief executive "to do something about the company's marketing." It was agreed that I would have a couple of months to familiarize myself with the company, the industry, the people involved, and the general situation. One essential task was to diagnose and formulate the problems involved. This seems to me to be an ideal way to work with a company because one has the opportunity to proceed beyond simple stereotyped views, both one's own and those of others. It becomes possible to establish relationships and become accustomed to each other. Researchers/consultants sometimes encounter a considerable degree of suspicion, and in my view, this is quite warranted: "What do these people actually understand about us? What do they know about our industry?" Many employees have been on the receiving end of pretentious reports written by consultants and researchers. I worked for three to four days a week on the project and spent most of my time at the company's head office or at one of the other units. I had ample opportunity to make use of both formal and informal access without which it would not have been possible to work on the assignment. This is not to say that I was always satisfied with the access that I had. There is naturally also the question of one's own ambitions as well as mental and physical stamina.

It is equally important when working with processes of change that the company and its staff find it easy to establish contact with the change agent. Researchers/consultants depend on initiatives taken by others and consequently should try to make themselves both physically and psychologically accessible.

Contacts with trade unions may give rise to special problems. When working with a large company that has factories and offices in different parts of a country, numerous local union branches may well have to be involved. In addition, representatives from the central organizations of various unions may also be involved. Trade union representatives frequently lack insight into areas such as strategic change, which is one of the most advanced fields in management. The actual state of relations between company management and trade unions, between the various union branch organizations, and between local union branches and their central organization could have a great bearing on the work of the change agent.

In his memoirs, Hans Rudberg, a former chief executive of a major Scandinavian foundry, gave an account of his experience of consultants when the company ran into a crisis. A proposal compiled by a major international consulting firm stated the following:

> The role of the consultant is first and foremost that of project leader. Through active participation in the project, the consultants will take on responsibility for meeting the stated objectives. We intend to bring in several of our most qualified consultants who are well equipped to provide the practical solutions to the tasks confronting the company.[44]

The CEO reacted in the following manner:

> These words are characterized by both an underestimation of the difficulties involved and an enormous overestimation of their own competence! . . . However, I have also reflected on and admired the completed different methods employed by Ulf af Trolle in his work as a consultant. At first sight, it might seem that he was playing one-man theatre. The opposite is in fact the case. He goes into a company and either takes on the role of chief executive or places himself at his side. He chooses to work *with the people in the company with consideration for the company's own natural conditions.*

The consultant mentioned accepts assignments only in the capacity of management-for-hire, a role that he justifies as follows:

> In the normal case, I would define my position as that of a deputy chief executive with special responsibility for company organization and strategy. My integration into the company management team was usually eased by the fact that the company had also taken on a new chief executive at the same time. As a result of the large number of emergency tasks confronting the new chief executive, it has been natural to divide up these tasks into those concerned with current operations and those related to the restructuring of the

company. . . . My position as a temporary reinforcement of top management has allowed me to proceed rapidly with the work and has helped to eliminate the efficiency gap that normally affects the relationship between the advisory consultant and company management.[45]

The above account highlights the fulfillment of three conditions that other consultants who do not have the same strong position of superstar consultant may find less readily attainable. First, he has direct access to the decision-making processes within the company's top management. Second, he has secured the unconditional support of the chief executive. Third, the demand for his services and the fact that he does not have any employees allows him to choose between assignments, not being dependent on any particular client for his livelihood. Hence, he is not in the same position as that of large consultancy firms that need to secure a workload for a substantial number of consultants. This has given him considerable professional integrity.

The same consultant has also said, "My patient companies have certainly not lacked the services of management consultants. . . . It appears almost axiomatic to me . . . that companies that were in a situation such as that confronting Boras Wafveri, Bahco, Mecman, Fagersta and Coronaverken could not be saved by normal long-term consultancy measures."[46]

In my view, the roles of change agent and senior executive (employee or management-for-hire) provide the most comprehensive access to strategic and organizational issues. Although these roles provide access, it is another matter as to what use is made of this access or how one actually performs in these roles. Clark has stated that actual participation in the chain of events will give the researcher/consultant *privileged access* that will facilitate the development of both theory and practice.[47] This does not mean that the role of the researcher/consultant is clear-cut and devoid of problems. In the section on action science in Chapter 4 and in Chapters 5 and 6, we will examine conditions in which research can be carried out through the role of consultant and the requirements that have to be met for a researcher/consultant to be called an action scientist.

Why is greater use not being made of the researcher/consultant role in academic research to obtain improved access? One factor is the practical difficulty of finding consulting assignments that are suitable for scientific research. Another reason is the scientific paradigm, which governs research. We will return to this latter explanation in Chapter 5.

A negative view of the researcher/consultant role is expressed by Carlson. He distinguishes between observation studies and reading as two mutually dependent ways of developing as a researcher.[48] He mentions participation in the form of a participant observer acting as a board director,[49] although he does not mention action research:

> No, consultancy is about as dangerous for research as it is of benefit to teaching. Research demands repetition, precision and contemplation while consultancy requires a spontaneous creativity, ingenuity and boldness. It is not just the lack of time or opportunity during a consulting assignment to secure all the observations and measurements required to analyze the specific case. Due to time pressure, one is corrupted to produce rather slipshod reports, a habit which could have serious repercussions for the scientific quality of the work.[50]

This quotation illustrates some of the difficulties that the action scientist may encounter when endeavoring to combine the roles of researcher and consultant. Carlson also places considerable emphasis on the importance of the written report. This is the customary approach with regard to the traditional academic role and the role of consultant/analyst.[51] Clark explains the negative attitude to action research in the following terms:

> The failure to exploit privileged access when it has existed in the past may be attributed to the inappropriate model for the scientific

process which has dominated research in the social and behavioral sciences during the past forty years. The behavioral sciences have become increasingly concerned with their professional status in relation to other established scientific disciplines. Consequently they have emphasized that the behavioral sciences are in many respects like the natural sciences. It follows that the methods of investigating that are wrongly assumed to typify the natural sciences should be adopted. It was claimed that knowledge is unified, analytical, abstract and lawlike—provided the theoretical frameworks could be sorted out. In research there was a strong preference for the detached position and an increasing concern for the experimental situation.[52]

Hence researchers have avoided using their own personal experiences, for fear of not appearing to be objective. According to Clark, this has made it more difficult for action research to gain acceptance:

> It is more than likely that a genuine mistake has arisen whereby actual examples of action research are misunderstood because the activities, interactions, and values that are most evident to the literature-based researcher do not conform to the idealized model of research purveyed in much of undergraduate teaching. . . . few academics have direct experience of action research. . . . absence of direct experience means that the values of those involved in action research are inadequately understood.[53]

Summary

In discussing access, I presented and illustrated my view of the concept of access. When dealing with processes of decision making, implementation, and change, it is essential to establish satisfactory access, and awareness of the access problem seems to be low. The next section dealt with the various roles in which the researcher/consultant could become involved. The possibilities for access associated with these roles were discussed. I concluded that the role of change agent created substantial opportunities for access and that it might open up useful research possibilities. The combination of researcher and change agent is known as action research or action science. This role/method has been used on only a limited scale in the scientific study of business firms. This is partly explained by the significant difficulties associated with the combination of the roles of researcher and consultant. The problems and potential of action science will be examined at greater length in Chapters 4, 5, and 6. Prior to that discussion, Chapter 3 will deal with the concepts of preunderstanding and understanding.

Notes

1. For an overview of the Fermenta case, see Kapstein, 1987; for a thorough analysis, see Sundqvist, 1987, and El-Sayed and Hamilton, 1989.
2. Geneen, 1984, p. 18.
3. According to a discussion with Professor Takahiro Miyao in Stockholm, November 1986.
4. Whitley, 1984, p. 375.
5. Warneryd, 1985, p. 11.
6. Henderson, 1984/85, p. 11.
7. This approach is similar to that employed by McGivern and Fineman, 1983, in their study of sixty-six British researchers and consultants.
8. Brown et al., 1976.
9. Ibid., pp. 7-36.
10. Ibid., pp. 11-13.
11. Ibid., p. 15.
12. Ibid., pp. 12-14 and 21-36.
13. Taylor and Bogdan, 1984, pp. 20-25.
14. Ibid., pp. 28-30.
15. Kulka, 1982, p. 50.
16. Taylor and Bogdan, 1984, pp. 20-27.
17. Barnes, 1977, p. 8.
18. Ortmark, 1985, pp. 133-38.
19. Blanchard and Johnson, 1984, p. 110.
20. See, for example, Schein, 1969, pp. 4-9.
21. Tilles, 1961, pp. 90-91.
22. Schein, 1969, p. 6.
23. Ibid., pp. 134-35.
24. Ibid., pp. 7 and 103.

25. McGivern and Fineman, 1983, p. 429, use the term "contingent consultancy" in an effort to get away from the notion that there is one definite best way of working as consultant. Asplund and Asplund, 1982, advocate a view that integrates the process and the expert consultant.

26. Other ways of presenting consultant roles are proposed by Hildebrandt, 1980; Johnsen, 1980, pp. 11-17; Lindberg, 1982, pp. 25-28; McGivern and Fineman, 1983; and Schein, 1995.

27. OD is treated by, for example, Beckhard, 1969; Kolb and Frohman, 1970; Fordyce and Weil, 1971; French and Bell, 1978; French, Bell, and Zawacki, 1978; Kotter, 1978; Beer, 1980.

28. French and Bell, 1978, p. 46.

29. Argyris, 1970, 1985, 1990; Argyris and Schon, 1974, 1978; Argyris, Putnam, and Smith, 1985; Schein, 1969; Schon, 1983.

30. Calder, 1977, pp. 357-58.

31. Ibid., p. 357.

32. See, for example, Dichter, 1979.

33. Imai, 1986, describes the way the Japanese engage everybody in continuing improvements of quality and productivity; Townsend, 1990, describes the way groups, quality teams, are used for the same purpose in an American service company.

34. Taylor, 1911. See also Tisdall, 1982, pp. 14-30, for a brief description of the origins of modern management consultancy.

35. See Kaplan and Norton, 1996; Edvinsson and Malone, 1997.

36. Argyris, 1970, p. viii and p. 2.

37. Ouchi, 1981.

38. Peters and Waterman, 1982, pp. 9-11.

39. French and Bell, 1978, pp. 16-18. Clark, 1972, p. 65, is against the use of the term "change agent" because "it is possible for change to arise from a variety of sources and to be planned or unplanned." Beer, 1980, p. 9, discriminates between clinical methods in which researchers attempt to minimize their influence and intervention methods in which they are not restricted.

40. McGivern and Fineman, 1983, p. 427.

41. Statskontoret, 1980, p. 112. See also Greiner and Metzger, 1983.

42. af Trolle, 1979, pp. 28-38.

43. Ibid., pp. 28-38.

44. Rudberg, 1979, p. 219.

45. af Trolle, 1975, p. 1053.

46. Ibid., p. 1052.

47. Clark, 1972, pp. 125-28.

48. Carlson, 1983, p. 13.

49. Ibid., pp. 160-61 and 173-77.

50. Ibid., pp. 139-40.

51. See, e.g., Lindberg, 1982, p. 47, who says, "The result of a consulting assignment must always be documented in a written report."

52. Clark, 1972, pp. 126-27.

53. Ibid., p. 126.

Three

Taking Off and Landing: The Route from Preunderstanding to Understanding

Preunderstanding refers to things such as people's knowledge, insights, and experience before they engage in a research program or a consulting assignment; *understanding* refers to their improved insights emerging during the program or assignment. I have classified this as the researcher's/consultant's Number 2 problem.

In my assessment, academic researchers give insufficient consideration to the significance of preunderstanding in choosing their scientific approach and methods. The purpose of this chapter is to examine the concepts of *preunderstanding* and *understanding* in greater detail.

The first section discusses positive and negative aspects of preunderstanding. In the next section, two types of preunderstanding and understanding are presented: firsthand, through personal experience, and secondhand, through intermediaries. A brief discussion on the role of insights and personal attributes takes place in the third section, and the final section is a summary of my conclusions.

Preunderstanding: Aid or Hindrance?

Odman defines preunderstanding in the following terms: "In response to frequent or everyday occurrences, individuals have developed a *preunderstanding* in order to avoid having to bother themselves with the interpretation of these events. Sense impressions, interpretation, understanding and language merge instantaneously, making it impossible to identify separate phases."[1]

A lack of preunderstanding will cause the researcher/consultant to spend considerable time gathering basic information (e.g., about an industry or the decision-making process). Most of this information will not be obtainable outside a company. Thus, the researcher/consultant will have to become familiar with the actual processes of decision making, implementation, and change within a specific organization. For this reason, I consider it vital for academic researchers to have personal experience from a position in which they were responsible for making and implementing decisions.

My interest in the concept of preunderstanding began with an essay written by the Swedish novelist and Texas philosophy professor Lars Gustafsson, titled "Knowledge behind the Words."[2] He starts by quoting from the Encyclopedia Britannica's description of a tennis serve:

> Stand behind the base line with your feet at an angle of about 45deg to the line. Drop your weight back on your right foot. Toss the ball well above your head and slightly to the right in advance of it. Swing your racket up and forward with one rhythmic movement, at the same time shifting the weight forward toward the left foot. Meet the ball as high above your head as you can comfortably reach. The racket face is outside, or on the right side of the ball, and

slightly over it. It travels from right to left. Swing directly through this, imparting a twist to the ball to spin it from left to right. This tends to hold the ball in court.[3]

Gustafsson continues:

> Read this passage again! It is undoubtedly written by a leading expert. It contains absolutely nothing incorrect or misleading.
>
> I can picture a little fat boy wearing thick-set glasses who has learned the definition by heart and then wanders out to the base line.
>
> He will discover of course that the perfect combination of body movements, that rare double rowing-stroke in invisible water which in 0.61 seconds sends a Connors, Bjorn Borg or Kenny Rosewall serve into the far corner of his opponent's service area is more than just a series of exercise movements. The knowledge that underlies the ability to execute a perfect tennis serve is quite different from the knowledge acquired from the encyclopedia definition. It is knowledge that exists in the back, arms, feet, a message that is sent to the dark side of consciousness where there are no words. It is something that one simply allows to happen. Life is full of this type of knowledge.[4]

Sir David Nicholson, former chairman of London-based P-E Consulting Group, claims that management consultants cannot understand the problems of strategic and structural change unless they have practical experience of running a company.[5] A lawyer once told me about the judge who often presided in traffic cases. This judge did not have a driver's license, and moreover, he did not know how to drive a car. I thought this peculiar. How could he understand the behavior of those involved in a car accident? "Would you require the judge of a murder case to be himself a murderer," replied the lawyer. This poses a dilemma. Probably a judge with firsthand experience of not only one but several assassinations would better understand a murder case. On the other hand, we would not trust him in court. In his amusing biography,

Frank Abingdale,[6] a master imposter who finally got caught, tells about his life in jail and his plans for a life when he would be released. One of his tricks had been to forge checks, and he was aware of the weak points in banking systems. During his time in jail, he started out as a consultant to banks on security, advising them on how to stop bad checks. This later became his profession. He had gained his knowledge through direct experience and involvement.

It has become increasingly apparent to me that the central role played by experience in the development of understanding and insight is a frequently recurrent theme among philosophers, authors, and others. For instance, the former Chinese leader Mao Tse-Tung has stated that if "we want to know how a pear tastes, we must change the pear by eating it ourselves."[7] I also recall a popular song of the 1950s, sung by Louis Armstrong and Ella Fitzgerald, called "Can Anyone Explain?" This, of course, is a singularly appropriate question for researchers and consultants. The song is about the kiss, and it concludes that you don't know what a kiss is until you have experienced it yourself.

Philosopher Bertrand Russell[8] deals with the problem of understanding with the aid of the concepts *knowledge by description* and *knowledge by acquaintance*. Research and education in management take place largely by means of description and not by acquaintance. This represents a weakness that receives scant attention in the theoretical and methodological literature of management.

The term *preunderstanding* is used in a wider sense than just *knowledge;*[9] preunderstanding also implies a certain *attitude* and a *commitment* on the part of researchers/consultants. It involves their *personal experience* as an essential element in the process of collecting and analyzing information. Moreover, researchers/consultants must demonstrate *theoretical sensitivity*[10] and be able to change their paradigm—their basic worldview—if reality requires them to do so. The researcher/consultant would thus be able to generate new concepts, new models, and new theory.

In psychology, the term *selective perception* is used to indicate an individual's propensity to perceive only selected parts of reality.

Hence, in the context of the academic researcher or management consultant, the problems confronting a company may be viewed through different glasses that restrict the field of vision to certain phenomena. This may be illustrated by an example that shows how different types of consultants reacted to a company's insufficient profitability:[11]

> *The advertising agency:* "You must improve your advertising, thereby securing increased sales volume."
>
> *The marketing research institute:* "You must know your market better. Only then can you direct your marketing efforts properly and increase sales."
>
> *The management consultant specializing in cost reduction:* "You should be able to lower your salary costs by 15% through new order entry routines."
>
> *The management consultant specializing in corporate strategy:* "The long-term objectives of your company concerning products, markets, and growth must be explicitly stated."
>
> *The business lawyer specializing in tax problems:* "The legal structure of your firm is not optimal from the taxation point of view."

Selectivity is essential when we are confronted with an overwhelming mass of stimuli. Theories, models, checklists, and so forth help to select both the phenomena to be studied and the phenomena to be excluded. The danger is a belief that one has selected what is of general relevance and that one has observed all that is required to be seen.

Creativity philosopher Edward de Bono has put forward the concept of *lateral thinking* as opposed to *vertical thinking*. He says that it is

> not possible to dig a hole in a different place by digging the same hole deeper. Logic is the tool that is used to dig deep holes deeper and bigger, to make them altogether better holes. But if the hole is in the wrong place, then no amount of improvement is going to put it in the right place. No matter how obvious this may seem to every digger, it is still easier to go on digging in the same hole than to start

all over again in a new place. Vertical thinking is digging the same hole deeper; lateral thinking is trying again elsewhere.[12]

The term *blocked preunderstanding*[13] refers to knowledge and approaches that are selective because they are closely associated with a specific paradigm and the theories, models, and procedures that emanate from this paradigm. Knowledge may be detailed and comprehensive but still function as a prejudice: One continues to dig in the same hole; one becomes an *expert ad absurdum*. In trying to force reality into received theory, reality becomes distorted rather than explained.

Mythology provides us with relevant metaphors. One behaves like Cinderella's wicked stepmother who cuts a toe off of one of her daughters and a heel off of the other so that their feet might fit Prince Charming's shoe. In Greek legend, a robber called Procrustes had an iron bed, known as "Procrustes's bed." He had the unpleasant habit of forcing his victims to lie on the bed, demanding that they fit perfectly. If they happened to be too tall, Procrustes cut their feet off; if they were too short, he had them stretched.[14]

Science that is guilty of such behavior is called *procrustean science*. This refers to the misuse of established and acknowledged theories, concepts, and models for formulating hypotheses to be tested through empirical research. When such hypotheses are used as a point of departure in research, they govern the way questions are asked and the way answers and other observations are interpreted. Thus, they allow certain data to be included while excluding others; they allow certain ways of processing the data, rejecting others. The consequence is that of Procrustes's bed; what does not fit is cut off and excluded, maybe not even noted, and what does fit may be stretched to fill a larger space than it is suited for. Procrustean science limits the scope for innovation and development; it preserves the status quo.

Glaser and Strauss warn especially of the risk of being biased by existing theories:

Many of our teachers converted departments of sociology into mere repositories of "great man" theories and taught these the-

ories with a charismatic finality that students could seldom resist.
. . . some theories of our predecessors . . . do not fit, or do not work,
or are not sufficiently understandable to be used and are therefore
useless in research, theoretical advance and practical application.[15]

Glaser has further stressed this in a book subtitled *Emergence vs.
Forcing.*[16] He points to the necessity of letting reality have a say on
its own terms. The researcher must not force preconceived categories and concepts on reality, even if these are well established in
extant theory. An example from business and economics is the
ubiquitous comparison between nations of consumption, productivity, and industrial development. Nation-states, however,
may not be meaningful categories for comparison.[17] Today's economic activity, rather, develops in regions and cultures, irrespective of nation-state borders. One example is the industrialized and
rich northern Italy and the agricultural and poor southern Italy.
Economically, northern Italy belongs to the mid-European industrial regions, southern Italy to North Africa. Furthermore, Terza
Italia (the third Italy) in the middle has based its wealth on small
businesses functioning through families and networks in a similar way to Asian traditional businesses such as the Chinese
guanxies.[18] Averaged data from these three regions provide no
meaningful information for comparing Italy's economic health
with that of other nations. Another example is large multination-
als who deal with global segments of, for example, teenager life-
styles. Communications factors such as increased traveling, the
Internet, mobile phones, satellite TV, and global branding—
McDonald's, Disney, Coca-Cola, Microsoft—have made certain
types of teenager consumer behavior borderless.

The emergence-versus-forcing issue can also be described as
inductive versus *deductive* research. Deductive research starts with
existing theories and concepts and formulates hypotheses that are
subsequently tested; its vantage point is received theory. Inductive research starts with real-world data, and categories, concepts,
patterns, models, and eventually, theories emerge from this input.
(I prefer to use the expression "real-world data" and hesitate to
talk about "empirical data" because this term has acquired the

meaning of quantitative data in business school research. Originally, the Greek word *empeiria* meant "knowledge based on experience and observation"—that is, all data emerging from real-world situations.)

In practice, only the starting point for research separates deductive and inductive research—but this is a very significant distinction. Deductive research primarily tests existing theory, whereas inductive research primarily generates new theory. The fear is sometimes expressed that inductive research will reinvent the wheel. This is unwarranted. Only bad inductive research will work that way—but so will bad deductive research by just producing more of the same and already accepted "knowledge."

After the initial stages, all types of research become an iteration between the deductive and the inductive. This is sometimes referred to as *abductive* research.[19] The term may be useful to stress the combination, but it is misleading if perceived as a third type of approach. For example, grounded theory research starts inductively, but Glaser and Strauss would not characterize their methodology as either inductive or deductive.[20]

Academic researchers who profess to a certain paradigm are certainly engaged in digging the same hole deeper—that is, testing and modifying existing theories, models, concepts, and categories. Interesting research undoubtedly can emerge within this framework. Unless the researchers are on their guard, however, their preunderstanding may act to block innovative thinking.

During an American Marketing Association conference on attitude research, a speaker requested more "hypothesis-free research" and said that the "scientific method as we use it usually consists of testing hypotheses. However hypothesis formation often reflects the biases of the researchers and marketers—the research that is done then reflects the bias built in by the hypothesis."[21] Glaser and Strauss even suggest that "an effective strategy is, at first, literally to ignore the literature of theory and fact on the area under study."[22] Even Sherlock Holmes warns his assistant Dr. Watson against bias in "A Scandal in Bohemia."[23] When Dr.

Watson exclaims, "This is indeed a mystery . . . What do you imagine it means?" Holmes replies, "I have no data yet. It is a capital mistake to theorize before one has data. Insensibly one begins to twist facts to suit theories instead of theories to suit facts."

In contrast, others seem to advocate a directly opposite view. According to Carlson, "The more advanced knowledge that one has of the area under study, the greater the potential value of a study visit or an interview."[24] Economist and Nobel Prize winner Tjalling C. Koopmans claims that "fuller utilization of the concepts and hypotheses of economic theory . . . *as part of the process of observation and measurement* promises to be a shorter road, perhaps even the only possible road, to understanding."[25]

Maybe these quotations are not contradictory after all. If we claim that scientists should have preunderstanding but also that they should have the innocent mind of a child when searching for data, we may end up populating our business schools with a bunch of schizophrenic professors. We should not require split personalities but rather dual personalities: Those who are able to balance on the razor's edge *use their preunderstanding but are not its slave.*

Capra uses Taoism to explain this: "The Chinese philosophers saw reality, whose ultimate essence they call Tao, as a process of continual flow and change" and "gave this idea of cyclical patterns a definite structure by introducing the polar opposites yin and yang. . . . It is important, but very difficult for us Westerners, to understand that these opposites do not belong to different categories but are extreme poles of a single whole." Neither is associated with moral values: "What is good is not yin or yang but the dynamic balance between the two; what is bad or harmful is imbalance."[26] So it is a matter of "both-and" instead of "either-or." We could probably say that sticking to established and accepted knowledge is yin and ignoring it and letting our mind freely expand in any direction is yang and that the ideal state should be an oscillation between the two.

Management consultants often exhibit blocked preunderstanding when churning out existing models and checklists irrespective of the nature of the problem. It may be a question of solving all of the problems by means of, for example, customer satisfaction surveys, computerized information systems, standardized training packages, or business process reengineering. An example of how fashion can act as a blocking mechanism was mentioned previously. Later on, we will discuss the importance of being able to devote time to diagnosis, for formulation of the problem, and the choice of approaches and methods. It is quite conceivable that researchers may choose to work with a certain type of theory and methodology rather than adopt too many different approaches. At the same time, they may consistently work on problems to which their standardized approaches are well suited and stay away from other kinds of problems. Hence, blocked preunderstanding relates to the consistent application by researchers/consultants of their favorite preconceptions in the belief that they have universal validity.

Someone has said that "for he who has a hammer, every problem is a nail." In this spirit, we may call the use of a single, packaged solution to multiple types of problems a case of the *hammer-and-nail syndrome*.[27] The consultants' preunderstanding and their models and methods are assets as long as they sell their services solely in situations in which they match a current client problem. There is a risk that the commercial side of consultancy will predominate with the result that they "milk the client," leaving questions of professionalism far down the list of priorities. By the same token, there is a risk that the academic researcher's first priority will be to exploit opportunities for research funding.

Hence, it is essential that preunderstanding be subject to change, that researchers/consultants be aware of paradigm, selective perception, and their own personal defense mechanisms. Moreover, they must also take into account the fact that their own possible insecurity or other personality factors may influence their development. Obviously, the researcher/consultant must be mature, open, and honest.

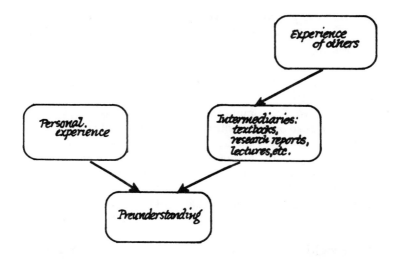

Figure 3.1. Sources for Preunderstanding

Preunderstanding, Firsthand and Secondhand

Figure 3.1 shows factors that contribute to the growth of preunderstanding. The individual's *own personal experience* from both private and working life is shown on the left-hand side of the figure. The knowledge that has been obtained via *intermediaries* appears on the right-hand side of the figure. The combination of one's own and other people's experiences constitutes a store of knowledge that represents the individual's preunderstanding at the start of a research project or a consulting assignment.

The traditional researcher's preunderstanding is primarily formed on the right-hand side of Figure 3.1—that is, on the basis of the experience of others, which is communicated through books, lectures, and so forth; this is knowledge by description, to use Russell's terminology. To emphasize clearly the difference between knowledge based on the individual's own experiences and knowledge based on the experience of others, I will use the terms preunderstanding—and understanding—*firsthand* and *secondhand*.

Secondhand preunderstanding has positive features and negative features. The positive features are summarized by Russell in the following manner:

> The chief importance of knowledge by description is that it enables us to pass beyond the limits of our private experience. In spite of the fact that we can only know truths which are wholly composed of terms which we have experienced in acquaintance, we can yet have knowledge by description of things which we have never experienced. In view of the very narrow range of our immediate experience, this result is vital, and until it is understood, much of our knowledge must remain mysterious and therefore doubtful.[28]

This would apply, for instance, to a process of change within a large multinational company. Actually to experience this process in terms of both time (over several years) and space (from the reactions of management down as well as from the parent company to subsidiaries and other representatives in, say, fifty countries) is impossible. Nor are we able to turn the clock back and experience what has already occurred.

IBM's unprecedented success during more than half a century is often attributed to continuous employee training and education: "There is no saturation point in education."[29] At IBM, learning through intermediaries was coupled with personal experience. The instructors were selected from among the most successful sales and systems people but only for a period of 18 to 24 months and as part of a career plan.[30] When personal computers, software, and services became more important than IBM's traditional core products, hardware and mainframes, a new situation occurred. IBM had to rethink and redirect its efforts, a turnaround process that involved double-loop learning and a new type of training and education.

The negative aspects of learning through intermediaries include the risk of misunderstanding or only superficially grasping the information communicated by others or of being forced to accept incorrect information. Geneen states,

As a public accountant . . . I was given all the time that I needed to check the books or the inventory. I spent days in counting the coal bins for one company and then certified the "fact" that there were so many filled coal bins, so many tons of coal. As I rose to comptroller, I had to rely upon the veracity of someone else's audit. When I became president of ITT, I had to rely on hundreds of different reports, full of "facts" and the decisions that I had to make were crucial.[31]

Consequently, the more important his conclusions became, the less opportunity he had to make sure that the "facts" were right. The same applies to consultants and academic researchers who build on others' reports and statistical calculations. How close to reality have they come?

British historian Paul Johnson,[32] in analyzing the "heartless lovers of humankind," gives examples of people—among them many intellectuals—who represented strong beliefs and ideas but had no intention of getting acquainted with them through personal experience. Karl Marx inherited considerable sums of money and never had less than two servants. He was a ruthless exploiter of his family and friends, among them the socialist philosopher Friedrich Engels. He "was unwilling to do any on-the-spot investigating himself," and he never visited a factory; he had to rely solely on written reports and other types of knowledge through intermediaries. "Lenchen [the family maid] was the only member of the working class that Marx ever knew at all well"; she became his mistress and gave birth to their child. Marx never paid her a cent and tried to persuade Engels to acknowledge the child as his. Stalin never endeavored to find out what the ordinary citizen wanted but was an enthusiastic consumer of statistics. Lenin was a library socialist—"an embodied theory"—who never set foot in a factory until he became the Soviet leader.

Karl Marx used to classify his own work as scientific and call his enemies unscientific. Recent history reveals the disastrous effects of the ideas of Marx, Lenin, and Stalin; reality has caught up with them, and their "theories"—deductions based on secondhand knowledge—have been invalidated.

There is considerable scope for misunderstanding information received through intermediaries. For instance, I never distribute a consultancy report until after I have had an opportunity to present its contents to the client face-to-face. One author recommends the "exhaustive" approach: "An overall appraisal of the case study shouldn't be the prerogative of the researchers and the actors. If the reader is going to have a chance to participate in the interpretation of the report, the case study will have to be presented in its entirety."[33]

It is undoubtedly important to provide a comprehensive and rich description of a case study, although I don't believe it is possible to replace the individual's own experience with that of a report that has passed between two levels of intermediaries. It is, however, a way of diminishing the disadvantages of secondhand knowledge.

Furthermore, the researcher runs the risk of entering the *vicious circle of academic research* where researchers quote each other, have the "right" references, publish articles in the "right" journals, and present papers at the "right" conferences. It takes on the form of *distance research*[34] that has only a limited contact with the actual subject of the research—for example, through a database. This type of research assumes that one is able to simulate change processes at the research institution, something that is clearly not possible.

Figure 3.2 illustrates the *development of understanding* in relation to a specific project. Researchers/consultants approach a project with a certain preunderstanding. By means of access as participants in a process, they are able to gain certain insights of their own. At the same time, they possess the methods that allow them to analyze and interpret the experiences of others. In scientific theory, reference is made to the *hermeneutic circle* that can be illustrated by the following statements: "no understanding without preunderstanding" and "an understanding of the parts assumes an understanding of the whole." The hermeneutic circle more accurately ought to be called the *hermeneutic spiral*.[35] It is an iterative process whereby each stage of our research provides us with knowledge; in other words, we take a different level of preunderstanding to each stage of the research (Figure 3.3).

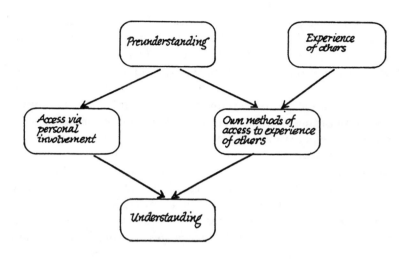

Figure 3.2. Sources for Understanding

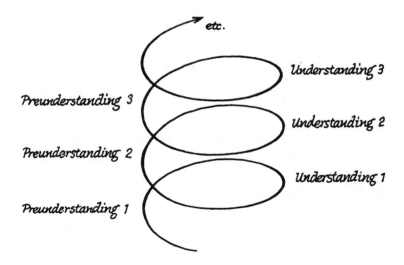

Figure 3.3. The Hermeneutic Spiral

The relationship between preunderstanding and understanding is influenced by our conscious as well as unconscious *intentionality*. Is our objective to undertake research into phenomena of considerable scientific interest? Or are we trying to find an opportune means of reaching a more senior academic post? Or is the consultant trying to earn as much money as possible ("I am in the invoicing industry," as one consultant has put it)? Or is it a mixture of all of these intentions—and others? Intentionality affects our selective perception and our path along the hermeneutic spiral. Bergstrom and Soderman[36] assume that *integrity* characterizes the academic researcher, whereas *efficiency* is typical of the consultant. They also discuss the desirability of bringing integrity and efficiency together to form a greater degree of professionalism among both academic researchers and management consultants. They consider, however, that professionalism is obstructed by certain malignant features of the working environment. The academic environment stimulates the growth of "esoteric" researcher types ("overgrown schoolboys who are difficult to understand and whose contacts are limited to a small group of the already initiated"), while the consultant's environment encourages prostitution ("short-term revenue, neglected long-term development").

Knowledge and Personal Attributes

This section will be concerned with the influence of knowledge and personal attributes on preunderstanding. Although there exists a rich literature on epistemology—the theory of knowledge—and psychology, I have chosen to rely on my own experience in this section. This is summarized in Table 3.1.

1. General Knowledge of Theories. Theories, including concepts, models, and approaches, help us to identify, diagnose, define, and analyze major factors and relationships. Consequently, we are better able to provide context and structure to a given situation and at the same time be well placed to convey this understanding

TABLE 3.1 Types of Knowledge and Personal Attributes

Type	Content
General knowledge	1. Theories, models, concepts 2. Techniques, methods, tools
Specific knowledge	3. Institutional conditions 4. Social patterns
Personal attributes	5. Intuition, creativity, vitality, social ability

to others. Above all, this is a question of intellectual understanding, and the researcher is well endowed in this respect; after all, this is the primary concern of a university training and a scientific environment.

2. General Knowledge of Techniques. This type of knowledge comprises techniques, methods, and actual tools of operation, such as the use of computer programs. The type of knowledge required to plan, implement, analyze, and report a mail survey of consumer opinion would fall into this category. So would the use of key indicators to assess a company's financial performance or the ability to plan and carry out sales calls. In the absence of this knowledge, operations will be time-consuming and lack focus. Academic researchers may have a certain amount of training in the use of techniques and above all can develop these skills in their projects.

3. Specific Knowledge of Institutional Conditions. This category comprises knowledge of technical conditions, customary practice, key decision makers, and other specific mechanisms and factors relating to a particular industry, company, market, product, service, and so forth. McKenna tells the story of Tektronix, manufacturer of electronic instrumentation, that hired MBAs to make the firm more marketing oriented: "They came to Tektronix armed with charts and theories, but they only made matters worse. They had no understanding of the peculiarities of the electronic-instrumentation business and they never made much effort to learn."[37] This quotation illustrates the MBAs' lack of institutional preunderstanding and their consequent difficulty in getting access to essential information. It illustrates the hammer-and-nail syndrome; a reliance on methods that were not applicable to the reality with which they were confronted. Institutional knowledge enlivens the models and techniques and allows them to be applied to a particular company or industry. This is a highly detailed type of knowledge that is acquired mainly through experience. The knowledge of a particular industry that can be acquired by an external researcher is limited to structural data and other fairly generalized types of information. Researchers try to come to grips with a problem on the basis of theories, models, and general techniques, whereas the practitioner approaches the problem from an institutional standpoint.

4. *Specific Knowledge of Social Patterns.* Each company creates its own cultural value system of rules (often tacit) of cooperation, social intercourse, communication, and so forth. There exist social relationships between colleagues that can be friendly, indifferent, or antagonistic; there are informal hierarchies and networks, and different types of personalities. It is indeed very difficult for researchers/consultants to gain a deeper understanding of the social patterns within a company that is new to them. The preunderstanding that researchers/consultants bring to a company is based on experience acquired in many different environments, both professional and private. This experience has enabled them to develop a certain receptivity to signals in the social environment and to patterns of behavior. Each particular assignment, however, requires specific knowledge that can be acquired only over a period of time. The only means by which this can be achieved is to actually spend time in the company. It is essential for the researcher/consultant to develop an understanding of the company's specific culture both in relation to institutional conditions and to patterns of behavior within its institutional constraints. The researcher/consultant will also want to gain insight into the opportunities available for changing the company's insti-

tutional environment. The researchers' ability to gain access will depend to a considerable extent on whether or not they succeed in establishing good personal rapport. The theories and techniques used by the researchers will have to be adapted to the company's own environment. That they have to be adapted to the intellectual and analytic characteristics of a problem may be well understood (except for cases of the hammer-and-nail syndrome), but there is equally a need to adapt the models and techniques to the social code.[38]

5. *Personal Attributes.* In addition, consideration must be given to the personality of the researcher/consultant, which in many instances will prove to be of decisive importance to the outcome of the assignment. Personal characteristics such as intuition, creativity, vitality, and human understanding are essential for the change agent. They work in conjunction with the four types of knowledge and may support or impede their implementation.

In my view, these types of preunderstanding, knowledge, and personal characteristics are essential to fully understand processes in an organization. The problems confronting the change agent are not solely a matter of intellectual awareness of theories and techniques. Knowledge of institutional conditions and social environment (points 3 and 4 above) are not as easily accessible and consequently do not present the same opportunities for advance preparation. Specialization in a particular industry considerably simplifies the acquisition of institutional knowledge. A preunderstanding of things such as particular products, customers, and distribution channels allows the consultant to concentrate on the company itself and its specific social pattern.

Process consultancy may be seen in part as a means of getting around the problem of preunderstanding. One of the assumptions underlying the process consultant's method of operation has been expressed as follows by Schein: "A consultant could probably not, without exhaustive and time-consuming study, learn enough about the culture of the organization to suggest reliable new courses of action. Therefore, he must work jointly with members of the organization who *do* know the culture intimately from having lived within it."[39] No demands are actually made here with respect to expertise in business and knowledge of institutional conditions; the consultant is solely concerned with releasing the client's own understanding.

As was pointed out in Chapter 2, my own experience tells me that process measures often lack in impact. This can be illustrated by two examples. The first is drawn from my experience of an assignment in the computer industry and the following presentation made at a marketing strategy conference:

> The TXD concept is planned to be introduced on the market in the spring and is expected to move into an expansionary phase when the DDP system has become firmly established on the market. The 110 series (which is part of TXD) is not compatible with the equipment of other suppliers. However, the development of standardized modems, particularly for Ethernet, is expected, at least in the long run, to improve the compatibility of TXD products with these and other standardized modems. The actual TXD concept would not appear in itself to have any major advantage sufficient to allow it to secure a market share. It is feasible that certain special applications would provide it with advantages in some sectors—for example, in banking. The primary factor that would give us a competitive advantage in the market for DDP and office automation equipment would appear to be the following: A total concept for DDP *and* office automation using the same hardware and offering opportunities for cost-effective link-ups with advanced communication systems such as the new generation of digital PABXs.

Here the researcher/consultant is confronted with the need to learn the terminology, acronyms, and technical relationships. This takes time and cannot normally be achieved through textbooks.

The other example is my personal account of a meeting in which a chief executive introduced a team of consultants and proceeded to talk about the work ahead:

> At the first meeting that I attended, the chief executive presented his thoughts concerning the changes that needed to be made in the company. He did this in a most stimulating and informative manner. To assist with this task, he had engaged a team of consultants.

The divisional director A, who was both oldest and head of the largest division, smiled and nodded in agreement with the chief executive's proposal. Several comments were made on the proposal. For example, B, who had just been promoted to divisional director, stated that he thought that it was important that the divisions now be left in peace to get on with their work, undisturbed by organizational changes. In his view, the company had gone through a long period of uncertainty and it was now a question of "full steam ahead." The chief executive replied that B should of course proceed at full speed but pointed out that he expected B to give his loyal support to the necessary measures that may have to be taken for the company as a whole. Moreover, he stressed that unless the company was able to break even within two years, there was a considerable risk of redundancies, and in the worst event, of a closure. The others present remained silent and it was impossible to know what they were thinking. Afterwards everyone quickly disappeared to their rooms.

In the absence of a knowledge of the individuals concerned and their social relationships, it is not possible to interpret the silence at the meeting. Did the chief executive exert his authority over his divisional heads by inviting in a team of consultants? Did Divisional Director A agree, or was he simply anxious to express loyalty. Would he also prove to be loyal when it came to action? What was the significance of B's statement and the chief executive's reply? The questions can be posed and speculations can be made regarding the answers, but there are no shortcuts to an understanding of the social interplay within a company.

I have worked on several long-term strategic and organizational projects (one to two years) within the transportation, textile, computer, and telecommunications industries. A principal difficulty has been a lack of preunderstanding of the products, services, and particular cultures that prevail in these industries and companies. In the academic research I undertook into the marketing of professional business services,[40] I had a considerable preunderstanding of the mechanisms that operate in relation to marketing, purchasing, and implementation of certain management consultancy services. I had acquired this knowledge both through study and experience. In addition, I had worked as a consultant to two advertising agencies, had been involved in producing advertising campaigns myself, and had also been a client of advertising agencies. Although my preunderstanding of the conditions under which advertising agencies operate was considerable at the outset of the research project, I was still not altogether satisfied. In one assignment, where I worked with a firm of consulting engineers within the building and construction industry, I had only a superficial knowledge of the industry's specific characteristics, such as technology, purchasing procedures, pricing, and the engineers' value systems. In the research project, I carried out a number of case studies on the marketing and purchasing of consultancy services based on interviews with both buyers and sellers. After the completion of the project, I worked an average of one day a week for about three years with one of the largest building consultants. The assignments were concerned with training in marketing and also to a certain extent with strategy and organization. Access was obtained through written reports and interviews and through project work as well as through the role of catalyst and discussion partner. These methods did not give me an understanding for building consultancy that made me feel entirely satisfied. I would have liked to have established a closer, more intimate relationship with the industry.

Preunderstanding can be illustrated by means of some further quotations from Rudberg's memoirs. On the subject of consultants, he says that "they frequently got hold of the wrong end of the stick."[41] He makes the following comments on Beijerinvest's takeover of his foundry:

What did Wall [the buyer's CEO] know about the company for which he was taking over responsibility, what should he know, and what is he able to know? He was almost certainly acquainted with the contents of the accounting firm's report. . . . He was himself without any type of knowledge regarding the reality with which he was now confronted.[42]

. . . [He had] an unfamiliarity with the complicated conditions of heavy industry. An inability to penetrate the concrete reality with which he was now confronted. An amateur's belief that standard methods of financial control, which may be well suited to trading corporations, wholesalers, and conglomerates like Beijerinvest itself, automatically will lead in the right direction. A lack of awareness, perhaps not so much of his own incompetence but of the disastrous consequences to which it could lead.[43]

Certified public accountants had been commissioned to analyze the long-term prospects of the foundry. This was secondhand knowledge, collected with the aid of annual reports, internal documents, and interviews with the chairman of the board, the present and past chief executives, and the present and past directors of finance.[44] For the reader of the report, it became thirdhand understanding.

Rudberg also describes how a person with substantial specialist experience and firsthand preunderstanding of the industrial manufacturing process was called into the company:

> Alde Nilsson's visit was quickly arranged. He visited the company on a couple of occasions and offered invaluable advice. Naturally his experienced eye was quickly able to establish where the shoe was pinching. The production flow was functioning properly. Alde expressed the problem in more or less the following terms. In any well balanced production system, there should always be a pull from the final stages of the production process. This pull should be felt throughout the entire production process. It will be even better if this pull is combined with a feeling of dissatisfaction over a lack of material. At present your company is like a choked engine. It is suffocating from work in progress, just like a petrol engine when the fuel mixture is too rich.[45]

Conclusions

A lack of preunderstanding means that the work of the researcher/consultant becomes liable to serious shortcomings and may indeed be misleading. In particular, I would wish to point to four problems.

First, the researcher/consultant is often able to list a great number of factors and relationships in a certain problem area. What is considerably more difficult is to attach weights to these factors and relationships—that is, to decide on their relative importance and which to give priority.

Second, the researcher/consultant risks choosing a method for access that does not provide the opportunity for the informants to give relevant answers or reactions. This was illustrated by the examples at the beginning of Chapter 2.

Third, the researcher/consultant runs the risk of never being aware of the consequences of inadequate access and preunderstanding and instead concentrates on, for example, advanced statistical analyses of weak empirical material.

Fourth, the researcher/consultant becomes highly vulnerable to modish concerns within management and a tendency to believe that these comprise the "correct" methods or solutions.

Researchers/consultants can, however, develop their preunderstanding in several ways over a longer period. By working on many different change processes, their experience grows over time. This assumes, however, that these projects are not of a purely repetitive nature. It is essential to be able to work under the guidance of and together with experienced researchers/consultants. By having previously worked in companies, the researcher may have developed a feeling for corporate environments and for the relevant issues.

Participation in courses and studies of the literature also provide opportunities for development. They are, however, subject to diminishing marginal utility if they are not combined with opportunities for trying this knowledge in a real-life situation.

In my experience, the best opportunity for researchers/consultants to develop their preunderstanding is to operate as *active* participants in a process rather than as interviewers or detached observers. Consequently, the role of change agent, as defined in Table 2.1, would seem more likely to lead to access and an improved level of preunderstanding than the other roles available to the researcher/consultant.

On the other hand, the traditional system of postgraduate research and the structure of rewards within the academic system often do not encourage researchers to develop their preunderstanding along the lines suggested above.

My conclusions may be summarized as follows:

The most difficult task facing the researcher/consultant is the acquisition of institutional knowledge and knowledge of the social interaction processes. Hence, it is in these areas that researchers/consultants must seek to improve their competence.

Preunderstanding and access receive little attention when the quality of academic research is assessed. A balance is required between knowledge from firsthand experience and secondhand knowledge through intermediaries. At present, researchers and, often, consultants as well are victims of secondhand preunderstanding.

Satisfactory access to a company is a necessary condition for the development of preunderstanding and understanding and for the consequent improvement in the expertise of the researcher/consultant.

Finally, a reminder: Although this chapter is about the need for preunderstanding, I have warned against blocked preunderstanding. It creates bias and does not allow creativity and innovation. Openness for new information—even if disturbing and uncomfortable—is imperative. Therefore, the use of strict application of an inductive approach, advocated by grounded theory, may be necessary in the starting stages of research programs and consultancy assignments.

The issues of access, preunderstanding, and understanding will be followed up in the subsequent chapters.

Notes

1. Odman, 1979, p. 45.
2. Gustafsson, 1977, pp. 52-55.
3. *Encyclopedia Britannica*, 1965, p. 936 H.
4. Gustafsson, 1977, pp. 52-55.
5. Tisdall, 1982, p. 123.

6. Abingdale, 1982.
7. Mao Tse-Tung, [1937] 1969.
8. Russell, [1912] 1948, p. 59.
9. The distinction between words such as *preunderstanding, frame* (of reference), *paradigm,* and *knowledge* is not particularly clear. Within hermeneutics, the term preunderstanding is used, and because I am inspired by hermeneutic literature, I have chosen to use this word.
10. Glaser, 1978, talks about theoretical sensitivity as a basic qualification for the scientist.
11. Gummesson, 1979, p. 8.
12. de Bono, 1971, p. 22.
13. Lindholm, 1980, p. 115; Lindstrom, 1973, p. 18.
14. My attention was drawn to Procrustes's bed by Aredal, 1986, who uses the metaphor in a study.
15. Glaser and Strauss, 1967, pp. 10-11.
16. Glaser, 1992.
17. Ohmae, 1995.
18. Fukuyama, 1995, pp. 97-111.
19. Coffey and Atkinson, 1996, pp. 155-56.
20. This has been confirmed by Glaser in our discussion in November 1997.
21. *Marketing News,* 1986, pp. 6, 8.
22. Glaser and Strauss, 1967, p. 37.
23. Doyle, [1891] 1985b, p. 210.
24. Carlson, 1983, p. 134.
25. Koopmans, 1947, p. 162.
26. Capra, 1982, pp. 17-18.
27. The expression "hammer-and-nail syndrome" is taken from a story that psychologist Alfred Friman told me.
28. Russell, [1912] 1948, p. 59.
29. Rodgers, 1986, p. 92.
30. Ibid., pp. 75-76.
31. Geneen, 1984, p. 94.
32. Based on Johnson's article "The Heartless Lovers of Humankind," 1987, and his book *Intellectuals* from 1989 (quotations, pp. 69 and 80).
33. Johannisson, 1980, p. 36.
34. Gustavsen, 1982, p. 17. The author further develops reasons why "distance research" is not realistic in connection with social processes. See also Gustavsen and Palshaugen, 1984.
35. Odman, 1979, p. 83.
36. Bergstrom and Soderman, 1982, pp. 13ff.
37. McKenna, 1985, p. 110.
38. Gummesson, 1982, p. 35.
39. Schein, 1969, p. 8.
40. Gummesson, 1977.
41. Rudberg, 1979, p. 218.
42. Ibid., pp. 276-77.
43. Ibid., p. 321.
44. Ibid., p. 268.
45. Ibid., p. 222.

C H A P T E R

Four

Case Study Research

The change agent works with *cases.* The use of the case study for research purposes is also becoming increasingly widespread in management. In many universities, doctoral theses dealing with marketing, strategy, organization, and so forth are often based on case studies.

The purpose of this chapter is to emphasize the necessity for access, preunderstanding, and firsthand experience of decision making, implementation, and change processes to produce useful academic research and management consultancy.[1]

A wide range of information-gathering techniques can be used in case studies. A thorough analysis of a particular process will require the use of the researchers' personal observations that result from their presence, participation, or even intervention in the actual process to be examined. *Participant observation* constitutes the core of anthropology / ethnography, and participation with active intervention is known as *action research* or *action science.* In terms of information gathering and analysis, both participant observation and action science depend largely on qualitative methods, although quantitative methods can sometimes play a considerable role.

The chapter is divided into four main sections. The first section deals with some basic principles of case study research and then goes on to examine three aspects of the method that I find particularly intriguing and misunderstood. The first concerns the issue of generalizing from a limited number of cases; the next is a critical review of historical analysis and futures studies as tools for understanding the dynamics of a company; the third aspect concerns the existence of taboos and the manner in which these are handled.

The second section deals with the meaning of the concept of action research/action science and the opportunities for integrating the roles of researcher and consultant. Qualitative methods of data collection and analysis, particularly informal, in-depth interviews and observation and their application to scientific research and consultancy are discussed in the third section. The final section discusses a puzzling question: What is a fact, and can fiction be more factual than facts? The chapter concludes with a brief summary.

For and Against Case Study Research

Case studies vary in character, but here, two types are of particular interest. The first one attempts to derive *general conclusions* from a limited number of cases. For example, one can examine the marketing process in a single or a few manufacturing companies to come to conclusions regarding business-to-business marketing. The second type seeks to arrive at *specific conclusions* regarding a single case because this "case history" is of particular interest.[2] The quotation in the previous chapter from Rudberg's account of the crisis at the foundry provides an example of this type of approach. It is a matter of interpreting a particular set of events in a believable manner.[3] Both types, however, may produce results of general interest.

Case studies are also used in education when students are invited to put forward solutions to actual or imaginary cases, using models and theory from literature together with their own experience. This is an alternative to traditional learning from textbooks; it's an effort to create a "management lab" in the classroom. The use of case studies in a classroom situation will not be examined in this book; I will deal solely with case studies for research purposes.

Yin[4] distinguishes between three types of uses of case study research: exploratory, descriptive, and explanatory. Researchers in business-related subjects traditionally limit case studies to the *exploratory* use: a pilot study that can be used as a basis for formulating more precise questions or testable hypotheses.

The *descriptive* case study is an attempt to describe, for example, what happens when a new product is developed and launched on the market. Description, often contrasted with prediction and prescription, is usually considered less prestigious in scientific circles. "That paper is only a description!" In *Description as Choice*, Sen states that the reason description is considered the simplest form of science rests, at least in part, "in the idea that description is largely a matter of mere observation and reporting, or reading other people's reports and summarizing—at best, systematizing. Whether a descriptive statement is acceptable could be thought to be dependent on its correctness and that could be resolved simply by observing."[5] Sen points out that this is an absurd argument.[6] In making descriptions, we have to make choices, and these choices are guided by our paradigm, access, and preunderstanding. There is no description without analysis and interpretation.

Although it is an unwarranted attitude, exploratory and descriptive case studies are traditionally given low status; they are viewed primarily as ancillary to other methods. The third use of case studies, as *explanatory* research, is looked on with skepticism, or sometimes even horror, by mainstream business school professors. In my view, however, case research is a useful strategy for studying processes in companies and also for explanatory purposes.

Kjellen and Soderman[7] point to some further uses of case research: to *generate theory* and as a means for *initiating change*.

According to the authors, if a change process is going to succeed, the researcher must have a fundamental knowledge of the studied organization and its actors, must have an ability to develop a language and concepts appropriate to the specific case, and must concentrate on processes likely to lead to understanding—*Verstehen*[8]—rather than conducting a search for causal explanations.

As has already been pointed out, the terms and concepts we use may be illuminating in one context but blur our sight in another. I am not happy with the distinctions referred to above—exploration, description, explanation, theory generation, initiation of change—when these are misused for ranking research strategies in alleged order of scientific excellence. They are hard to see in isolation: Exploratory studies as well as descriptions can be theory generating, descriptions may be explanatory, and so forth.

An important advantage with case study research is the opportunity for *holistic view* of a process:

> The detailed observations entailed in the case study method enable us to study many different aspects, examine them in relation to each other, view the process within its total environment and also utilise the researcher's capacity for "Verstehen." Consequently, case study research provides us with a greater opportunity than other available methods to obtain a holistic view of a specific research project.[9]

Holism may be viewed as the opposite of *reductionism*.[10] The latter consists of breaking down the object of study into small, well-defined parts. This approach goes all the way back to the seventeenth century and the view of Descartes and Newton that the whole is the sum of its parts. This leads to a large number of fragmented, well-defined studies of parts in the belief that they can be fitted together, like a jigsaw puzzle, to form a whole picture. According to the holistic view, however, the whole is not identical with the sum of its parts. Consequently, the whole can be understood only by treating it as the central object of study. In this context, case research seeks to obtain a holistic view of a specific phenomenon or series of events. This is a time-consuming job, and it is generally not possible to carry out more than one or a very limited number of in-depth case studies in a research project.

Case studies can be of particular value in the applied social sciences where research often aims to provide practitioners with tools. Alloway states that case research is particularly useful "when the audience are managers who must implement findings."[11] This is the typical situation for a management consultant. He goes on to say,

> Research addressed to practitioners . . . carries the additional burden of drawing recommendations from the findings which are, one, understandable and two, implementable. The familiarity of a managerial audience with the language, data format and analyses used in case research is, alone, a major advantage. Further, the conceptual and descriptive richness of the data gathered enables the practitioner to assess for himself the applicability of the findings to his circumstances.[12]

A frequent criticism is that case research is inferior to methods based on random statistical samples of a large number of observations. During recent years, case study research has received growing recognition among groups of management researchers. For example, in the area of marketing, researchers from Northern Europe make greater use of case studies than American researchers who concentrate more on quantitative methods.[13] There seems, however, to be a trend toward more case study research in the United States.

In medical research, case studies are considered to have only limited scientific value; they are characterized as "anecdotal" and often scorned but can nevertheless be accepted as a source of ideas, circumstantial evidence, and a basis for formulating testable hypotheses.[14] Medical doctors' understanding is largely built on their ability to learn from single cases; Hippocrates, known as the founding father of medicine, based his landmark work on only a few cases.

One author views case study research as an emergency approach:

Obviously, case studies, irrespective of how well they are planned, lack the scientific weight and general applicability of conventional research methods. However, in certain areas they represent the only possible research strategy. Moreover, if a sufficiently large number of cases are examined, they can serve as a basis for fruitful theoretical developments and also provide guidelines for therapeutic advice.[15]

The above quotation begins with the word *obviously*. Personally, I cannot accept anything as "obvious" in science, particularly because conventional research methods are scarcely applicable to studies of processes of decision making, implementation, and change in companies.

The criticism of case studies as a scientific method can be summarized under the following three headings:[16]

- Case studies lack statistical reliability and validity.
- Case studies can be used to generate hypotheses but not to test them.
- Generalizations cannot be made on the basis of case studies.

The next section will examine these points, especially the question of making generalizations on the basis of one or several case studies.

Generalizing from a Limited Number of Cases

Both researchers and consultants may feel a need to generalize knowledge: researchers, to develop and test theories, and consultants, as a means of improving their expertise. There is an implicit assumption that it is desirable to make generalizations. Although this was also my initial standpoint, I have become increasingly dubious of the meaning of *generalization*. It no longer seems so "obvious" that a limited number of observations cannot be used as a basis for generalization. Nor is it obvious that properly devised statistical studies based on large numbers of observations will lead to meaningful generalizations.

In business schools, we are taught how statistical sampling should be used to allow scientific generalizations. This seems to be the only aspect of generalization that is taught, and obviously, many people, including researchers and consultants, believe that there are no other possibilities. I even hear graduate students say things such as, "out of the twenty possible cases to be investigated, we drew two by random sampling," thus believing that this procedure, in some magic way, would increase the scope for generalization. Researchers who base their work on one or a few cases state in their reports that "naturally, these observations are too few to allow generalizations; this study should be seen as an exploratory search for hypotheses that will subsequently be tested; the evidence is only anecdotal." Generalizing from statistical samples is just one type of generalization, however; it is not general—and it is rarely applicable to case study research. Generalization from case studies has to be approached differently.

My own views on this question have been influenced by Normann, who has himself made use of case studies in consultancy and research:

> If you have a good descriptive or analytic language by means of which you can really grasp the interaction between various parts of the system and the important characteristics of the system, the possibilities to generalize also from very few cases, or even one single case, may be reasonably good. Such a generalization may be of a particular character; it might be possible to generalize a statement of the type "a system of type A and a system of type B together comprise a mechanism which tends to function in a particular way." On the other hand one cannot make any generalizations about how common these types of systems and interaction patterns are. But the possibilities to generalize from one single case are founded in the comprehensiveness of the measurements which makes it possible to reach *a fundamental understanding of the structure, process and driving forces* rather than a superficial establishment of correlation or cause-effect relationships.[17]

Generalization has two dimensions in this quotation. On the one hand, quantitative studies based on a large number of observations are required to determine how much, how often, and how many. The other dimension involves the use of in-depth studies based on exhaustive investigations and analyses to identify certain phenomena—for example, the effects of a change in corporate strategy—and lay bare mechanisms that one suspects will also exist in other companies.

In the field of marketing, particularly in the United States, the research tradition is highly limited to statistical and mathematical methodology combined with survey techniques from the behavioral sciences. Since the 1980s, however, focus groups—a kind of qualitative group interview—have gained considerable ground.[18] Bonoma[19] advocates a greater use of qualitative methods in marketing theory and research. He warns, however, that qualitative researchers must be aware that generalizations in marketing theory may not be very general and that they must be willing to deal with discomforting new data to change or modify their conclusions.

To me, this is very much a matter of the attitude to research inherent in the researcher's/consultant's paradigm. I have already claimed that "science is a journey, not a destination." The phrase can be expanded to "science is a journey, and the existing theory is not its destination." In this light, new data are never discomforting. They never "destroy" existing theory; they expand and improve it.

In the same spirit, philosophers of science describe research in social areas as a continuing, eternal process of understanding that never actually reaches the final "truth." They come to this conclusion from many different points of departure. According to Popper,[20] the first priority is not to verify theories; it is to formulate them in such a way that they can be tried for falsification. In this fashion, theoretical development is an ongoing process in which the creators of a theory keep working to test their creation in order to destroy it and replace it with something better.

Physicist/philosopher David Bohm says that science is "primarily an activity of extending perception into new contexts and into new forms, and only secondarily a means of obtaining what may be called reliable knowledge."[21] According to Shipman,

"Each social researcher is a pioneer because the data that he collects is likely to change the theoretical model that, overtly or covertly, forms the basis of the work. New data exhaust old theories."[22] He takes the example of Boyle's Law on the relationship between the pressure and volume of a gas. Repeating the experiment is unlikely to produce anything other than confirmation of the law, since all conditions can be controlled.

Human beings like business situations are unique, however; there are uncontrolled elements, such as customers and competitors, that create unexpected results. The research conditions in business are such that conceptualization and the operational definitions used for measurement and observation are rarely subject to the same control as those in the natural sciences. Consequently, there is a considerable likelihood that existing theory will prove to be inadequate in the new investigations. Shipman further points out that in economics the focus is on generalized behavior; the economists aggregate and simplify human behavior with no reference to human idiosyncrasies: "On the test of ability to predict, economists have a poor record. If prediction was reliable, economists could confidently work the stock market. In practice this remains the preserve of amateur, but mainly rich stockbrokers."[23]

Generalization is closely related to *validity*[24]—that is, the extent to which researchers are able to use their method to study what they had sought to study rather than (often without being aware of it) studying something else. The favorite criterion of science, however, is *reliability*. Simply put, this means that two or more researchers studying the same phenomenon with similar purposes should reach approximately the same results. A study with high reliability can thus be replicated by others. Reliability fulfills three functions:

1. A police function: Curb dishonest research and nail the villain!
2. An intelligence test: Are the scientists clever or stupid and is their reasoning logical?
3. A substitute for validity when validity seems to be beyond reach; reliability then plays the part of a "validity crutch." The researcher establishes reliability and assumes validity.

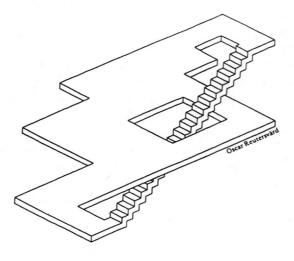

Figure 4.1. The Reutersvard Staircase 1
SOURCE: Impossible Figure by Oscar Reutersvard, 1984, p. 37. Used by permission.

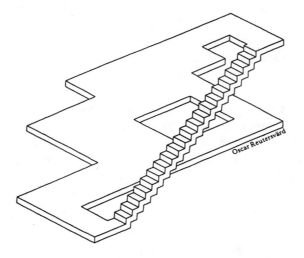

Figure 4.2. The Reutersvard Staircase 2
SOURCE: Impossible Figure by Oscar Reutersvard, 1984, p. 61. Used by permission.

[7] Validity means in essence that a theory, model, concept, or category describes reality with a good fit, just as a good map properly describes Earth or an architect's blueprint is useful for erecting a functioning building. If the map did not reflect the terrain, most people would trust the terrain and abandon the map. Scientific training, however, all too often seems to blind a person to nature, and the scientist may give up the terrain rather than the map.

Take a look at the drawing by Oscar Reutersvard in Figure 4.1. If an architect presented such a blueprint and a builder tried to construct the staircase, reality would soon declare it to have zero validity. The architect would have a difficult time getting his invoice paid. But how many of the theories, models, concepts, and categories presented in management subjects are "Reutersvard staircases"? Management theories are usually not exposed to such unambiguous testing of validity as is the architect's blueprint; they are exposed to situations in which the variables are difficult to control and effects are difficult to follow up.

Suppose we give the model back to the designer and get a new one. Maybe it would look like the staircase in Figure 4.2: a new and graphically neat solution but still lacking validity.[25]

I found further support for the above arguments in an analysis of validity and generalization of case study research. Validity is seen "as a continuous process that is integrated with theory and that requires the researcher to continuously assess his assumptions, revise his results, retest his theories and models and reappraise the given limitations that have been set for the study." But there are also dangers:

> This process of validation places great demands on the researcher. Inadequate research can easily result from a lack of clearly defined principles and rules for validation processes of this type. Hence a more open discussion of the weaknesses surrounding a particular approach, its results etc. will help to improve the quality of this process of validation.[26]

Theories in management are validated in action. If we read the memoirs of Carlzon (SAS, Scandinavian Airlines), Gates (Microsoft), Geneen (ITT), Iacocca (Chrysler and Ford), McCormack (IMG, International Management Group), Sculley (Pepsi and Apple), Sloan (General Motors), or other successful business leaders, we find that they have ideas about how to run a company and they have a proven record of turning one or several businesses around. Whether their descriptions, conclusions, and recommendations are correct and generally valid, we do not know, but they possess insight, they ring true, they gain credibility. Their books "smack with validity," to borrow a phrase from Shipman.[27]

It was not until I closely studied Glaser and Strauss's book *The Discovery of Grounded Theory*,[28] read their later research, and discussed its contents with Barney Glaser that I felt that I was on more solid ground. Although emanating from sociology, the above-mentioned book has attracted considerable attention among researchers in management areas, probably more so in Europe than in the United States.

The clear distinction that the authors draw between *theory generation* and *theory testing*[29] is particularly fruitful. I read subsequently in a work by Hunt[30] that the unconscious inability to distinguish between research designed to generate theories and that intended to test theories is a basic reason for academic disputes on the quality of scientific reports.

Glaser and Strauss's book is concerned with the generation of theory, the attempt to find new ways of approaching reality, the need to be creative and receptive in order to improve one's understanding. This contrasts with the testing and refinement of existing theories and models, which is the primary concern of mainstream researchers. This difference between theory generation and theory testing and refinement can be illustrated by referring to the developments that have taken place within marketing in Scandinavia and other parts of Europe during the last decade.[31] New conceptual developments of service management, services marketing, industrial marketing, and relationship marketing have been grounded in empirical data gathered in case studies. This is in contrast to the mainstream marketing research focused on the testing of the traditional consumer goods-oriented "marketing-mix" theory.[32] The adoption of a different approach to the collection and assembly of data has yielded new insights into marketing.

This example illustrates one of the cornerstones of the Glaser and Strauss method: Theories and models should be grounded in real-world observations rather than be governed by established theory as was discussed in the comparison between inductive and deductive research. But can theories and models that purport to have some degree of general applicability be based on a limited number of cases? Their answer in the affirmative: "Since accurate evidence is not so crucial for generating theory, the kind of evidence, as well as the number of cases, is also not so crucial. A single case can indicate a general conceptual category or property; a few more cases can confirm the indication."[33] For example, Fleck[34] used the single case of how the Wassermann reaction is related to syphilis in order to show the emergence of a "fact." From this one case, he drew conclusions about the way scientists work and how scientific results are created.

In establishing the number and types of cases needed, Glaser and Strauss use comparison[35]—that is, they choose cases that represent different aspects of reality. This is known as *theoretical sampling.* It is an ongoing sampling process in which the researchers simultaneously collect, code, and analyze their data and decide along this journey what to collect next and where it may be found. For example, cases may be chosen because of suspected intrinsic differences between them. A study of services marketing may, for example, involve cases taken from banking institutions, cleaning companies, travel agencies, consultancy firms, medical clinics, and others. The cases are then compared, and attention is drawn to differences and similarities. In this example, pricing policy will be seen to vary markedly between the various service sectors. Hence, a large number of cases will be required to make any general statements about pricing decisions in service companies. The study of only one or a very few cases, however, will be sufficient to establish that irrespective of service industry, the interaction between the customer and the individual who delivers the service will have a decisive impact on the way the customer perceives the quality of the service.

The actual number of cases needed in a specific study will be determined by *saturation*[36]—that is, the diminishing marginal contribution of each additional case; the researcher will have no need to continue with further cases when the marginal utility of an additional case approaches zero. In a similar vein, Patton uses the term *purposeful sampling*, within which he lists sixteen variations.[37]

The question of generalization can be extended one stage further: Is it at all meaningful to generalize in a social context?[38] "To generalize is to be an idiot," exclaims one author.[39] The opposite of generalization is *particularization*,[40] meaning that social phenomena are part of a specific situation and are far too liable to change to allow meaningful generalization. The contingency theory of organizations actually claims that there is no "right" organizational structure for a company; it all depends on the circumstances. A paradigm shift from traditional marketing management theory to relationship marketing means departure from a general mass marketing with its focus on the average consumer in favor of the particular, the consumer as an individual.[41] Theory becomes *local theory*; knowledge in a social context arises when one is able to deal with a specific situation. In a discussion on action science, Gustavsen and Sorensen[42] also place considerable emphasis on the importance of local theory; in their view, it is perhaps the only type of theory that can be created in social situations. Cronbach states that "when we give proper weight to local conditions, any generalization is a working hypothesis, not a conclusion."[43] In a true holistic sense, Argyris et al. "seek both generalizability and the attention to the individual case."[44]

The argument that our knowledge consists of a series of hypotheses that can be used to provide guidance rather than act as a commitment to a particular standpoint concurs with the theoretical sensitivity displayed by Glaser and Strauss.[45] When confronted with new data, they have exhibited complete freedom in seeking to *transcend*[46] the existing theory, creating a new theoretical formation without regard to previous results, established truths, and the prestigious, leading professors in the field. Hence, there is a substantial risk that generalizations in a social context act as a prejudice that effectively blocks understanding rather than constituting supportive preunderstanding.

This section started with a discussion of the advantages of generalization and concluded with an expression of doubt and skepticism about the meaning of the concept. As long as you keep searching for new knowledge and do not believe you have found the ultimate truth but, rather, the best available for the moment, the traditional demand for generalization becomes less urgent.

Historical Analysis and/or Futures Studies?

In the study of major changes in companies, historical analysis is often presumed to be an important analytical tool. Historical analysis, however, has not been integrated into the science (or even art) of management in the same way as studies of the future. The literature on planning frequently recommends a model that contains a section titled "Position Audit," a further section titled "Forecast," and often a section called "Background," sometimes containing a rather shallow historical account.

Companies make forecasts, scenarios of the future, market studies, and so forth that are part of long-range strategic planning and annual budgeting. At the same time, they experience considerable uncertainty in the use of these methods. The interest in forecasting and planning seems to come and go and also to change in approach; strict, well-structured planning is superseded by visionary, qualitative speculations into alternative futures, only to be replaced by new success formulas of rigorous planning.[47] In the 1980s, the president of a major European bank shattered planning at least temporarily when he declared that futures studies were often meaningless and that it was even difficult to be sure about the present position.[48]

The time horizon for planning is also the object of changing fashions. Former Soviet Premier Gorbachev went from the traditional communist five-year plan to a 500-day plan for the transition from planned economy to market economy. The Japanese are known to look very far ahead; there are even rumors of a visionary plan that stretches 240 years! An American consultant told me that he was hired by a Japanese company to assist in its short-term planning. He had yearly budgeting in mind but learned that the client's mind was on a 10-year plan, the shortest time they planned for. In contrast, presidents of companies in the United States and to some extent in Europe are haunted by investors and financial reporters every three months, or even every month, to show enhanced profits and continuous growth.

There is no similar tradition within management for using historical analysis systematically. Of course, company histories have been written, often in connection with an anniversary. These range from solid scholarly works to superficial journalism and public relations stunts. They are not usually written to create a basis for company survival and turnarounds.

The following discussion is based on the views of a number of authors who have argued in favor of a greater use of historical analysis (so far, I have found none openly arguing against). This is followed by my own personal evaluation of historical analysis based on both my personal experience from consultancy work and my own reading.

Historical analysis is not just a simple retrospective study but a reflection of the view that history is always present and that new history is always in the process of being created from current social, political, and economic reality.[49] History can be viewed as a means of interpreting both the present and the future—"a hermeneutic bridge."[50] Human and social problems must be studied in their historical and social context,[51] and organizational research is still largely nonhistorical. A company's history is frequently used merely as superficial background material rather than as an operational tool. The purpose of systematic historical analysis is not, however, to derive some form of "historical truth" but rather to reflect historical diversity as a stimulus to action.[52] With this purpose in mind, the historical analysis may fulfill the following functions relevant to strategic and organizational issues:

> To contribute to an awakening from organization slumber; to raise self-confidence at a time when company morale is low; to create

new knowledge by studying earlier processes of intellectual development; to develop new, special types of competence; to break a vicious circle; to seek to understand the roots of growth.[53]

Kjellen and Soderman argue strongly in favor of a historical approach to case study research. Their view is based on the belief that

it is not possible to understand the actual state of an organization without an insight into the company's history, i.e. the processes that have led up to the company's present condition. Moreover, it is inherent to the nature of organizations and other social systems that some of their principal characteristics cannot be readily observed at a surface level. It is difficult to arrive at any conclusions without studying their behavior over a fairly long period of time.[54]

They make the following practical proposals. First, they suggest the use of a "milestone classification" for the major changes that have occurred in the company's environment, ownership structure, production process, product/market mix, organization, and management. Second, they propose an analysis of "critical events," their background and consequences.

The role of the business historian is described by Smith and Steadman in the following terms:

Business historians undertake several important jobs: first, to understand a company's history in great detail; second, to convey this history to present-day managers; and finally to act as agents of change. For these functions, the historian's training as scholar and teacher is essential. By stretching managers' awareness of the company beyond their immediate experiences, the historian enhances their ability to direct and cope with change.[55]

The most spectacular case against the value of historical analysis is the failure by historians, political scientists, economists, statisticians, politicians, reporters, diplomats, and other Soviet "experts" to foresee the collapse of Marxism-Leninism in 1989; they did not even speculate on the possibility.[56]

For one who is already a disbeliever, these recent cases could easily and triumphantly give the kiss of death to historical analysis. Unfortunately, the issue is more complex than that.

The financial turmoil in Asia, starting with the collapse of the Thai economy in July 1997, was not foreseen by international financial authorities. Furthermore, at a meeting of the International Monetary Fund (IMF) in Hong Kong in September 1997, nobody even asked about the stability of the Indonesian economy, which was soon thereafter to break down—the general credo was that Indonesia was the country you need least to worry about.[57]

In 1978, India-born Texas economics professor Ravi Batra foresaw the downfall of communism before the year 2000, but his prophecy was met with scorn and skepticism. He has proved to be correct so far, but he also predicted the downfall of capitalism, which in 1999 is yet to be seen.[58] The immediate bankruptcy of the Soviet Union was predicted by U.S. financial analyst Judy Shelton in the late 1980s.[59] She participated in a research program to find out the *real* debt figures of various countries (official statistics from many countries have low validity, and they are often deliberately deceptive, which most researchers and consultants seem to disregard). Her analyses indicated that the Soviet Union's debt was twice as high as the official records stated. She believes that the reason the experts were wrong was that "financial people usually go into business, while economists and political scientists do research."[60]

From a totally different viewpoint, brain surgeon David Ingvar[61] has studied the relationship between the biological functioning of the brain and the nervous system on the one hand and our behavior in an organizational setting on the other; he calls it *neurobiological management*. One of the findings is that the individual registers—in physically identifiable sectors of the brain that can even be photographed—the *past*, the *present*, and the *future*.

"The future is dark, the present burdensome; only the past, dead and finished, bears contemplation," says Elton in *The Practice of History*.[62] The past is our preunderstanding, the present is the stimuli that we perceive right now. For businessmen, the present may be the latest sales figures, price-cutting activities by the competition, or a conflict with the bank. They compare what they perceive with past experience and future expectations. They may feel comfortable in this context, or they may feel uneasy. If they feel something is wrong here and now, they may get excited by the challenge or feel anxiety that leads to illness; ulcers and high blood pressure are not uncommon among executives. Recent brain research shows that a specific part of our brains is used in planning the future; it contains a "futures program."

An organization consists of individuals who in the past have been more or less successful in creating a common identity of shared values, a history, and a corporate culture. In the present, events occur that raise hopes or misgivings for the future. If our comprehension of the past, the present, and the future, both as individuals and organizations is deficient, we exhibit disturbed behavior and stress expressed as alienation, aggressiveness, fatigue, and so forth. If we lack understanding of the company history—founding fathers, traditions, symbols, systems, processes—we may feel deprived. The same is true if we lack understanding of the present and the future.

With reference to the previously mentioned authors and a discussion between professors and businessmen,[63] the case in support of history may be summarized in the following manner:

* History is a diagnostic instrument that helps us to put a problem in its context and environment. It supplies a thread and helps us to create order among a mass of data; it provides patterns. No two sets of circumstances are ever identical, although certain patterns may recur frequently.

* Communication in a process of decision making, implementation, and change is facilitated if there is agreement on the factual and historical background.

* History helps us both to create analogies and to select the pertinent analogies. It provides a fixed point for triangulation between the past and the present position of a company and the position of competitors; it provides opportunities for comparison.

* History helps us to place facts and events within a shared memory, it presents the heritage and roots, the tradition that helps to create company spirit and pride. Shared values is one of the McKinsey Seven Ss of management,[64] where heritage and symbols, such as anecdotes about the founders, are emphasized as common characteristics among successful firms. History gives a sense of perspective, helps us to see where we fit in, and it adds meaning to our lives.

* History helps us to avoid reinventing the wheel.

* "History is interesting only because it teaches us that everything is perishable," a Buddhist guru once explained to me. The Western cynic says that all we ever learn from history is that we never learn from history. A more positive approach is to say that we can learn from history what we cannot learn from it—that there are no simple formulas, that history does not provide solutions but a thought process, and that we have to realize and accept ambiguity and complexity.

* History can help us to change things before we have to, which is actually the basic purpose of strategic thinking: Foresee changes, act before they hit us, and prepare to benefit from the new situation.

This all sounds sensible, but it could also be turned against you. The case study, when used as an educational tool, is history from which the student is supposed to learn by analogy. The case study is important in the curriculum of many business schools, but it is also criticized. Marketing consultant Regis McKenna says that for many new markets there are no analogies: "Personal computers don't follow the same rules as stereos or consumer electronics. They don't even follow the same rules as big computers. The textbook has to be rewritten every day in emerging industries."[65] Iacocca says that young MBAs "seem to think that every business problem can be structured and reduced to a case study"[66] without understanding the time pressure and complexity of the business world. Iacocca's employer at that time, Henry Ford, took a negative stand to history:

> Henry used to boast that he never kept any files. Every now and then he would burn all his papers. "That stuff can only hurt you," he'd tell me. "Any guy who holds on to his files is asking for trouble. Eventually the wrong person will read them and you and the company will pay the price." He was even worse after Watergate . . . "See?" he said. "I was right—look what can happen to you!" . . . He lived by his grandfather's motto: "History is bunk."[67]

The business executive has been compared with a car driver who looks in the rearview mirror and decides how to drive on that information. When the computers came, they just took over the extrapolations from the driver. Budgeting and strategic planning are often historical, based on past results that are extrapolated, with no allowance made for discontinuities, quantum leaps, and alternative futures. Traditional statistical and mathematical forecasting looks for patterns and projects a trend. As a reaction to those historical methods, technological forecasting and futurology emerged and included more qualitative techniques, challenging the past and making their own assumptions about the future. Scenario writing is a systematic way of speculating about possible futures and determining what actions have to be taken if one of these occurs. The balanced scorecard offers an approach to accounting that stresses the future instead of the traditional historical focus for accounting. It also includes intellectual capital—that is, other types of capital than the financial capital, such as the customer base and its future potential.

Preunderstanding in the shape of paradigm, historical knowledge, concepts, hypotheses, and theories is essential but can also be biased and block a person's sensitivity. Finding that historical patterns repeat themselves can be helpful. It may also be the case that repetition is purely in the mind of the researcher/consultant as suggested by the hammer-and-nail syndrome and procrustean science. For the business executive, discontinuity may be the problem—that is, the ability to see when a new situation arises and not to get stuck in the past. Even if the long-term trend is the same in one market, the cyclical deviation may be sufficiently large in the short term to require new action.

One executive[68] said that we often do not even know where we are and that it is hard to find out where we were. Thus, in real business life, we lack the ability to identify the necessary platforms from which to project the future. To quote a former marketing director of IBM, "Buck" Rodgers,

> I have observed that progressive managers no longer want to deal with information of a historical nature—other than to look at the past for its heritage value. Today the emphasis is on what I call occurrence management, which concentrates on identifying a potential problem and taking action before it happens.[69]

Smith and Steadman claim that historical analysis can be a tool to create a vantage point for development. They suggest the following output of historical analysis:[70]

- Studies of the fundamental strategic and structural development of the company
- Case studies of corporate successes and failures suggesting effective and ineffective courses of past action and their determinants
- Studies of specific past policies, strategies, or decisions to determine their relevance in current contexts
- Studies of the causes of evolution of specific contemporary problems
- Studies of the abiding and transient features of the corporate culture

A necessary requirement of historical analysis is that the company has proper documentation and well-organized records. With the flow of data in today's multimedia society, such record keeping is unrealistic, however.

Case studies can be concerned with different functions, relationships, or events. They may also involve a study of historical, present, or future conditions or a mixture of them all. Company history has not hitherto been one of my major concerns. At the same time, many have emphasized the importance of historical analysis and have considered my nonhistorical attitude to be unfortunate. I have therefore tried to extend my knowledge of the value of historical analysis and have also been influenced by these studies.

I had little interest in company history and was of the opinion that an understanding of history had not been of much assistance to those trying to alter a company's strategy. They rather seemed to use history to explain why things were as they were and, in effect why they should remain that way. They are unable to free themselves from what they have been doing for one or several decades: "Would I have taken the wrong decisions and acted wrongly?" History, then, represents a fixed point that creates security, whereas deviations from established practice may create anxiety. History becomes a defensive routine that prevents adjustments being made.

Consequently, I avoid history and instead try to uncover the future. I believe that my attitude stems from my early days as a marketer rather than an organizational theorist. In marketing, the company's external environment is always much more important than the internal. The real decisions are made in the world outside—among consumers, middlemen, competitors, politicians, legislators, and trade organizations. The external environment is neither particularly knowledgeable nor interested in the company and its development. Hence, my own starting point in relation to company strategy and organization is to ask the question: "What is going to happen in the company's external environment and what measures can be taken to adjust to these changes and to influence the market?"

On the other hand, I find it interesting to study a company's culture and view it in relationship to the requirements of the marketplace. This interest in business culture has developed enormously in recent years in management studies.[71]

Consultants found corporate culture a novel approach to selling their services; they have even been called "corporate culture vultures."[72] Their new service was cultural engineering—the alleged ability to change the culture of a company. A culture may have been built over a long time, tens of years, even hundreds. The oldest corporation still in business in Sweden, Stora, celebrated its 710th anniversary in 1998. Can you really change such cultures, and what is it that you change?

This takes us back to a definition of corporate culture. It is often referred to as shared philosophies, ideologies, values, assumptions, attitudes, norms, symbols, and so on that hold a group together.[73]

In practical business life, however, when major changes in corporate strategy are required, it is always necessary to change several of the leading management positions. It is essential to bring in those who are without history, those who don't know how and why things were done previously and do not feel the need to defend previous decisions and measures.

A company does not consist of one unified culture. There can exist a very strong basic culture with variations from groups, professions, functions, or countries. But there can also be subcultures from different companies that have been acquired over the years. Working in a consulting assignment, I once came into the office of a public relations director who had six banners on his desk. On my inquiry as to what they represented he said, "They show the logos of the parent companies of this subsidiary during my time." This subsidiary had never really merged with anyone in the mind of the public relations guy. When the electrical giants Asea and Brown Bovery merged into ABB, later joined by Combustion Engineering and other companies, a group was formed consisting of some 1,300 subsidiaries. How do you implant a shared culture in this behemoth?

During my work with change processes, I frequently interview company employees who, without my prompting, give me a description of episodes from the company's history, often in terms of personnel changes, changes of owners, chief executives, or products. Once contacts have been established on a more personal basis, employees are often prepared to give a more confidential account of the reasons for the departure or promotion of various leading figures. I have not found this to be of any particular help because the purpose is to adjust the company's strategy to the present and future market and technology. Given that my starting point is that of the marketing executive, my interest is directed to what we are going to do tomorrow to ensure that things go well rather than think about what we did yesterday and why it went badly. In my view, there are two broad approaches to the subject of change. These are illustrated in Figure 4.3.

Figure 4.3 Looking Back or Ahead?

Two types of actors pull in different directions. The opponents of change refer to the company's history ("we have been in existence for a hundred years and have never been involved in exporting"), tradition ("this would never have been allowed to happen when A was chief executive"), and present structure of authority ("we can't move B from the executive floor because it would only lead to bad feelings"). New ideas, methods, and so forth are rejected as unrealistic and viewed as the product of passing fashions rather than as sources of information on which to base future trends and scenarios.

On the other hand, the supporters of change refer to business development, new technology, and survival in the future. If one assumes that the market is uninterested in the company's history, that the company's operations must reflect market requirements, and that the latter are subject to continuous change, attention naturally becomes focused on the future and the company's role in a changed environment. The latter considerations are a central part of my own approach to corporate strategy.

Figures 4.4, 4.5, and 4.6 illustrate three different approaches to the historical process. Figure 4.4 describes my present methods of operation—working with current processes but at the same time keeping an eye on the future.

Figure 4.5 shows the approach adopted by change agents who also have an interest in history; here, the object of study is a change process that encompasses past, present, and future.

Figure 4.6 illustrates a study that has been made from outside of the change processes but that concentrates on a longer period comprising past, present, and future. A study of this type has been carried out by Johannisson[74] with reference to the glass industry.

Figure 4.4 Focusing on the Present and Future from the Inside

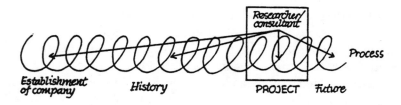

Figure 4.5 Focusing on the Past, Present, and Future from the Inside

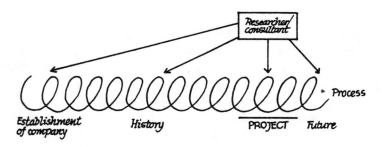

Figure 4.6 Focusing on the Past, Present, and Future from the Outside

carried out by Johannisson[74] with reference to the glass industry. Here, the author's aim was to act as an agent of reconstruction and observation, not as an agent of change for the glassworks on which the study focused. Figure 4.6 can also serve to illustrate other research roles—for example the analyst who stands outside the actual processes of change but whose task is nevertheless to propose specific measures.

My own views on the role of historical analysis in case study research have taken on a new dimension after having read and considered opinions of the above-mentioned authors. It is almost certainly the case that previous events in the company have created "sediment"[75]—that is, layers of behavior that no longer fulfill any useful purpose but nevertheless remain part of corporate culture. A historical study can help to uncover the process of sedimentation. Before coming to any definite conclusions on this issue, however, it will be necessary to evaluate the usefulness of historical knowledge in concrete situations. In certain cases, it is quite conceivable that I make use of historical analysis without doing so in a consciously systematic manner; this is partly a consequence of my earlier demands regarding preunderstanding. It is, however, rather a question of "recent history" covering a period of only a few years.

Let me pose the following question:

∗ What are the practical opportunities open to the researcher/ consultant regarding the use of historical analysis as an aid to understanding processes of change?

In trying to answer this question, I find that there are, unfortunately, substantial difficulties. I would very much like to believe that employees, given an insight into the changes confronting them and being able to do this in a historical context, would themselves be able to tackle and solve corporate problems. This is part of the organizational development approach to which I previously indicated a certain amount of skepticism. At the same time, an actual change in a company's current situation depends on an awareness of "company pathology" (the ability to identify its problems) by at least one influential company executive.

In a wider frame of reference encompassing the interests of society at large rather than just those of the company, historical analysis can be of undoubted value. Given the more limited perspective within which the change agent operates, a number of difficulties curtail the use of historical analysis:

* Efforts have to be concentrated on the difficult task of trying to establish what is currently going on and what is likely to happen in the future.

* How can one come to grips in practical terms with historical processes and how should one assess the validity of the analyses?

* I have a marked distrust of interpretations based on written company records and on external documentation, such as journal articles and stock exchange reports. The Fermenta case referred to in Chapter 1 is an extreme example of the low validity of media reports. These are of a highly random nature, sometimes informative, sometimes misleading. Moreover, memos and minutes avoid sensitive comments—the taboos. Nor can companies in the age of increasing electronic communication maintain systematic records that provide a basis for a future-oriented historical analysis.

* During the 1990s, information technology began to offer the Internet, the World Wide Web, e-mail, mobile phones, and global satellite TV transmission as commodities. Through home shopping and home banking, consumer-initiated buyers' clubs, instant access to price information for comparisons, and so on, the traditional *physical marketplace* is partly taken over by the *intangible marketspace*, a market that is everywhere, any time of the day and night. This is causing a paradigm shift in many markets; both consumers and suppliers are thrown into an unknown situation with no previous correspondence.[76] How can history predict and assist when conditions are so radically altered?

✳ Innovations in industries are often introduced by those who do not have knowledge of a particular industry, those "without history" who are not committed to a "this is what we do in our industry" approach but are instead prepared to meet and adjust to the requirements of the present and future customer.

✳ To use historical analysis in practice, there is a need for techniques that provide implementable procedures.

Taboos and Anonymity

Certain phenomena are not considered acceptable subjects of study or should not be put in writing. They might be embarrassing to those involved and even trigger the anger of powerful people. Consequently, there is a tendency to avoid these phenomena, although they may be of decisive importance for a particular process. They become taboo.

I should like to emphasize two types of taboos. The first concerns the taboos of the research process as such. Although the traditional model of the research process is an idealized model, when confronted with reality, the process is characterized by complexity and intractability. According to McGrath, this leads to the conclusions that "the researcher, like the voter, often must choose the lesser among evils," and that "there is no such thing as flawless research."[77] This is not the picture of reality presented to students. "Students trying to learn how to do research are constantly faced with gaps between the rational model of many of their texts and teachers and the realities of how research actually is conducted. They must learn the 'street-smarts' of the research process."[78] This is learned in a haphazard fashion: "They decipher rules of thumb from throwaway lines in conversations with faculty, asides in methodology textbooks, and embarrassed footnotes in journal articles . . . from the gossip, anecdotes, and folklore that pervade research units—and from their own experience."[79] The human problems, "the sociology of science," are rarely made explicit in research reports; the reader is presented with "rational rhetoric."

Taboos can concern prejudices among members of promotion committees and research funds or among journal referees; references to researchers at a competing university or to a professor's antagonists; or the misuse of power within a research institute.

The second type of taboo concerns the content of research. In management, such taboos can be the stupidity of a leader, bribes (a well-known phenomenon in international business but never touched on in marketing textbooks), sex, drug abuse and alcoholism, or industrial espionage. In his study of business cultures, Hofstede stated,

> Sex was the taboo of the Victorian age. At least in the organization literature, power was the great taboo until the 1960s. Both taboos have been more or less lifted since that time. Culture in the organization literature may be the great taboo of today. In all three cases, the taboo is on something we are all involved in but not supposed to speak about.[80]

The view that culture is taboo is supported by Hall's anthropological studies:

> Years of experience in trying to communicate the basic discoveries about culture have taught me that the resistance one meets has a great deal in common with the resistance to psychoanalysis which was strong in its early days. Though the concepts of culture . . . are abstract . . . they touch upon such intimate matters that they are often brushed aside at the very point where people begin to comprehend their implications.[81]

Hofstede concluded that sex is no longer a taboo subject, but Burrell is of a different opinion. "The issue of sex is one which organizational analysis has avoided for too long." He continues:

> Poetry, novels, and biography are all redolent, for the most part, with sexuality and its manifestations. In this regard, at least, novels and fiction do present this feature of organizational life much more readily than much of organizational theory. Few would or could deny the existence of sexual relationships in organizational settings

but yet their presence is not described let alone explained by much of the sociology of organizations.[82]

Books on this "blindspot of organization studies" are now available.[83]

In 1984, a high-class escort service, illegal according to local laws, was busted by the police in New York. It turned out that it was run by Sydney Biddle Barrows, a young female member of a well-known American family, and naturally, this made the news for a long time. The newspapers were hardly looking for the true story behind the operation but, rather, speculated in invented details, eventually hoping to make a sensation by revealing names of wealthy clients. It could have remained at that, but the young madam had the drive and courage to write a book on the actual management of her service company, treating it as a business operation. The book, *Mayflower Madam*,[84] was coauthored with the same man who helped Chrysler president Iacocca write his story. The usual approach would have been to revel in the more bizarre details about the delivery of the service. But this is actually a book on the mechanics of running a small-scale service operation. The approach created a bestseller; the public was obviously receptive to it. The impact of masculine and feminine qualities as well as homosexuality for general management, organizational structure, design of products and services, and so on is slowly being recognized. Gender research is becoming a new discipline in universities, and the media and the legal profession have found a growing market in the upsurge of interest in sexual harassment in working life.[85]

Areas that have still gone almost unnoticed in management research and theory are both organized crime (organizations specifically set up with a criminal "business mission") and criminal behavior in legitimate organizations.[86] Mafia-like organizations exist around the world. They seem to be gaining market share and control some economies. Examples are the former Soviet Union states in general, certain local markets in trades such as restaurants and retailing, and of course, the narcotics and prostitution trades. Money laundering, transfer of money for tax evasion, and computer crimes are some of the growing areas that directly affect general management, accounting, and marketing and cause mal-functioning of market economies. Some of the areas are a threat to the global society, such as uncontrolled trade in nuclear arms and waste and uncontrolled gene manipulation and cloning. Reasons for the avoidance of these areas by management researchers is both insufficient perception of the problem and considerable iner-tia. But there are also high personal risks involved because re-search may require unorthodox methods, and there is the risk of punitive action from the organizations under study.

In an in-depth study of a newspaper publisher, it is suggested that taboos also exist in relation to more public events:

> On one occasion when I discussed the results of my investigations with a number of senior newspaper executives, they shook their heads in disbelief and said that the results were just an exceptional case. It was not until I referred to arguments that they had them-selves used in a panel discussion a few hours before, that they were prepared to admit that my findings had been correct. It is a simple matter to deny what goes on around us—particularly if it is subject to a taboo. In the same way as it is "forbidden" to talk openly about for example sexual organs, it was also considered unacceptable to discuss the activities undertaken by newspaper companies to se-cure government subsidies. It would seem to be only permissible to talk about the grants received by other industries.[87]

One example from my own experience concerns the chief ex-ecutive of a company:

> He had a very quick temper, and it was difficult to predict whether one was going to be praised or told off. His staff therefore tended not to keep him informed unless it was unavoidable. He was con-tinually suspicious that conspiracies were being hatched. Indeed, a fairly certain way of gaining his approval was to pass on such ru-mors. He surrounded himself with a subservient management group composed of those managers who had not been able to find alternative employment and who were able to live with the role of informer. Individuals who could have achieved something were immediately suppressed and left the company, usually following a violent row. The chief executive proceeded to slander these

individuals and in certain cases went so far as trying to stop other employers from employing them. The chief executive went to great pains to charm powerful individuals such as visiting financiers and board members. Undoubtedly, these occasional visitors to the company received an impression of a somewhat crude but nevertheless hearty atmosphere at the company and a chief executive who knew how to keep an organization on a tight rein.

How could one go about making such a description in which the company and the individuals concerned were actually named? It is also striking that evaluations of individuals are seldom made explicit in case studies. It would lead to unpleasantness for the researcher and even give rise to a legal action in which the researcher was required to produce supportive evidence. Family ties, personal chemistry, even breaches of the law may have a decisive effect on a change process. Such considerations are taboo.

There are examples of reports of taboos from the business literature. Iacocca[88] provides a candid description of his boss's indulgence in wine and women and the way he mixed his personal expenses with those of the company. Araskog[89] tells about the "gargantuan bribe" offered by corporate raiders. In Ortmark's[90] book on financial power, events such as the suicide of the eldest son of a powerful family head is analyzed. These events are important for the understanding of a process, and if they were left out, the description would be deceptive. Such frankness is unusual in business literature and research reports, although it appears in novels, newspaper reports, and gossip columns. For example, during the 1990s, both *Time* and *Newsweek* exposed us to business tycoon Donald Trump's marital hardships, and their impact on his business empire has been analyzed.

Researchers are confronted with the problem of choosing between a presentation of anonymous cases in which they can be frank or case studies in which names are given but unpleasant aspects are excluded. To be able to understand and interpret a process, these taboos are of essential importance. The change agent can take account of them in his or her work, but the researcher cannot openly refer to them. On the other hand, the models used in business administration are not concerned with the assessment of personal qualities and relationships; they are "depersonalized and objectified."

Taboos come up during consultancy assignments, but the consultant may decide to ignore them either because they are difficult to do anything about or because the consultant is uncertain or has insufficient access. The case of the chief executive outlined above is such an example; it was essential to remove him from his post, but no one dared to take on such a controversial issue.

It is quite probable that the taboo problem cannot be solved independent of society's own general attitudes toward these issues. On the other hand, researchers ought to be required to show an awareness of the taboo problem and to point out that they have access to information that cannot be revealed.

Action Research/Action Science

Action research is the most demanding and far-reaching method of doing case study research. Definitions of action research differ somewhat between authors. Argyris et al.[91] suggest the term *action science* for the following two reasons. First, projects that have been labeled "action research" have often not properly fulfilled the requirements of scientific research but have been closer to consultancy or journalism. Second, action researchers often limit themselves to the use of traditional methodology that stems from the positivistic paradigm.

These arguments agree well with my own observations. Because my book has an objective similar to that of Argyris et al.—to improve professionalism in research and consultancy—the term *action science* will be given priority except when referring to or quoting from work in which the term *action research* was originally used.

What then is action science? Hult and Lennung[92] made a study of some seventy publications and found certain qualities that should exist in order to call something action research; later Argyris et al.[93] discussed at length the criteria of action science. Elden and Chisholm describe the basic classical model of action research in terms of five elements.[94]

My concept of action science deviates in some respects from the classical action research model usually accredited to Kurt Lewin.[95] It embraces Lewin's original notion—that action research is a way of learning about a social system and simultaneously trying to change it—but it takes the standpoint of management and the successful operation of a business. The tradition of action research is societal, a way of giving knowledge support to underprivileged groups, either in organizations, such as workers against management, or society in general, such as a racial minority against a racial majority. To make my vantage points more distinct, I suggest the division in two action science paradigms: *societal action science* and *management action science*. First, the societal action science concept will be introduced and then my management science concept will be discussed more at length.

Societal Action Science

The societal action science concept takes a social and political view. When, for example, a company is threatened with closure, employees, unions, and local governments may want the firm to continue, whereas banks and investors may not.

Socialist writers have often made the distinction between the "technocratic" approach that concentrates on the efficiency of the firm and a "progressive" approach that focuses on solidarity with underprivileged groups. The Frankfurt School, represented by, for instance, Habermas,[96] views research as a means of changing society for the benefit of its citizens. Sandberg has expressed this view in the following manner:

> Many different types of research can be termed action science. Technologists and economists have for a long time worked on research projects together with practitioners. However, this research has been conducted in conjunction with senior executives from business and government administration. The type of action science with which I am concerned seeks to develop a working relationship with relatively underprivileged groups far down the social hierarchy.[97] . . . Hence action science implies that the researcher

supports action that seeks to introduce changes in line with the wishes and demands of employees.[98]

One branch of action science—*participatory research*—advocates that all those affected by a study should be involved and contribute to the outcome. According to Tandon, it can be defined as follows: "Participatory research attempts to present people as researchers themselves in pursuit of answers to the questions of their daily struggle" and "it rejects the myth of professionally trained experts as the only legitimate pursuers of knowledge."[99]

The paradigm of participatory research claims that an elite control of knowledge is used to suppress others. That may sound like socialist gospel, but even philosopher Francis Bacon said that "knowledge is power" as far back as the sixteenth century. Cleansed of ideological slogans, a pragmatic core remains. It is in contrast to the elitist Western relationship between the expert professional and the ignorant layman, earlier referred to as the doctor-patient relationship, in which the active and knowledgeable doctor cures the passive and ignorant patient by prescribing "scientifically" verified therapies.

Participatory research usually refers to suppressed people in the Third World. In developed countries, however, the fear that the knowledge and information society of the future will create a new species of social outcasts—those who are poorly educated and are not connected to computer networks and databases—is certainly real.

Action science may also promote the changing of values and norms as the learning process proceeds. This may lead to a paradigm shift, the challenge of the status quo suggested by double-loop learning.

Management Action Science

Management action science is focused on the company as a business. The following ten points specify my management action science concept.

1. *Action scientists take action.* The concept of action science is reserved for the situations in which researchers assume the role of change agents of the processes and events they are simultaneously studying. In contrast to the mainstream scientist who is serenely detached, the action scientist is deeply involved. Applied to the study of business corporations or government agencies, the action scientist can be a person who is both an academic researcher and either an employee or an external management consultant.[100]

2. *Action science has dual goals: both to contribute to the client and to contribute to science.* If ever there was a role conflict in science, here is a juicy one. Action scientists must be able to balance a schizophrenic personality and get the best out of Dr. Jekyll as well as Mr. Hyde. It means that they must handle both the client's interests and the interests of science. They must contribute to the general and theoretical developments in business disciplines. This requires them to juxtapose their findings to previous research and literature and to disseminate them through reports, articles, and lectures. However, the pressures on action scientists do not end there. They are expected to produce not only knowledge but usable knowledge that can be applied and validated in action. It is not enough just to apply existing theory—that is, *applied research,* which could be an action strategy but does not necessarily contribute to science. Within action science, role conflict and ambiguity are part of the researcher's day-to-day life.

3. *Action science is interactive; it requires cooperation between researchers and client personnel and continuous adjustment to new information and new events.* The researchers interact closely with the people and the environment they are studying. Those involved—the researchers and the organization's personnel—solve problems and learn from each other and develop their competence. According to Argyris et al., "Becoming an action scientist involves learning to reflect on reflection-in-action, making explicit the theories-in-use that inform it, and learning to design and produce new theories-in-use for reflection and action."[101] This requires sensitivity and an ability to transcend existing theories into new and better theories. For the practitioner, this is a natural way

of working. According to Clark,[102] this may be an "uneasy part-
nership" for the scientist. For example, in redefining the business
mission of a company, information on customers and competitors
may be generated. The interpretation leads to conclusions and
recommendations that in turn lead to decisions and action. This is
an iterative, cyclical process. Mainstream researchers may feel uncomfortable with these adjustments because they interfere with
their original research design. It is obvious that the demands of
the positivist paradigm are not applicable to action science, and if
the researchers try to apply them, they will become bad consultants and consequently also bad action scientists.

4. *The understanding developed during an action science project
aims at being holistic, recognizing complexities.* Case study research is
done to get access to complex realities and realities that belong to
the hidden part of the iceberg, the 90% under the surface. The
mainstream scientist would single out one or a few factors and
study these in detail. The action scientist must focus on the totality
of a problem, but still make it simple enough to engage those involved. The research strategy is to be "optimally incomplete."[103]

5. *Action science is applicable to the understanding, planning, and
implementation of change in business firms and other organizations.*
Change processes are often complex, influenced by a multitude of
factors that are interconnected in seemingly chaotic patterns; verbal and nonverbal cues abound, and the informal is as important
as the formal. Being a resident in the organization and an actor on-
stage gives the researcher a unique access to change processes.

6. *It is essential to understand the ethical framework and the values
and norms within which action science is used in a particular project.*
Because this is a management action science concept, it does not
per se focus on the societal issue of solidarity and aid to underprivileged groups. There are areas of common interest, however.
For example, corporations progressively begin to understand the
need to use the capacity and motivation of all employees. Training
and education of staff is on the agenda, and we speak about the
importance of learning organizations. To handle customers
smoothly, empowerment and enablement of frontline personnel
is required, particularly in service operations. Total quality man-

agement (TQM) values recognize everybody's participation as indispensable to achieve continuous improvements of quality. Change processes, however, concern many stakeholders who do not share each other's values and goals. Especially in U.S. public companies, investor value and stock price are getting undue short-term attention at the expense of long-term customer and employee relationships and future-oriented development projects. Deciding what norms should govern the research depends on the purpose of the project. Action science can also prompt the changing of values and norms as the learning process of the project proceeds.

7. *Action science can include all types of data-generating methods but requires the total involvement of the researcher.* To understand the nature of action science, it is necessary to examine other methods of access. Qualitative, informal, in-depth interviews and the ethnographic methods of observation and participation are also important as part of action science. A variety of existing material as well as quantitative survey techniques and other statistical methods may also be useful. Action science adds the dimension of the researchers who become active participants influencing the process under study; they become change agents.

8. *Constructively applied preunderstanding of the corporate environment and the conditions of business is essential.* Graduates of business schools, as well as their professors, are often accused of being too theoretical and too quantitative. Researchers in intervention processes often assume the role of midwives—not pregnant mothers—and assist only in the process of birth. They don't provide specific expertise on a technical issue as such, but they provide specific expertise on how to inspire processes of change. Others are experts on specific issues, such as manufacturing systems or key account management. Whichever role they assume, preunderstanding of corporate environments and the conditions of business is mandatory. This preunderstanding can be based both on firsthand understanding through personal experience and on secondhand understanding through reports and other intermediaries. Preunderstanding is a resource to be used when called for, not a filter to bias an investigation.

9. *Management action science should preferably be conducted in real time, but retrospective action science is also an option.* The literature requires the researcher/consultant to consciously and systematically be doing action science in the course of the daily work in a project. We have, however, a wealth of information stored in the minds of people who have lived through important and often dramatic changes. They did not at the time see themselves as researchers but afterward started to reflect on what they had been through, asking themselves the question, Could this be of general interest to the disciplines of management and economics? As complementary to *real-time action science*, I would like to introduce the concept of *retrospective action science*. To deserve this tag, the studies should be systematic and relate to theory and other research; they should not result in mere memoirs and ego-boosting monuments. The experience of having lived the processes should be triangulated by using additional methods such as document studies and interviews with other actors. The great advantage of retrospective action science is absolutely unique access and preunderstanding that should not be wasted by the scientific community. Note, however, the perils of blocked preunderstanding and preconceived notions that may force unwarranted conclusions on the data. An example of successful retrospective action science is the memoirs of a former secretary of finance in the Swedish government, who, with a background as Ph.D. in economics, wrote an exceptionally candid and reflective book.[104] Another example is a Ph.D. dissertation on work processes in parliament, authored by a former member of parliament.[105] Two Ph.D. dissertations in which I have been involved apply retrospective action science. One was written by of an ex-partner of a publishing house, exploring the meaning of knowledge for leadership and corporate strategy.[106] The other author had followed the process of entrepreneurial activity as a former CEO and chairman of the board of an innovation company.[107] These authors all had privileged access to events that no scholar could ever dream of attaining from a university position.

10. *The management action science paradigm requires its own quality criteria.* Action science should be governed by the hermeneutic paradigm, although elements from the positivistic paradigm may

be included. Management action science cannot be evaluated by the same criteria that currently dominate research at most business schools and other research institutions. Furthermore, it cannot be evaluated solely by the criteria emanating from the scientific paradigm; equal consideration has to be given to the practical consequences for the client organization and the consultant paradigm. Different paradigms and their quality criteria will be further explored in the next chapters.

Is Action Science Doable?

Action science is more demanding on the researcher's personality than any other approach (see further on personality traits of consultants in Chapter 5, particularly Tables 5.3 and 5.4). In practice, it is hard for the management action scientists to score high on all the ten points listed above. But the same problem exists with all approaches, not least statistical techniques.

The basic problem is whether action science is at all feasible in practice. This is indeed a major problem, although it hasn't received much attention in the literature. Schmid states that "action science claims to unite research practice with the actions of practitioners and that this occurs *without either form of practice predominating over the other*. Hence the action scientist professes a loyalty to *both* knowledge *and* to the objectives of the practitioner." Action scientists "seek to integrate two essentially different forms of practice which inevitably produce contradictions, ambivalence and problems of cooperation. This combination of different forms of practice leads to the predominance of one form over the other, i.e. places a limit on the operation of the other."[108]

Sandberg[109] tries to solve this problem by replacing action science with the concept of *praxis research* in which a separation is maintained between the roles of researcher and consultant at the same time as there is an interaction between the roles. He distinguishes between *reflection* on the one hand, and *dialogue and action* on the other. In the former, the researcher maintains a distance from a change project, analyzes it within a more *general, long-term framework and develops concepts, categories, models, hypotheses, and theories.* Regarding dialogue and action, the researchers involve themselves in *dialogue* with the company—its personnel—taking *action* and *intervening* in the specific project. An *interaction* takes place between the researchers' reflection and their work as change agents.

This does not, however, necessarily take place within one single project but rather over a longer period of time and several projects: "Dialogue and action involve the use of previously acquired scientific knowledge as well as experience gained from dialogue and action in an ongoing research process."[110] This reflects the hermeneutic spiral of preunderstanding-understanding-preunderstanding and so forth in a never-ending chain. As far as reflection is concerned, the action scientist is governed by the rules of the scientific game, whereas in dialogue and action, the demands and requirements of the client are uppermost. Gustavsen[111] presents a closely related aspect of action science in which he suggests that a single research project should not be assessed in isolation. Instead, its scientific qualities should be valued within the context of a larger research program comprising several projects.

Action science requires an assignment concerning processes of change. In Chapter 2, I pointed out that the mere presence of a researcher/consultant—for example at an interview or when a report is presented—can exert an influence on processes of change. This is undoubtedly correct in many instances, but it is a rather passive and insufficient influence to be called action science.

It is not a simple matter to find assignments suitable for action science. A researcher can hardly state, "I have chosen my subject, and I intend to engage in an action science project." It is not enough that the researcher has obtained financing for the project. An organization must also have a problem that gives the researcher scope to go in and act. Traditional case studies can usually be carried out more or less according to the researcher's wishes, provided that traditional data collection methods are used.

One can also follow the opposite approach: A consultancy assignment is available and seems to offer the opportunity for action science. For example, a major consultancy assignment was concerned with increasing the profitability and efficiency in a group of companies with which I was involved. The parent company demanded the use of a specific type of strategic decision model. I had used this type of model on previous occasions and had become uncertain about the quality of the advice offered in the literature and about whether the description of the model was sufficiently realistic. As a result of these doubts, I decided to take the opportunity to study the process of model usage with an action science approach.[112]

I have discussed action science as a method for conducting case study research and as a means of integrating the work of the researcher and the consultant. The great advantage of action science is that it provides the researcher with substantially improved access. The great problem is how to unite the roles of researcher and consultant. I have also stated that the ideal action science project can rarely satisfy all demands within one and the same project. There is also a moving borderline in relation to participant observation and other methods. These will be discussed in the next section.

On Interviews and Observation

To understand the nature of action science, we have to examine closely related methods of access. Qualitative, informal, in-depth interviews and the anthropological / ethnographic methods of observation and participation are also important as part of action science. Quantitative survey methods such as questionnaires or structured personal interviews may also be useful. Action science adds the dimension of the researcher who, like the consultant, intervenes and becomes a change agent in the process under study. In contrast to the mainstream scientist who is detached, the action scientist is involved. An action scientist is both an academic researcher and a management consultant taking on the role of change agent.

The established classification of methods contains distinctions that seem relatively unimportant to me but that tend to create conflicts. For example, the traditional distinction between *field research* (data obtained through questionnaires, interviews, obser-vations, and participation) and *desk research* (the study of existing documents) seems to me to be increasingly artificial and is of little substance to the action scientist. Those engaged in the latter find themselves surrounded by a continuous flow of data: answers to questions, informal conversations, discussions at meetings, and the examination of existing documents and those that emerge out of an ongoing process, such as budgets, plans, memos, reports, slide presentations, letters, faxes, Internet messages, and press commentaries. The fact that some of this data appears on paper, film, or on a computer monitor while other data is communicated orally or by body language is not particularly important. It is the conversion of this data into information and conclusions that is of interest. The action scientist is also surrounded by a flow of both *quantitative* and *qualitative* data, another artificial demarcation line that creates unnecessary conflicts among scientists.

All methods for data collection give rise to both advantages and disadvantages. An interesting question when working with qualitative methods is whether methods that do not lead to *objec-tive*, maybe not even *intersubjective*, but to very personal, *subjec-tive*, interpretations can be considered acceptable in science and in consultancy. This may well lead to difficulties in satisfying main-stream scientists' requirements; they may have difficulties in un-derstanding that the researchers themselves are the most impor-tant scientific instruments.

There is a substantial risk that informal methods of obtaining information may lead to superficiality. According to one colum-nist, "Researchers chat to company employees and then go off and write worse stories than those that regularly appear in the news-papers."[113] One article quotes the head of a corporation on the sub-ject of a research reports:

> The authors claim to have worked closely with the corporation . . .
> over a period of five months. However, this does not accord with
> our own understanding. The authors have met shop stewards from
> the metalworkers' union on two occasions and white collar union

representatives on two occasions. They have also met senior management on two occasions.[114]

During informal interviews, questions are not put in any preestablished order. The selection of questions is governed instead by the actual situation confronting the interviewer; it is a probing technique. Sometimes the interviewers may limit themselves to asking the questions they feel appropriate to ask on the spur of the moment, whereas on other occasions, a particular conceptual model or checklist will govern the choice of questions. The interviewer may also put forward a preliminary proposal to test reactions. The latter resembles a projective test in which the respondents provide quick and spontaneous reactions and a convenient source of alternative approaches and suggestions for improvements. Moreover, actions are taken and decisions are made that give rise to reactions. One listens attentively and tries to obtain the reactions of others by means of short questions or statements. Particular attention is paid to what the informants consider to be important. One has total freedom to change the form of the interview during a sequence of interviews and exclude or add to the areas of inquiry. One can ask to borrow or to copy written material that appears relevant. Close attention is paid to the body language—posture, gestures, facial expressions, dress—of the persons being interviewed; an attempt is made to evaluate these observations as being just as significant as the verbal statements.

One can also offer professional advice on what may be right or wrong about a particular aspect. The following example serves as an illustration. During an interview, I found that a company had engaged an advertising agency to set up a campaign designed to improve the company's image. The media cost of the campaign was expected to be around $300,000. In my judgment, the campaign was meaningless; the company lacked business mission, goals, and strategies and hence had no corporate image to communicate. After a brief examination of the project, I got in touch with the chief executive and proposed that the campaign ought to be stopped. It turned out to be possible to cancel the contract with media. The chief executive was satisfied because he wanted to cut costs.

The example illustrates that information gathering, analysis, conclusions, recommendations, and implementation can take place more or less simultaneously. This contrasts with the stage-by-stage approach (albeit partly iterative) recommended in scientific research. Care has to be taken here, however. There is a considerable risk that without an understanding of the institutional conditions, consultants and researchers may put forward naive, standard solutions.

Two methods of documenting an interview can be contrasted to each other. When using the first method, the intention is to try to preserve the interview in its original form without any form of editing or comment. The interviewer may make rapid notes or use shorthand. The conversation can be recorded on tape, which would preserve the purely verbal part of the interview or group discussion, although the symbolic language, including body language, would not be captured by this method. The use of a video camera, however, would in some situations allow the researcher to solve at least part of that problem.

In the second method, the interviewers write down all the obvious data—for example, frequency of customer calls, quantity of goods sold, specific events that have occurred—and then supplement their own notes with reference to the available documents. They make a note of their own tentative conclusions and ideas but do not try to establish any kind of comprehensive account of the interview. Hence, a two-hour interview can result in anything from a few lines of notes to several pages.

The first method provides a basis on which to assess the researcher's conclusions because it offers a complete account of the researcher's material. However, the material will not shed any light on the following items:

- Nonverbal communication between the interviewer and the informant from the company
- Whether or not the researcher has spoken to the right people

- Whether or not the researcher has obtained all the available and relevant archival material
- Informal contacts between the interviews

The first method allows the researcher to return to the verbal part of the interview situation as often as necessary. Using the second method, the researcher draws conclusions from certain selected observations made during the interview, meaning that a reexamination of the material would require a new interview. This would have to take place at a new point in time. Consequently, the interview would not necessarily be the same because a lot might have occurred during the intervening period.

The use of the second method is preferred by change agents because it can be difficult to combine the first method with the consultant's role as an active force for change. Hence, it will not be possible for an outsider to follow the course of the interview stage by stage. In my view, however, the first method also allows only a limited opportunity for others to examine a change process. A pile of written material may create magic by looking impressive, but due to its limitation to verbal statements, it may completely lack rational significance. It is essential in both cases that the researcher/consultant is honest and does not deliberately deceive the reader. At the same time, without being aware of it, there is the risk of showing bad judgment or omitting or misinterpreting vital aspects of the process under consideration.

The quantitative data collection methods used in research, such as questionnaires and structured interviews, merely rely on verbal statements. According to Hall, nonverbal language is of equal importance:

> Most Americans are only dimly aware of this "silent language" even though they use it every day. They are not conscious of the elaborate patterning of behavior which prescribes the handling of time, spatial relationships, attitudes toward work, play and learning. In addition to our verbal language, we are constantly communicating our real feelings in the language of behavior.[115]

In an article, aptly titled "The Sounds of Silence," the Halls say that nonverbal communication is the "only language used throughout most of the history of humanity. . . . You use this preverbal language, consciously and unconsciously, every day to tell other people how you feel about yourself and them. This language includes your postures, gestures, facial expressions, costume, the way you walk, even your treatment of time and space and material things."[116] In the same spirit, Nash decodes the runner's wardrobe as "the silent language of clothes."[117]

Primitive tribes know this. Babies are forced to use nonverbal communication to survive. Everyone active in business is aware of nonverbal language. Only researchers and sometimes consultants behave as if they did not have this knowledge, seemingly paralyzed by their elegant and detached research methodology and quantifications. In a chapter titled "Reading People," sports star promoter Mark McCormack advocates the use of *aggressive observation:*

> I will often fly great distances to meet someone face-to-face, even when I can say much of what needs to be said over the phone. . . . I want to form impressions based on what I observe even more than what I hear. After all, the impressions you have from meeting someone in person are often quite different from that formed in speaking over the phone.[118]

Related types of observation are the *unobtrusive methods.*[119] These are unconventional methods and measures used discreetly in order not to disturb the object of study. They are also referred to as *nonreactive;* that is, there is absolutely no interaction between the researcher and the individuals being studied and there is also no intervention. With the approach taken in this book—that the researcher/consultant has to become more deeply involved in the change process—unobtrusive methods might at first glance appear to be out of place. Instead, they should be seen as methods of access to data that supplement interactive methods, just as observations of gestures and clothing can supplement verbal statements. The data gathered can be grouped in physical traces, archives, and observations.[120]

Sherlock Holmes, who often impressed visitors by telling them something about themselves or about objects, can serve as an example of unobtrusive methods. In the case of "The Blue Carbuncle" Holmes had received a hat from a client. He showed it to Dr. Watson who said there was nothing to be learned from the hat. Holmes:

> On the contrary, Watson, you can see everything. You fail, however, to reason from what you see. You are too timid in drawing your inferences. . . . The man was . . . fairly well-to-do within the last three years, although he has now fallen upon evil days. He had foresight, but has less now than formerly, pointing to a moral retrogression . . . probably drink. . . .

On Watson's expression of astonishment Holmes explained:

> This hat is three years old. These flat brims curled at the edge came in then. It is a hat of the very best quality. . . . If a man could afford to buy so expensive a hat three years ago, and has had no hat since, then he has assuredly gone down in the world. . . . Here is the foresight, said he, putting his finger upon the little disc and loop of the hat-securer. They are never sold upon hats. This man ordered one, it is a sign of a certain amount of foresight, since he went out of his way to take this precaution against the wind. But since we see that he has broken the elastic, and has not troubled to replace it, it is obvious that he has less foresight now than formerly, which is a distinct proof of weakening nature.[121]

Webb et al. state that unobtrusive methods constitute a reaction against the almost exclusive reliance on questionnaires and interviews in social research:

> We lament this overdependence upon a single, fallible method. Interviews and questionnaires intrude as a foreign element into the social setting they would describe, they create as well as measure attitudes, they elicit atypical roles and responses, they are limited

to those who are accessible and will cooperate, and the responses are produced in part by dimensions of individual differences irrelevant to the topic at hand.[122]

Observation is an essential method of data gathering in anthropology/ethnography.[123] In its widest sense, anthropology is a study of a series of cultural phenomena such as customs, beliefs, behavior, and the social organization of humankind. Actually, consultants work much like anthropologists, although the latter seem to have defined their domain to that of primitive tribes in Papua New Guinea or social dropouts in slum districts. Today, however, there are "corporate anthropologists" who have entered business firms as consultants in the United States.

Ethnography is the branch of anthropology that is of prime interest to the management researcher/consultant. The ethnographic approach is concerned with descriptions of social patterns. The ethnographer learns from others about their culture and thereby must exhibit empathy, open-mindedness, and sensitivity. The prevailing method of access is participant observation, a highly empirical and inductive method of data gathering. In the course of participation, systematic observation is made through watching and in-depth interviews, documented not only in the form of memos but also photographs, films, and tape recordings.

Sometimes it is also the observation and even collection of artifacts—that is, objects that may play a significant role in a culture. The classic symbols of corporate power are room size, floor location of a room, the size and thickness of the carpet, admission to an executive dining room, and even the key to special restrooms.

Traditional survey methods such as questionnaires together with the study of archival material are also used. Characteristic of the anthropological approach is the long period over which a culture is studied; this is in comparison to the one- or two-hour interviews used in many management studies.

Van Maanen makes the following characterization:

The result of ethnographic inquiry is cultural description. It is, however, the type of description that can only emerge from a lengthy period of intimate study and residence in a given social setting. It calls for the acquired knowledge of the always special language spoken in this setting, first-hand participation in some of the activities that take place there, and most critically, a deep reliance on intensive work with a few informants drawn from the setting.[124]

As change agents, researchers/consultants must have a close relationship with major decision makers and other line and staff representatives in the company with which they are working. They must be able to enter a new environment and a new culture as strangers, but they must be "professional strangers."[125]

It takes time to become an accepted member of an organization and to be able to understand what is happening. The length of time that it takes depends, among other things, on researchers'/consultants' preunderstanding, their professionalism, and the help they get from gatekeepers such as executives who can allow or refuse entry to an organization. Barnes states: "A social scientist may well find that gaining access to the people he wants to study may be as difficult and lengthy a process as gaining financial support for his work."[126] He goes on to explain refused access:

The rationale for refusal was usually that the anthropologist was not an initiated member of the tribe and that, therefore, he lacked the qualifications essential for access to the secrets, or that, even if he had acquired the necessary qualifications, he would pass on the secrets to the unqualified world at large through his publications.[127]

When access is refused, or when the researcher's/consultant's presence may be a disturbance, *covert* inquiry is sometimes used (raising, however, some tricky ethical issues) "where the scientist seeks information which he believes the citizens would wish to keep secret from an outsider but which they may be willing to impart to a newcomer who identifies himself with them. Several studies of rule-breaking in industry and commerce have been made in this way."[128]

Participant observation is direct, without intermediaries, but the degree of participation can vary. As an illustration, we will examine the approach adopted in an ongoing study of leadership and development processes in a construction company.[129] In the view of the researchers, *direct observation* is the principal method to be used in studies of change processes:

> Research into the role of leadership during processes of change comprises the study of actions, reactions and interactions, i.e., an examination of how the interrelationships between the various actors can change over time. Hence direct observations can be considered to be a perfectly adequate method of investigation. Interviews and questionnaires could also be used to obtain additional data on the motives for action, the perception of other people's motives and the experiences gained from periods of change. It is naturally quite impossible—even with unlimited resources—to capture the entire development process that takes place within a company during a particular period. In practice, we are limited to observations of specific aspects of certain selected fragments of an extremely complicated process.[130]

The methods of observation used in this study, which extended over a period of two years, are described in the following manner:

> We attend meetings, conferences, seminars, training courses, follow development projects, visit construction sites as well as participate in special events. We carry out observational studies of senior members of management during one working week. Questionnaires are distributed to all of the office staff as well as to senior site foremen in order to gather information on the creative climate within the company. We also examine different types of data concerning the company and its construction operations.[131]

Altogether, four individuals have been involved on the study, three external researchers and a member of a corporate staff unit ("in charge of development projects"). The fact that two or three members of the team usually attend meetings is considered to have improved the reliability and coverage of the data. This may

well be true under certain circumstances, but I would hardly recommend it as a general method. It is expensive in terms of resources as well as being highly dependent on the competence and
degree of cooperation between the individual researcher/con-
sultants. In the worst case, the presence of a team could actually
"disturb" the processes:

> We are aware that human systems that are the subject of observa-
> tion and study are liable to be influenced. . . . However, this influ-
> ence tends to decline as confidence is gradually built up between
> the researchers and those who are affected by the study. The possi-
> bilities of establishing a spirit of trusting cooperation are particu-
> larly favourable in relation to longitudinal studies, provided that
> the researchers have succeeded in persuading all the parties in-
> volved that it is in their mutual interest.[132]

This research project also makes a slight move in the direction
of action science:

> On separate occasions, we have reported our observations to the
> management group and representatives of the staff union, to a
> meeting of all of the staff, and on another occasion to the manage-
> ment group alone. We have particularly tried to keep these ac-
> counts free from our own personal judgements. The direct link with
> the company has also naturally been maintained through the con-
> tinuous cooperation with the staff member responsible for devel-
> opment projects who is part of our research team. The
> investigations have therefore included a certain element of action
> science methodology. In other respects, the researchers have acted
> as neutral observers.[133]

It is not clear to me how one can be a "neutral observer" in a social situation, and this is also a problem for professional anthropologists. The latter would like to be "a little fly on the wall," thus
being inconspicuous but still able to move freely around. Even in
the realm of the natural sciences, where heavy emphasis is placed
on the neutrality of the observer, problems may arise. I am think-

ing here of Heisenberg's principle of uncertainty, which states that under observation an electron changes its behavior.[134]

Direct observation, however, is often time-consuming, requiring resources not available to the researcher/consultant. It can be difficult in the sense that you cannot physically be at the place of an incident because you do not know where and when it will occur. Even if you can figure out that an incident is likely to occur, it may be infrequent and your presence may interfere with the incident. You would need the patience of the paparazzi photographer squatting outside the home of a celebrity for months hoping she will strip without drawing the curtains.

The critical incident technique (CIT) is a method for coming close to direct observation but avoiding some of its hardships. An example of the application of the method is given by Bitner, Nyquist, and Booms[135] in the investigation of the "service encounter," that is, the occasion when a service is delivered in interaction with a customer. In three service industries—hotels, restaurants, and airlines—131 employees were interviewed, producing 355 usable incidents. The respondents were instructed to do the following:

Think of examples when their or their fellow employees' interactions with customers were difficult or uncomfortable.
Describe the circumstances of the incident.
Provide details until the interviewer could visualize each incident.

The authors summarize the advantages of CIT in this way: "CIT generates data with the level of detail and richness that puts the researcher close to the realities of the process being studied; it is almost direct observation."[136] It is an inductive method in which no hypotheses are needed and the incidents, as they appear in the answers, are allowed to form patterns that the researcher can develop into concepts and theories. The method allows more incidents, minicases, to be collected than would be possible through direct observation, and it gives plenty of room for researchers'/consultants' "theoretical sensitivity." It will not, however, provide them with the same intense feeling of an incident that they would get through direct involvement and observation; it is still access through intermediaries and understanding second-hand. Moreover, the incidents have to be fairly brief and well defined—a requirement that a process of change—for example, a company turnaround—hardly can fulfill.

What methods of access are recommended in consulting handbooks? Kubr[137] refers to three basic sources—records, events and conditions, and memories ("all the information stored in the minds of people")—that can be drawn on by the traditional methods of questionnaires, interviews, observations, and studies of archival records. Like Block,[138] Greiner and Metzger concentrate on traditional methods and recommend the questionnaire as "the consultant's most powerful tool for yielding maximum information in the most efficient manner."[139] Schein, however, considers questionnaires a less useful instrument for the study of processes and suggests that a combination of interviews and direct observation would be an optimal approach.[140] These writers also describe a large number of tactical rules that can be used to interpret social interaction, social atmosphere, and so forth. The same type of tactical rules sometimes appear in textbooks on scientific method. In my judgment, long experience and good preunderstanding are required to be able to apply these rules. I have already expressed the opinion that those researchers/consultants who have acquired knowledge by acquaintance have a superior preunderstanding that helps them to get better access in new projects.

The purpose of this section was to discuss and compare methods of access to data. But what are data worth? When do they become reliable and truthful; when do they become facts? This will be discussed in the next section.

On Facts and Fiction

A problem for researchers and consultants alike is to determine what data to use. Are there any "facts" in management? A widely circulated book on management consultancy gives the following advice:

> All sound consulting work is built on facts. Operating consultants need a considerable number of facts to have a clear picture of the situation, arrive at precise problem definition and relate their proposals to reality. Facts are also needed for assignments which try to develop something very new and involve a great deal of imagination and creative thinking. Facts may be difficult to obtain and in some cases fact finding may be the most tiring phase of the consultant's work, but there is no alternative.[141]

My first impression on reading the above was that it was either based on ignorance of the consultant's real world or that it was a public relations boast that sought to promote the credibility of the consultancy profession. It seems to be based on the idea that objective data constitute social "reality," a belief that historically is ascribed to the natural sciences. It also gives an impression that facts can be found, even though considerable effort is required. However, no definition of "facts" is provided.

The obsession with the one and only true fact scarcely has any foundation with an experienced change agent or action scientist. Moreover, it is not grounded in today's natural sciences either. Elton compares historical research with the natural sciences and states that "phenomena once regarded as objectively true [in the natural sciences] are now seen to be only a statistical abstraction from random variables."[142] Instead, natural scientists use phrases such as "more probable," "more accurately descriptive," "more aesthetically satisfying," or "more intellectually satisfying."

A study on "the soul of a fact" was made by Fleck in *Genesis and Development of a Scientific Fact*.[143] Although the report was presented in 1935, it did not attract attention until recently. A scientist reacted to the title by exclaiming: "How can such a book be? A fact is a fact. It has neither genesis nor development."[144] The general idea is that a fact is definite and permanent, independent of subjective interpretation, and independent of paradigm. According to Fleck this is an illusion.

It is therefore particularly important to examine the methods that are used by the researcher/consultant to assemble facts. A couple of examples will be used to illustrate the connection between facts and research approach.

In strategic planning, both academic writers and management consultants recommend that the firm make a "position audit" in which the present status of a firm's product line, customer segments, competitive situation, finances, and so forth are established before they go on to make predictions and prescriptions about the future. Wallander[145] has pointed out that predictions and forecasts in business are overrated. We know so little about the future that these forecasts rather decrease our ability to adapt to a changing environment. But he goes one step farther and states that *we are often not even able to describe our present position.*

Successful business leaders have always lived with ambiguity, chaos, and complexity. Within the positivistic and scientific paradigm, such "disorder" is a token of weakness, failure, and need for further research. The statistics and mathematics forming the base for "rigorous, empirical research" require rational, logical, and simple cause-effect relationships with operationalized independent and dependent variables. In an article and commentaries on how implementation is treated in research in marketing, Piercy, Cravens, and Gummesson[146] question the role of theory and scholarly research. Gummesson concludes:

> It is a paradox that the mathematics promoted in marketing is the *old* mathematics, based on mechanical, algebraic and geometric models from the 14th century and earlier. They have been upgraded over the years, and today with high speed computers, equations can be solved that took too long to solve before, and data can be processed with more sophistication. The preoccupation with the old mathematics is a paradox because the *new* mathematics, deriving from the 20th century and much of it from the past few decades, opens up new opportunities. It includes systems theory, chaos theory and dissipative structures, fractal geometry, autopoiesis with self healing and self organizing systems, and others. They are all geared to accepting and addressing complexity, dynamics,

indeterminism and ambiguity. They are not looking for simplistic and partial cause and effect links, but for patterns and wholes. They dissolve the artificial demarcation line between qualitative and quantitative; in fact, the new mathematics is more qualitative than quantitative.[147]

Simultaneously, my impression is that there is a strong urge for *management by fact*—more reliance on data and less on opinion. At face value, this may seem contradictory, but in my view, two or more contradictory "facts" could very well coexist. In fact, contradiction, chaos and ambiguity *are* facts, but not facts in the positivistic sense.

In a consulting assignment concerning a client's business mission, goals, and strategies, I scanned through several feet of shelf containing reports on future developments in the computer and electronics markets. These reports had been prepared by some of the world's leading consultancy firms specializing in projections regarding future changes in technology and markets. Two questions presented themselves here.

First, how had the data contained in the reports been assembled? They were based on questionnaires and interviews, but the information provided to the reader on methods of sampling, qualifications of interviewers and analysts, and the proportion of nonrespondents was incomplete. How should the reader handle these uncertainties? Could these data be considered facts?

Second, could this material be considered to provide an adequate basis for decisions because it represented only a limited range of data? It could of course be supplemented by additional data, although at a cost.

In hindsight, when the answers are there, I can conclude that my search for useful prediction in the high-priced and prestigious reports was wasted. They did not forecast the future except in haphazard terms, and if they ended up right on the content of some issue, the timing was wrong. We have heard predictions of the paperless office (offices today have more paper than ever before; the launching of the Xerox copying technology and computers *caused* the amount of paper to increase, not to decrease) and more recently that traveling to international conferences would be replaced by Internet conferences (the Internet has *caused* traveling to increase, not to decrease). In 1977, founder and leader of Digital Equipment, Ken Olsen, is reputed to have said that "There is no reason anyone would want a computer in their home," and Bill Gates, Microsoft's leader and computer wunderkind, claimed in 1981 that "640 kilobyte memory capacity ought to be enough for anybody" (today personal computers come with one or several gigabytes—that is, a couple of million kilobytes).

Hence, it may be concluded that decisions are largely based on intuition, experience, willpower, and what might be considered socially acceptable in a given situation. This is also a kind of "fact," but it is difficult to determine using traditional methods. In phenomenology, a statement by a person is considered a fact about this person's interpretation of a phenomenon—for example, why the competitors are gaining market share—but it is not a fact about the phenomenon itself; that is, it is not necessarily the true explanation to the company's loss of market share.

TQM practices include consumer surveys with the purpose of establishing the right level of quality for goods and services. In these surveys, consumers are asked about their opinions. Consumer opinions are a blend of subjective feeling and objective appraisal which, through some "black box" processing, are set in relation to their felt needs and the size of their purse. The outcome is customer-perceived quality, which becomes a fact in the context in which it is used. The conclusion is important: *A fact is not an absolute truth; it is a context-dependent truth.*

Geneen devotes several pages of his memoirs to discussing the meaning of facts. He wants *unshakable facts,* but he says they are hard to come by. Instead we tend to regard a whole series of derivations as facts: "apparent facts, assumed facts, reported facts, hoped-for facts, accepted facts," and others. He further says that the "truth is that the so-called facts are almost always coloured by the bias of the man presenting them."[148]

What could we do to make certain that we are getting as close to the facts as our ability, time, and resources allow? Geneen recommends that facts should be gathered from a wide range of sources.

This would allow the manager to "strip away the biases, including his own, and to try to get a true picture of what is involved."[149]

This is the same recommendation as is made to researchers under the label of *triangulation*.[150] Used in navigation, land surveying, and civil engineering, triangulation is "a technique for precise determination of distances and angles for location of a ship's or aircraft's position, and in such endeavors as road building, tunnel alignment and other construction." If one side and two angles of a triangle are measured, the entire triangle is established: "By constructing a series of such triangles, each adjacent to at least one other, values can be obtained for distances and angles not otherwise measurable."[151] In the social sciences, the term *triangulation* is used for the application of two or more methods on the same research problem to increase the reliability of the results. For example, a statistical, quantitative survey of consumer needs could be supplemented by in-depth personal interviews with a small number of consumers and by focus group discussions. If all these point to the same results, the chances are increased that "facts" have been obtained. If the results are contradictory, we realize that the use of a single method could have misled us. The use of multiple methods, however, has to be carried out with "distance" between he methods. Unfortunately, as pointed out by McGrath et al., *"we characteristically use in our next step, the very methods that we and others have used before on the same problem,"*[152] thus creating methodological redundancy instead of complementarity.

Iacocca says that managers get stuck in their decision making, "especially those with too much education," and he once commented to his successor, "The trouble with you, Phil, is that you went to Harvard, where they taught you not to take any action until you've got *all* the facts." The business environment is also changing, and as Iacocca says, "I'm writing these words in 1984 and we're already planning our models for 1987 and 1988 . . . even though I can't say with any certainty what the public will want next *month*."[153]

Kaldor[154] advocates the use of *stylized facts,* which are approximations that help us to communicate without getting lost in too many details. These facts may not be accurate in a strict sense but draw our attention to important phenomena. "Averages," for example, are stylized facts. "Average income" may not apply to any single individual but can be used to compare the living standards in different parts of the world. Stylized facts can be attractive through their simplicity but at the same time can be dangerously deceptive. For example, average income does not say anything about the distribution of wealth between individuals.

Doctorow claims that novelists

> compose false documents more valid, more real, more truthful than the "true" documents of the politicians or the journalists or the psychologists. Novelists know more explicitly that the world in which we live is still to be formed and that reality is amenable to any construction that is placed upon it.[155]

The statement that false documents could be more true than true documents certainly sounds confusing. This subject has also been discussed by scientists Milton Friedman and Paul Samuelson, both Nobel Prize laureates in the economic sciences. They have adopted contradictory positions in an argument on true and false assumptions.[156] In Friedman's view, theoretical assumptions must not be judged by their realism but by their predictive usefulness: "Truly important and significant hypotheses will be found to have 'assumptions' that are widely inaccurate descriptive representations of reality and in general, the more significant the theory, the more unrealistic the assumptions (in this sense)." Samuelson emphatically refutes this standpoint.

Philosopher Thomas Nagel, in *The View from Nowhere*,[157] describes the dilemma between our individual, subjective outlook on the world and our efforts to free ourselves from this subjectiveness in favor of an objective view, a view that positivistic scientists claim to be able to create, just given time and resources. He finds science pretentious and says that it is true that the world consists of stones, tables, houses, and atoms, but that it is just as true that it consists of billions of individual subjective perspectives. These are just as much "facts" as are the physical objects, but because of their complexity they are left out of (allegedly) scientific reports.

Sen's conclusion is that there

> is no reason why descriptive statements in economics have to aspire after mechanical accuracy even when it conflicts with comprehension and absorption. There is of course an obvious objection to presenting non-facts dressed up as facts, but there is no need to do this once non-facts are accepted as legitimate descriptive instruments themselves. Such a description of something will be good in the sense of being useful, but . . . must not be confused with its being a good—or realistic—description of that thing.[158]

Sen considers fiction "a general method of coming to grips with facts. There is nothing illegitimate in being helped by 'War and Peace' to an understanding of the Napoleonic Wars in Russia or by the 'Grapes of Wrath' to digesting aspects of the Depression."

So facts are not that unambiguous, and the ability of science to find facts is challenged. When witnesses are sworn in, the U.S. courts require them to repeat the phrase: "I swear to tell the truth, the whole truth, and nothing but the truth, so help me God." It is interesting to note that in search of the truth they ask God for help. One might have thought that in our century the wording would have been changed to "so help me science." But as we have seen, there are good reasons for not changing this.

The ordinary journalism that surrounds our daily life hardly fulfills any of the criteria of scientific inquiry. A *Newsweek* reporter says,

> Distortions often get a head start on truths through a peculiar combination of laziness and hype. . . . Serious news, too, is often treated with the gullibility and lack of follow-through that allows a prankster to thrive. . . . When a story fades, it fades almost entirely, and the media's saturation coverage skips on to the next event, often passing over whatever new details that may fundamentally change the "old" stories.[159]

However, one brand of journalism, *investigative journalism,* can be interesting to compare with scientific research; there are differences as well as similarities. Both are carried out with the same basic methods: interviews, observation, participation, and study of written archives.[160] Furthermore, investigative reporting is characterized by the following.

First, the colloquial term *muckraking*[161] tells us that reporters are looking for something that people deliberately or unconsciously conceal; they are penetrating a taboo area. The Watergate scandal in the beginning of the 1970s is often referred to as the most significant case of investigative journalism in modern times.[162] Reporters Bernstein and Woodward became celebrities by uncovering illegal data gathering carried out by then-President Nixon's staff to gain political advantages. Another famous example of investigative journalism is Ralph Nader's[163] investigation of General Motors and the denied designed-in defects of cars that caused repeated accidents. *Newsday* editor Bob Greene[164] has dug up cases any academic researcher would envy him—among them, the distribution system for heroin from Turkey to Long Island and corruption in the state of Arizona.

Second, investigative reporters are not necessarily waiting for something to happen; they are not geared toward daily events and tight deadlines. They may investigate the deals of a business leader, a company's or a whole industry's product line and its effect on the environment, or a government agency's connections with the building and construction industry. They may investigate something that has caught their attention as inexplicable or just interesting. They may carry out research for months without writing a single line for publication.

Third, they are challenging the tenet of old-style journalism that says "you can't fight city hall"—that is, the belief that how something complicated really works, symbolized by the city hall, cannot be found out and thus is not amenable to research.[165] The investigative reporter searches for "problems that officialdom ignores"[166] and his or her "persistent questioning of accepted mythology upsets the high priests,"[167] making for "high-risk journalism[168] . . . where [the reporter's] reward is about equal parts of pain and pleasure."[169]

Investigative journalism is often much more daring than academic research. Reporters are trained to get access to people in high office, and they are not scared of phoning them in the middle of the night. They demonstrate more stamina together with unorthodox methods of access.

The distinction between investigative journalism, memoirs, novels, documentary films, and scientific research is not clear; sometimes they merge into some kind of "factual fiction" or "faction." Some of the world's best-selling writers dwell in a borderland between these species of writing. Let's look at a few examples illustrating different types of access, preunderstanding, datagathering methods, and formats of presenting the results.

Fictional works by Arthur Hailey—for example *Airport, Hotel,* and *Strong Medicine* (on the pharmaceutical industry)[170]—are based on extensive interviews, observation, and archival material and on an aspiration to penetrate the business he has chosen as the arena for his plot. It is presented as fiction—but it could have been true! A similar example based on a different type of data gathering is Jeffrey Archer's *First among Equals,*[171] a fiction on political rivalry in Britain's Parliament. Being himself an ex-member of Parliament, he has firsthand preunderstanding of the political game and has had privileged access to information. Vance Packard (e.g., *The Hidden Persuaders* on advertising, *The Waste Makers* on designed-in obsolescence of products)[172] and Anthony Sampson (e.g., *The Sovereign State* on the unknown life of ITT, *The Arms Bazaar* on the arms trade, *Empires of the Sky* on the international airline business, and *The Midas Touch* on money)[173] are examples of investigative journalism that deals with aspects of business life, with a strong inclination to reveal new facts and present taboos.

Most case studies used for research purposes in management are based on interviews of one or two hours' length with each respondent.[174] Serious investigative reporters seem to put in more effort, and what they achieve is often much more revealing than the output from academic research. One example is an interview with Fidel Castro published in *Playboy;*[175] getting access to the respondent is an achievement in itself, and most academics would have given up. It took diplomatic contacts to get the interview. It took patience to wait for the calls from Castro's office to indicate that he was ready for a new session: "Few interviews could have been as bumpy in the making as our eight day marathon with

Fidel Castro." The eight days resulted in 25 hours on tape, some of it recorded in seven-hour sessions ending at four o'clock in the morning.

Successful business leaders write their memoirs with the assistance of professional writers. Previously, these writers were referred to as ghost writers and were kept in the closet, but today they at least get recognition with their name on the book's cover, usually in small letters. Geneen's book is a good demonstration of the joint effort of the experienced writer and the executive. In the introduction to the book, coauthor Alvin Moscow writes:

> I met Harold Geneen in the spring of 1980 through the introduction of Richard Curtis, the literary agent who conceived the idea of our collaboration on a book. . . . A year later, in April 1981, we went to work together. . . . It turned out to be a happy collaboration which took two and a half years. . . . We would meet after his normal business day and work from six to eleven o'clock, sometimes to midnight, sometimes on weekends. Our tape-recorded sessions which must have run to millions of words, were dutifully transcribed.[176]

In his description of Ford Motor Company, Iacocca uses his own experience as the source. In a different type of book on Ford, Lacey moved with his family to Detroit for two years, made some two hundred interviews, including two with Henry Ford II while Iacocca refused to receive him, and he worked briefly on the assembly line.[177]

Another example of investigative journalism presented in a novel format is Graham Greene's book about a former Panamanian head of state, General Torrijos.[178] The book is a cross between a sociological and political report and a novel. He calls the book *Getting to Know the General* with an emphasis on "know" and with the subtitle *The Story of an Involvement*. He had no problem with access; he was invited on the initiative of the general. He visited and lived with him and his staff on several occasions.

Gunter Wallraff, the German investigative reporter, uses disguise to get access to new environments, so-called *covert inquiry*. One of his books[179] reports how he disguised himself and impersonated a Turk, took the jobs he could get, and lived as a member of the guest worker community for two years, day and night. Through this involvement, he found out about aspects of corporate life that no mainstream scientist would have been able to uncover with interviews and observations. His method raises some ethical issues, but on the other hand, there seems to be no alternative but to abstain from the topic and classify it as "not amenable to research."

I have come across some books that describe the development of new products in the information technology industry illustrating two types of access. *The Soul of a New Machine*[180] is a detailed and dramatized account of the development of a new computer at Data General. The author gets access as a participant observer living with the development team. *A Switch in Time* and *The Mobile Phone Book* are written by an engineer at Ericsson,[181] manufacturers of telecommunications equipment, with the assistance of a copywriter from an advertising agency. They describe the birth of the new electronic, digital telephone switches and the emergence of mobile telephony. The author had worked in the company for 35 years and been personally deeply involved in the events he describes.

Rand Araskog, the successor of Harold Geneen as CEO of ITT, has written a book based on his experience:

> In the midst of the raiders' attack on ITT, I decided to record my actions and thoughts and, later, to share the experience of an American corporation under siege, especially now when the frontal assault on mainstream businesses is one of the central facts of this decade.[182]

This is a type of action research; Araskog was the lead actor in the drama, and he recorded and interpreted the process. He probably did not do this in a manner that would be accepted as scientific, but he certainly had a privileged access.

Two professors of economics, under the pseudonym of Marshall Jevons,[183] have written a combined mystery novel-textbook on economics and account for the work of a fictional promotion and tenure committee. Their professional knowledge of the subject of economics and their own experience of the process of assessing candidates for academic promotion could have been presented in the traditional academic format, but the authors chose to dress it up in a murder intrigue. Their presentation of the sociology of the promotion committee, although fictional, communicates the mechanisms inherent in the process better than any traditional research report.

None of the examples above would pass as scientific research, although some of them could have been designed to do so. But would that be desirable? Shipman says that "control over research methods and their publication for scrutiny would be unwelcome to a journalist and would ruin a good novel."[184] John Gardner, novelist and teacher of creative writing, says that if one is "persuaded that certain things must never be done in fiction and certain things must always be done, one has entered the first stage of aesthetic arthritis, the disease that ends up in pedantic rigidity and the atrophy of intuition."[185]

Novels, memoirs, short stories, and movies have shown themselves to be better able to explore and expose taboos. It is perhaps the case that memoirs, novels, and so forth are able to provide a more realistic picture of processes within companies. Or to quote from an interview with an international consultant and researcher: "I read a lot, particularly fiction. I get much more from reading Marguerite Yourcenar than from reading a research report. Her novel 'Memoirs of Hadrian' provides wisdom and understanding."[186] Others also point to the value of drawing on fiction when conducting research. For instance, one writer states that "case studies are often just imagination dressed in the grey suit of reality and that novels are less imaginary than we tend to believe."[187]

This section has exposed the reader to a number of examples of the connection between facts, fiction, and method as presented by different categories of professionals: scholars, investigative reporters, and authors of memoirs and novels. I would like to conclude with some comments on the media used to communicate with an audience.

The best known statement on the connection between medium and content is probably that by McLuhan: "The medium is the message."[188] Expressed in a somewhat simplified way, it means that you cannot separate content from the way the content is conveyed. The same "fact" presented in a person-to-person conversation, in a scientific report, in a lecture, on a theater stage, or on television will not be received in the same way because the media are different. In the late 1990s, French philosopher Pierre Bourdieu, directed a harsh attack on TV as a meaningless medium, distorting information and communicating only flashes of ideas and loose statements without commitment and context. For that reason, he never accepts to be interviewed on TV. Postman elaborates this further in several examples. In one of these, he tells the story of the doctoral candidate who in his dissertation referred to a statement by saying in a footnote, "Told to the investigator at the Roosevelt Hotel on January 18, 1981, in the presence of Arthur Lingeman and Jerold Gross." This disturbed the assessors who claimed that quotations should emanate from written sources: "You are mistaken to believe that the form in which an idea is conveyed is irrelevant to its truth. In the academic world, the published word is invested with greater prestige and authenticity than the spoken word."[189] This of course is disputable. What happens if a future scholar quotes this dissertation and the statement? He can then refer to a written source and the content of the very same statement gets increased factual status.

Maybe it's a fact that there are no facts.

Summary

This chapter has dealt with case study research. It has stressed that the change agent, the consultant as well as the researcher, works with a limited number of cases. It has further discussed some areas of case study research that I find particularly intriguing: generalizations from one or a few studies, the usefulness of historical analysis, and the problem of taboos. It has presented action science as a method for case study research and the opportunities and difficulties inherent in the method. It has also commented on the use of interviews and observation as techniques for data gathering. The last section raised the question of the meaning of facts and the distinction between facts and fiction and between science and other forms of research and presentations.

The scientists' use of methods and the consultants' modes of operation raise the difficult question of assessing quality in research and consultancy. This question will be dealt with in the next chapter.

Notes

1. For a further review of the case study as a research method, see, for example, Eisenhardt, 1989, and Yin, 1994.
2. Strauss and Glaser, 1970, pp. 182-93, call the first type "case study" and the second "case history."
3. How a case study can be interpreted using hermeneutics is described by Odman, 1979, pp. 106-84.
4. Yin, 1994, p. 13.
5. Sen, 1980, pp. 353-69.
6. Ibid., p. 353.
7. Kjellen and Soderman, 1980, pp. 30-36.
8. Ibid., p. 35. Within hermeneutics and phenomenology, the German word for understanding, *Verstehen,* has become accepted international jargon. See Weber, 1968.
9. Valdelin, 1974, p. 47.
10. Capra, 1982, p. 85ff.
11. Alloway, 1977, p. 2.
12. Ibid., p. 3.
13. Mattsson, 1982, p. 24.
14. Lindahl and Lindwall, 1978; Hesslow, 1979; Sjostrand, 1979.
15. Rubenowitz, 1980, p. 35.
16. Hagg and Hedlund, 1978, pp. 7-13.
17. Normann, 1970, p. 53.
18. See, for example, Krueger, 1994, and Greenbaum, 1998.
19. Bonoma, 1985a, p. 206.
20. Popper, 1979, pp. 40-41.
21. Bohm, 1977, p. 374.
22. Shipman, 1982, p. 26.
23. Ibid., p. 31.
24. Taylor and Bogdan, 1984, p. 7. For a presentation of different types of validity and reliability see, for example, Yin, 1994; Kirk and Miller, 1986; and Nachmias and Nachmias, 1987, pp. 167-76.

25. The staircases are reproduced in Reutersvard, 1994, pp. 37 and 61. For an analysis of the optical illusion of figures, see Ernst, 1992.

26. Hagg, 1982, pp. 95-99; quotations from pp. 97-98.

27. Shipman, 1982, p. 139.

28. Glaser and Strauss, 1967; Strauss and Glaser, 1970; Glaser 1978.

29. Glaser and Strauss, 1967, pp. 1-15.

30. Hunt, 1983, pp. 21-25.

31. Gummesson, 1977, 1999; Gronroos, 1990.

32. This refers to the traditional marketing education in several Western countries, including the United States where marketing education heavily relies on U.S. textbooks primarily concerned with consumer goods and the "marketing mix" theory.

33. Glaser and Strauss, 1967, p. 30.

34. Fleck, [1935] 1979.

35. Glaser and Strauss, 1967, pp. 45-77.

36. Ibid., pp. 61-62.

37. Patton, 1990, pp. 182-83.

38. Patton, 1980, pp. 279-83.

39. Ibid., p. 281, a quotation from Blake.

40. Ibid., p. 280.

41. Gummesson, 1999.

42. Gustavsen and Sorensen, 1982, p. 151.

43. Cronbach as quoted in Patton, 1980, p. 280.

44. Argyris et al., 1985, p. 84.

45. Glaser and Strauss, 1967, pp. 46-47.

46. Glaser, 1978, pp. 6-7.

47. See further, Mintzberg, 1994.

48. Wallander, 1994.

49. Arbnor and Andersson, 1977, p. 85.

50. Ibid., p. 94.

51. Ibid., p. 47.

52. Ibid., p. 93.

53. Ibid., p. 63.

54. Kjellen and Soderman, 1980, pp. 26-28, quotation from p. 27.

55. Smith and Steadman, 1981, p. 165.

56. Elson, 1990, pp. 52-53.

57. According to William J. McDonough, President and CEO of Federal Reserve Bank of New York, at a presentation at Svenska Dagbladets Executive Club, in Stockholm, June 1998.

58. Batra, [1978] 1990.

59. Shelton, 1990.

60. Nilson, 1989, p. 28.

61. Ingvar, 1984, 1985; Ingvar and Sandberg, 1985.

62. Elton, [1967] 1989, p. 11.

63. Smith and Steadman, 1981, 171; Kantrow, 1986.

64. Peters and Waterman, 1982, p. 10.

65. McKenna, 1985, p. 111.

66. Iacocca, 1984.

Case Study Research   153

67. Ibid., p. 105.
68. Wallander, 1994.
69. Rodgers, 1986, p. 122.
70. Smith and Steadman, 1981, p. 171.
71. See, for example, Deal and Kennedy, 1983; Hofstede, 1980.
72. Uttal, 1983, pp. 66-72.
73. Kihlmann et al., 1985, p. 5.
74. Johannisson, 1980.
75. See Danielsson's, 1977, discussion on "sediments," pp. 10-12.
76. Gummesson, 1999.
77. McGrath et al., 1982, pp. 76 and 101.
78. Martin, 1982, p. 19.
79. Kulka, 1982, p. 44.
80. Hofstede, 1980, p. 375.
81. Hall, [1959] 1973, p. 186.
82. Burrell, 1984, quotation from p. 97. See also the discussions in Holm-Lofgren, 1980.
83. See, for example, Heran et al., 1989.
84. Biddle Barrows, 1986, p. 132.
85. See, for example, Stockdale, 1996, and Alvesson and Billing, 1997.
86. See Gummesson, 1999, who talks about the law-based relationship and the criminal network; see also Falcone and Padovani, 1991; Fiorentini and Peltzman, 1995; and Eberwein and Tholen, 1997.
87. Issal, 1984, p. v.
88. Iacocca, 1984, pp. 114-15, 154.
89. Araskog, 1989, p. 14.
90. Ortmark, 1985.
91. Argyris et al., 1985, p. x.
92. Hult and Lennung, 1978a, 1978b, pp. 178-80.
93. Argyris et al., 1985, pp. 36-79.
94. Elden and Chisholm, 1993, pp. 126-30.
95. Lewin, 1946.
96. Habermas, [1968] 1987.
97. Sandberg, 1982, p. 29.
98. Ibid., p. 79.
99. Tandon, 1988, p. 7. See also other articles in the special issue of *Convergence*, "Focus on Participatory Research," 1988.
100. Coghlan and McDonagh, 1997, pp. 139-161.
101. Argyris et al., 1985, p. 82.
102. Clark, 1972, 62ff.
103. Argyris et al., 1985, p. 78.
104. Feldt, 1991.
105. Garthon, 1983.
106. Sveiby, 1994.
107. Rylander, 1995.
108. Schmid, 1982.
109. Sandberg, 1982, pp. 11-12.
110. Ibid, p. 84.

111. Gustavsen, 1982.
112. Gummesson, 1982.
113. Bergstrom, 1984.
114. Bendrik, 1978.
115. Hall, [1959] 1973, p. xiii.
116. Hall and Hall, 1977, p. 132.
117. Nash, 1977, p. 172.
118. McCormack, 1984, p. 23.
119. Webb et al., 1966; Webb and Weick, 1983.
120. Webb et al., 1966, p. 3.
121. Doyle, [1891] 1985a, pp. 282-84.
122. Webb et al., 1966, p. 1.
123. Taylor and Bogdan, 1984; Bjorklund and Hannerz, 1983.
124. Van Maanen, 1982, pp. 103-04.
125. *The Professional Stranger* is the title of Agar's 1980 book on anthropology.
126. Barnes, 1977, p. 8.
127. Ibid., p. 5.
128. Ibid., p. 11.
129. Edstrom et al., 1984.
130. Ibid., p. 14.
131. Ibid., p. 15-16.
132. Ibid., p. 16.
133. Ibid., p. 16.
134. Patton, 1980, p. 189.
135. Bitner et al., 1985, p. 50. See also Nyquist, Bitner, and Booms, 1985.
136. Ibid., p. 51.
137. Kubr (ed.), 1983, p. 127.
138. Block, 1981.
139. Greiner and Metzger, 1983, p. 223.
140. Schein, 1969, pp. 97-101.
141. Kubr, 1983.
142. Elton, [1967] 1989, p. 71.
143. Fleck, [1935] 1979.
144. From foreword by Thomas S. Kuhn in Fleck, [1935] 1979, p. viii.
145. Wallander, 1994.
146. Piercy, 1998; Cravens, 1998; and Gummesson, 1998.
147. Gummesson, 1998, p. 248. For discourses on ambiguity, chaos etc., see Peters, 1988; Prigogene and Stengers, 1985; Zohar and Marshall, 1993, p. 212; Stacey, 1996; Capra, 1997; and Morgan, 1997.
148. Geneen, 1984, p. 78.
149. Ibid., p. 93.
150. Taylor and Bogdan, 1984, pp. 68-70; Jick, 1983, pp. 135-48.
151. The *New Encyclopedia Britannica*, 1986, p. 917.
152. McGrath et al., 1982, pp. 108-12. Quotation from p. 110.
153. Iacocca, 1984, pp. 53-54.
154. Kaldor, 1960a, 1960b.
155. Doctorow, 1977, quoted and discussed in Van Maanen, 1985, p. 257.
156. Sen, 1980, p. 356.

157. Nagel, 1986.
158. Sen, 1980, p. 357.
159. Alter, 1986, p. 50.
160. Bolch and Miller, 1978; Williams, 1978.
161. Downie, 1978.
162. Bernstein and Woodward, 1974; Williams, 1978, p. x.
163. Nader, 1965.
164. Hygstedt, 1990.
165. Williams, 1978, p. xi.
166. Ibid. p. xii.
167. Ibid. p. xiii.
168. Ibid. p. xii.
169. Ibid. p. xii.
170. Hailey, 1965, 1968, 1984.
171. Archer, 1984.
172. Packard, [1957] 1971, 1961.
173. Sampson, 1973, [1977] 1985, 1984, 1990.
174. See, for example, the accounts for case study research methodology in Bonoma, 1985b, p. 204, and Kanter, 1983, p. 378.
175. "Playboy Interview," 1985, pp. 57-58.
176. Geneen, 1984, p. 5.
177. Lacey, 1986, p. xix.
178. Greene, 1984.
179. Wallraff, 1985.
180. Kidder, 1981.
181. Meurling and Jeans, 1985, 1994.
182. Araskog, 1989, p. xiii.
183. Jevons, 1986.
184. Shipman, 1982, p. 15.
185. J. Gardner, 1983, p. 3.
186. Interview with Richard Normann by Jeffmar, 1984.
187. Guillet de Monthoux, 1978, p. 40.
188. McLuhan, 1966, pp. 7-21.
189. Postman, 1985, pp. 20-21.

C H A P T E R

Five

Quality of Academic Research and Management Consultancy

"Quality is an unusually slippery concept, easy to visualize and yet exasperatingly difficult to define," concludes David Garvin in his book, *Managing Quality.* Quality "remains a source of great confusion to managers."[1]

Quality is confusing not only to managers but also to professors and others who review the quality of individual researchers, research programs, scientific reports, dissertations, scripts for journal articles, and conference papers. Ever since I first started working in management consultancy and then in academic research, problems of quality appraisal have been one of my principal concerns. That is the rationale behind writing this chapter.

The first part of this chapter deals with general aspects of quality from industrial manufacturing, consultancy and other services, and science. The next section examines the scientific paradigm and the quality criteria for academic research. The following section deals with the consulting paradigm and its quality criteria. Finally, a summary of conclusions is presented.

On Quality Appraisal

Industrial manufacturing and the development of mechanical and electronic products are subject to elaborate quality procedures.[2] The advent of modern statistical process control is usually ascribed to W. A. Shewhart, who introduced the quality control chart at Bell Laboratories in the 1920s.[3]

Mass production of goods requires highly systematic handling if a company is to survive in a competitive market. It is very evident to a customer when a product, particularly a piece of machinery, fails. Industrial manufacturing is quite amenable to quality control because it offers a controlled environment, allowing systematic quality work and the use of methods, techniques, and instruments to measure quality.

Beginning in the 1970s, Japanese competition has forced European and American industry to raise its quality standards. The Japanese, together with U.S. consultants, have also provided new approaches and methods for improvements in quality.

In comparison with the manufacture of goods, quality control of *computer software*[4] and *services* lags behind; both areas lack the quality tradition of hardware. Today, the "bugs" and "viruses" hidden in the intangible software make equipment and service systems vulnerable. For example, in January 1990, AT&T's long-distance telephone traffic in the United States was knocked out for nine hours—75 million calls were stopped, causing chaos at airlines, credit card companies, and others heavily dependent on information technology. "Software is the invisible Achilles' heel of the computer revolution," as *Newsweek* concluded in its account of the event.[5]

As the share of computer software in machinery continually grows and services account for two-thirds of the gross national product, these areas become of increasing importance with regard to quality improvements. These areas are undoubtedly learning from quality approaches developed in manufacturing, and both software and services are establishing their own quality approaches and methodology. During the 1980s, theories and models of service quality have emerged, and the interest in service quality is growing rapidly. It is still justified to label computer software quality a "juvenile delinquent." While this is written, users are crying out their frustrations over the unexpected hardships of installing and using the new software Windows 98, whereas the provider Microsoft claims that 98% of all installations are successful.[6]

To promote an interest in quality, Japan in 1962 established a prestigious quality prize named after their teacher, W. Edwards Deming; in 1987, the Malcolm Baldrige National Quality Award was established in the United States. To apply for these prizes is a demanding exercise; one of the winners of the Baldrige Award, Xerox, assigned twenty people to the task for six months. A variety of national and industry-specific quality standards are in existence in production and trade. In an effort to facilitate quality control and quality assurance, the International Standards Organization (ISO) launched the ISO 9000 quality standard series, which in 1996 had been acknowledged by 117 countries.[7]

At this point, an objection could easily be raised: "Hold on; research and consultancy are not the same as manufacturing goods. It's software and services, the areas where industry is having trouble. Research and consultancy are professional services, produced in knowledge-based organizations populated by 'knowledge workers.' What then can industry teach us about quality?" That is just the question I intend to raise here. There is no exhaustive answer, but I am ready to look for some tentative connections.

The extensive literature on total quality management (TQM) lists a large variety of quality definitions. The following definitions will be used as vantage points for discussion:[8]

Crosby:[9] Quality is conformance to requirements.

Juran:[10] Quality is fitness for use.

Gummesson:[11] The quality of a professional service is a matter of perceived quality; the customer is buying confidence and trust.

ISO 9000:[12] Quality is the totality of features and characteristics of a product or service that bear on its ability to satisfy stated and implied needs.

What do we find when these definitions are applied to problems of quality in research and consultancy? Using the first definition, we could say that quality of research and consultancy is the degree to which we live up to the specifications set up in our research design or in our contract with the client. We could then go through the specifications and state "complied with" and "not complied with" in relation to each item; we could go even further and create more refined scaling. This mode, however, assumes that the specifications are sufficiently clear and unambiguous and that standards are available for the appraisal of each item. Unfortunately, when dealing with processes in organizations, neither management research nor consultancy provides such generally applicable specifications and standards. Processes in companies are characterized by the opposite: the unexpected and the ambiguous.

To tell science from nonscience, the academic community has tried to establish criteria and standards for general application. These are mainly rooted in the positivist paradigm, and they resemble the specifications used for the incoming inspection at a warehouse when a shipment of standardized, mass-produced components is being checked. But scientific research is not the same as standardized components, and thus, problems arise in using such rigid criteria in a science context—they are useful only if it is clear what science really is. It is not just a matter of comparing the requirements specification with each research report and each candidate for academic promotion.

I have too often found critiques of academic work and memos written by members of promotion committees deplorable reading. It is frustrating when people want to display "rational" and "scientific" reasons for their very private prejudices, sympathies, aversions, fears, and ignorance.

Referees get power, and it is an old truth that power corrupts. I call this *the arrignorance syndrome,* the combination of arrogance through power vested in the function of a referee and ignorance of the object being evaluated.

This frequently becomes a taboo subject where the victims run into a credibility conflict when they contend the outcome. People tend to say that the victims are sore because of the rejection; they will feel sorry for them, call them bad losers, and refer to "sour grapes." If accepted, there is no personal reason to bring up the matter—rather, the opposite. So the quality appraisal becomes a closed system of single-loop learning, a vicious circle. To avoid favoring friends and renowned authors, professional journals blind review the submitted articles, neither party knowing the other's identity. This helps to some extent, but the parties can often guess who the other person is. Hiding in the safe house of anonymity may also induce arrogant and irresponsible behavior.

It is all very well to set up criteria and standards, but when they cannot be implemented and they just become "academic" (as the word is used in a depreciatory sense), it is not so good. In the moment of truth, when being confronted with a yes/no decision, it is unclear what criteria should be used and what weight should be given to them. This ultimately may turn into a psychological and social game, vividly described in Jevons's fiction *The Fatal Equilibrium*.[13] The university's promotion committee is examining a candidate's qualifications for tenure. The candidate is obviously an excellent mainstream scientist who tests hypotheses based on a rational, utilitarian view, getting a large quantity of papers published in the right journals. Some committee members question his "single-minded view of how human beings behave" but are corrected by another member, saying, "I don't think you can penalize a young scholar for adopting the paradigm of his profession."[14]

Actually, the specification is under debate, which leads to total confusion, and the candidate becomes the victim of the promotion committee members' own problems. It includes circular reasoning, the stretching of standards in favor of one already selected winner, misunderstandings, sloppy reading of the material, lack of knowledge of the subject, and liking or disliking of a candidate. My serious complaint is that these people try to hide their subjective speculations behind allegedly logical reasoning, professional judgment, and deep concern for keeping science "clean."

The "conformance to requirements" definition of quality, of course, cannot be valid if the requirements are unclear. Just as in industrial manufacturing, unclear specifications are a major irritant when the quality of scientific production is being assessed. Different perceptions of quality are often one cause of unclear specifications, and there is often a *perception gap* between those who produce research and those who assess it. This is taken into consideration in marketing management, where it is recognized that there exist gaps between the consumers' idea about what they are buying and the supplier's idea of what consumers want. The company then endeavors to find these gaps and narrow them. In recent models of service quality, several such gaps have been identified.[15]

To avoid ambiguity and uncertainty, one could decide to allow only a certain stereotype of science to be accepted. This is being done when in business school a promotion is granted solely to the mainstream scientist who follows a well-specified pattern from positivistic research, being regulated only by the thermostat of single-loop learning. This strict adherence to technical specifications, "specs," is condescendingly referred to in industry as "specsmanship." Of course, such a strategy is unfortunate in science because it excludes everything that is not amenable to quantitative hypotheses testing, thus leaving out, for example, change processes in organizations.

Looking at the second and third definitions, we can ask ourselves, Fitness for whose use, and who is the customer? If there were universal quality standards, the problem would be nonexistent. Because no such standards are available, we have to identify the individuals, the target groups, for our research and consultancy, what marketers term the "customer segments." In industry, the present norm for quality is usually that of *customer-perceived quality* and *customer satisfaction*. Market-oriented business firms adjust their quality to customer needs and wants but also educate customers to demand their products and services. It is not the case that all customers want the highest technical quality, because it could become too costly. It would be nice to have a Rolls Royce, but a customer may settle for an ordinary car because he or she finds it quite in agreement with personal quality standards. Quality is a total concept that comprises not only the technical performance of the car but also things such as insurance, warranties, and availability of service. It also takes into account our trust in the dealer and manufacturer; we are buying confidence. We assess whether the people selling us the car smile, willingly answer our questions, and show empathy. This leads us into the fourth quality definition: "the ability to satisfy stated or implied needs." Explicitly stated needs become obvious in our interaction with customers and can also show in surveys. Implied needs are not obvious; they require empathy and expert knowledge of the providers. Either the customer cannot express them—they are tacit knowledge; they are felt but short of words—or the customer feels embarrassed about them.

Both the researcher and the consultant need to pay attention to confidence, trust, and implicit needs. The needs may be part of the culture and the social game in an organization or examination committee. Has the researcher quoted the professor enough, has the script references to previous articles in the editor's journal? Such intangible and partly subjective elements have been clearly recognized in recent models of service quality.[16]

How does one define the market segments in relation to academic research and consultancy? For academic research, the segments are the university faculty, promotion and grant committees, and "invisible colleges," such as editors and reviewers of articles for journals.[17] The relevant segments for consultants are their existing and potential clients. Action scientists have an even more complex task because they must encompass both academic and business segments.

If we really want to be recognized, promoted, or make a profit, we have to make sure that the perceived quality is adequate. When we were students at the Stockholm School of Economics, Professor Bertil Ohlin told a story about an article that he submitted to a prestigious British journal. A polite letter from the editor informed him that the article had not been accepted for publication. A handwritten note had mistakenly gotten stuck between the pages of the returned manuscript, however. It read as follows: "This amounts to nothing and should be rejected. J. M. K." The referee was world famous economist John Maynard Keynes, and the article spelled out the ideas for which Ohlin was awarded the Nobel Prize in the Economic Sciences in 1977.

There are numerous examples of incorrect decisions taken by the established judges. Greta Garbo was turned down as a field artist during World War II for being "too tall" and "amateurish." In a book, aptly titled *Rotten Rejections,*[18] stories are told about the judgments delivered by publishers on some of the most successful authors: thriller champion John le Carré ("has no future"), Joseph Heller's *Catch 22* ("I have no idea what the guy is trying to say"), *The Good Earth* by Pearl S. Buck ("Americans are not interested in China"), superselling storyteller Jean M. Auel ("wouldn't sell enough to cover the printing costs").

One professor describes the reports from the promotion committee concerned with his tenure as "confusing." One of his major works was marked as nonscience by a member of the committee but another hailed it as progressive science.[19]

Because quality is in part both intangible and subjective, we need some influential friends among our satisfied customers. It is not required that we produce this year's model of the Rolls Royce of academic research or consultancy; on the contrary, it could mean that we have to produce the 1926 Ford Model T if that is what is favored by senior professors, grant committees, and client executives. If they are against convertibles, we have to produce sedans. If they favor thrift, the emphasis has to be placed on low fuel consumption. Even the ancient poet had to please his king to get food and not get beheaded. The customer still remains the king.

One strategy could be to try to change the views of our judges. As long as the change consists of a modification within the existing paradigm, we may be successful. If we aim at a more fundamental change—namely, the paradigm shift of double-loop learning—we are confronted with a riskier task.

In action science, the researcher/consultant is expected to produce "usable research," defined as research that could be applied in real-life situations and be helpful to the practitioner; Reutersvard staircases won't do. Quality is assessed in relation to the way research results are perceived to facilitate the solution of an actual problem.

Obviously, a host of criteria are used in the quality appraisal of researchers and consultants. There is no universal list of criteria because their application depends on the reference point provided by a judge's personal paradigm. Customer-perceived quality and customer satisfaction can thus be considered subjective as long as the choice of paradigm is subjective. Within the paradigm, the research could be evaluated more systematically—"objectively" or "intersubjectively"—and be considered to be of better or inferior quality.

Hence, contrary to the beliefs of the general public and many researchers, scientific methods do not lead to clear, objective, and undisputed knowledge. There is also a view that the natural sciences are more exact and objective than the social and behavioral sciences. However, a study carried out by Mitroff of forty-two scientists who had been working on material brought back from the moon by the Apollo space capsule, indicated "intense differences between the way scientists approach their work."[20] In relation to another research project, I have had cause to examine the approaches adopted in medical and nutritional research.[21] I came to the conclusion that these areas of research are just as liable to subjective assessments and conventions as business administration but that the scientists are both less aware of it and less willing to admit that such is the case. A professor of medicine writes:

> The scientists themselves usually lack insights into the scientific community and the forces that determine its behavior. One calls for, in vain, a debate about the structure of the scientific community, about its basic values. . . . One has to go back to the feudal societies to find a similar tacit resignation to those in power, or to the religious societies to encounter such a naive belief in authorities.[22]

Management philosopher Peter Drucker says that management

> is not and will never be a *science* as the word is understood in the United States today. Management is no more a science than is medicine: both are practices. A practice feeds from a large body of sciences . . . so management feeds off economics, psychology,

mathematics, political theory, history, and philosophy. But like medicine, management is also a discipline in its own right, with its own assumptions, its own aim, its own tools, and its own performance goals and measurements. And as a separate discipline in its own right management is what the Germans used to call a *Geisteswissenschaft*—though "moral science" is probably a better translation of that elusive term than the modern "social science." Indeed, the old-fashioned term *liberal art* may be the best term of all.[23]

Fleck, who builds his views on the theory of science on one single case from medicine, contributes an analysis of the sociology of science. He defines the *thought collective* as "a community of persons mutually exchanging ideas or maintaining intellectual interaction."[24] Today, it is growing more and more popular to see these collectives as networks, but traditionally, they are permanent "thought communities,"—that is, research institutions with their own name, hierarchy, buildings, and funding. The members of the thought collective share a *thought style,* including a shared preunderstanding between the members, which clearly facilitates internal communication but also includes constraints that prohibit every alternative mode of thinking. The thought community easily becomes a self-contained system of opinion. As Braben expressed,

> There are not only more layers to the onion, but there will be new vegetables to explore, whose flavour we have not yet tasted or even suspect. . . . The more strictly we tried to control the research enterprise, the fewer surprises it would hold and eventually the more sterile it would become.[25]

The strict adherence to quality specifications would only promote incremental research and not the quantum leaps, the revolutionary breakthroughs.

Behrman and Levin, in their criticism of business schools, say that

> given the thousands of faculty members doing it, the research in business administration during the past 20 years would fail any reasonable test of applicability or relevance to consequential

management problems or policy issues concerning the role of business nationally or internationally. . . . Research needs to be redirected away from the irrelevant exercise of methodological techniques on increasingly narrow data bases. The promotion and tenure system must cease rewarding these activities.[26]

Payne and Lumsden[27] conclude that the results from the academic community in terms of concept generation *and* subsequent wide-scale use of these concepts by the business community is somewhat disappointing. In contrast to this, one consultant[28] argues that academia is the R&D arm of the consulting profession but has not got proper credit.

Researchers may also be the object of political or religious pressure that influences the acceptance or rejection of research. A modern example is that of the Russian geneticist Trofim Lysenko who reported forged data and "proved" that acquired behavior was hereditary. The practical consequence of his "results" was this: If you train man and wife in socialist thinking their children will be born socialists.[29]

Lysenko used political arguments against his critics and with the support of Stalin and Khrushchev managed to suppress all serious genetic research in the Soviet Union for more than two decades. The story is usually presented as a warning to politicians and others against interfering with the autonomy of research. However, it is also an example of the fact that the integrity and organization of the scientific community is not sufficiently strong to resist pressure and opportunistic behavior. Today, the integrity and ability to resist pressure or to exhibit opportunism has not improved, only taken new routes. Gene technology is currently being exploited by research institutions and private companies, with megaprofits and fame as the prime drivers. There is little scientific knowledge of the long-term effects of gene manipulation. What exists is mainly positivistic and fragmented studies in laboratory environments, covered with a glazing of subjective guesswork and peer consensus. The political and public dialogue is not suppressed by the threat of Siberian camps but by the subtle means of social ties, public relations activities, silence, political lobbying, and media campaigns and by the less subtle means of lost research grants and failed careers.[30]

These situations will all be referred to as the *Lysenko syndrome*, to be found also in the area of management. For example, investigative reporter and economist Ake Ortmark[31] describes how he interviewed the virtually anonymous members of the Wallenberg industrialist family for a book on the nature of financial power. He experienced difficulty of access, and considerable pressure was exerted on him to omit certain events and to magnify others in the final version.

An American professor with whom I discussed a doctoral dissertation emphasized that there was a need "to play the doctoral game."[32] He viewed scientific research as a game with clearly defined rules. Like little Linus in the comic strip *Peanuts*, who carries a blanket around with him as a comforter, academic researchers find security in testing hypotheses by means of statistical and mathematical formulas. An idealized picture of the researchers has been created that fails to take into account their motives and needs. Broad and Wade express it in the following terms:

> Scientists are no different from other people. In donning the white coat at the laboratory door, they do not step aside from the passions, ambitions and failings that animate those in other walks of life. Modern science is a career. To be successful, a researcher must get as many articles published as possible, secure government grants, build up a laboratory and the resources to hire graduate students . . . strive to be awarded a tenured post at a university . . . gain election to the National Academy of Sciences and hope one day to win an invitation to Stockholm.[33]

This naturally affects the researcher's behavior and may lead in certain unfortunate cases to deliberate fraud.[34] C. P. Snow, scientist and novelist, has described this in his semiautobiographical book, *The Search*: "From that day I understood, as I had never before, the frauds that creep into science every now and then. Sometimes they must be quite unconscious: the not-seeing of facts because they are inconvenient, the delusions of one's senses."[35] He goes on to explain his struggle with his conscience when he discovers that a colleague and friend has presented biased results. "It was a deliberate mistake. He had committed the major scientific crime . . . had given some false facts, suppressed some true ones. . . . I scarcely think the ethics of scientific deceit troubled him; but the risks must have done. For if he were found out he was ruined."[36] The author finally ends up with the conclusion: "Let him win his gamble. Let him cheat his way to the respectable success he wants. He will delight in it, and become a figure in the scientific world; and give broadcast talks and views on immortality; all of which he will love."[37]

In recent years, it has been questioned whether Freud cheated in case reports, using procrustean science to make data fit his theories.[38] And did Einstein really develop the theory of relativity by himself, or was it largely the work of his wife?[39]

A series of results, from parapsychological phenomena (such as Uri Geller's claim that he could bend spoons by thought) to the possibility of cold fusion, have recently been the object of controversy. To reveal concealed manipulation of experiments and demonstrations, the famed magician James Randi has been called in by scientists.

It is not simply a question of following a specification and a clearly defined set of rules. At any given point in time, opinions on what represents good research tend to vary. Within the same university or university department, different groups of researchers representing different research paradigms may either actively oppose each other, or accept some form of coexistence.[40]

From this exposé of aspects of quality I am inclined to conclude the following:

Getting acceptance for scientific work is partially an intellectual achievement and partially an ability to communicate and handle the social and political interaction with superiors, peers, and others who exert an influence over your career. Both aspects of quality, the intellectual dimension and the social dimension, have to be handled satisfactorily and in combination. The literature on science deals with the intellectual dimension almost solely and therefore gives a false impression of the scientific process.

The thoughts and actions of academic researchers are subject to underlying paradigms that we will sum up with the term *scientific paradigm.*[41] In a similar vein, let us now invent the term *consultant paradigm.*

Quality assessments of consulting services are also highly subjective. In an earlier study,[42] I found that the client was primarily concerned with assessing the consultant's credibility. In other words, it was a matter of a trusting working relationship and perceived quality.

Feyerabend summarizes his attitude to science in the following terms:

> Thus science is much closer to myth than a scientific philosophy is prepared to admit. It is one of the many forms of thought that have been developed by man and not necessarily the best. It is conspicuous, noisy and impudent but it is inherently superior only for those who have already decided in favor of a certain ideology or have accepted it without ever having examined its advantages and its limits.[43]

Feyerabend's experience is in tune with my own experience: A considerable amount of management research has an almost blind faith in the value of its methods and in the relevance of its findings at the same time that it displays an ignorance of its own paradigm.

Consultants can also be "conspicuous, noisy and impudent" and claim unwarranted praise for the significance of their assignments. When SAS (Scandinavian Airlines) was successfully turned around, a large number of consultants were involved, several of whom openly stated that the success represented a vindication of their advice. The CEO, Carlzon, expressed a certain amount of irritation at these claims and in his book[44] mentions only two individual consultants by name. The following quotations further illustrate that some consulting firms have little doubt about their own excellence.[45]

> "The combination of specialist skills enable our solutions and recommendations to be more concrete and detailed than those of most

other consulting companies who work with more limited resources." [Advertisement]

"Together we will be able to solve most of the problems that arise in business life. Large or small, public or private, it doesn't make any difference." [Advertisement]

"The breadth of our consulting company enables us to solve any problem raised by our clients." [Interview statement by the president of a large international consulting firm]

On the other hand, we could accept the wisdom of Sherlock Holmes as expressed in *The Valley of Fear*:

Surely our profession, Mr. Mac, would be a drab and sordid one if we did not sometimes set the scene so as to glorify our results. . . . The quick inference, the subtle trap, the clever forecast of coming events, the triumphant vindication of bold theories—are these not the pride and the justification of our life's work?[46]

With the aid of Holberg's play, *Erasmus Montanus*, it is possible to present a striking caricature of the scientific and consultant paradigms. Montanus has just returned from the Academy in Copenhagen and becomes involved in a conversation with his brother Jacob who is at home looking after the farm.[47]

> **Montanus:** I dispute about weighty and learned matters. For example: whether angels were created before men; whether the earth is round or oval; about the moon, sun and stars, their size and distance from the earth; and other things of a like nature.
>
> **Jacob:** That's not the sort of thing I dispute about, for that's not the sort of thing that concerns me. If only I can get the servants to work, they can say the world is eight-cornered, for all I care.

Table 5.1 provides a summary of the major areas of research and consultancy work influenced by the respective paradigms. Special account has already been taken of some of these factors: access and roles (Chapter 2), preunderstanding and understanding

TABLE 5.1 Scientific and Consultant Paradigms

The scientific paradigm affects:	*The consultant paradigm affects:*
The researcher's *goals,* such as a desire to obtain new knowledge, to have an article published in a refereed journal, to be cited, or to be promoted	The consultant's *goals,* such as completing an assignment to the satisfaction of the client, and being offered new assignments
The researcher's *preunderstanding* and *understanding,* with focus on theory and support from practice	The consultant's *preunderstanding* and *understanding,* with focus on practice and support from theory
Choice of *research territory* and within this, *research projects*	Choice of a *specific field of consultancy,* such as corporate strategy, and *securing assignments* in that field
Choice of *methods* and *researcher roles* for gaining *access*	Choice of *methods* and *consultancy roles* for gaining *access*
Choice of *quality criteria:* the assessment of good and bad research by the *scientific community*	Choice of *quality criteria:* the *client's assessment* of consultant's work

(Chapter 3), and methods of access (Chapter 4). We have not examined the nature and contents of different scientific and consultant paradigms, however. In conjunction with an assessment of the quality of research and consultancy, it will be necessary to look at certain features of the paradigms that affect the actions of researchers and consultants.

Scientific Paradigms and Quality Criteria

In a book titled *Wondering about Society,* Asplund[48] draws a parallel between the heroes of the detective novel and researchers. In both cases, it is a question of discovering something, contributing to the solution of a problem. Detectives adopt different approaches. Some put forward hypotheses, systematically collect facts, and then deduce logical conclusions on causal relationships that lead to the discovery of the murderer. We have already met Sherlock Holmes—who was a private consultant in the field of crime—and he will provide further examples. In "The Case of the Silver Blaze" he presents his approach:

> It is one of those cases where the art of the reasoner should be used rather for the sifting of details than for the acquiring of fresh evidence. The tragedy has been so uncommon, so complete and of such personal importance to so many people that we are suffering from a plethora of surmise, conjecture and hypothesis. The difficulty is to detach the framework of fact—of absolute undeniable fact—from the embellishments of theorists and reporters. Then, having established ourselves upon this sound basis, it is our duty to see what inferences may be drawn and which are the special points upon which the mystery turns.[49]

Sherlock Holmes's scientific paradigm is usually perceived to be that of the natural sciences; it is a positivistic paradigm. His deductive and sequential logic inspired a textbook on the computer language BASIC, building entirely on the Sherlock Holmes stories.[50] If the authors had tried instead to convert the methods used by French Inspector Maigret into programming language, they would have failed miserably. Maigret adopts a different approach:

> As soon as he was back in his office Maigret took off his jacket and, standing by the window, filled his pipe. In spite of everything, he was not wholly satisfied, and Madame Maigret would have said he was on edge.
>
> And so he was. He had conducted his inquiries to the best of his ability, concentrating as much on the past as on the present. And with substantial results. And yet he had a nagging feeling that he had missed something. But what? He could not put his finger on it, and it worried him.
>
> "Would you get me the police station at Sancerre, please, Miss. I'd like to speak to the man in charge, if he's there. . . . If not, give me one of his assistants. . . ."
>
> He began pacing the room restlessly. Within the next two weeks, he told himself reassuringly, the case would be solved, and he and

his wife would be able to go and relax in their house at Meung-sur-Loire, which, incidentally was not so far from Sancerre.[51]

This description of Maigret mixes feelings, intuition, chance, and atmosphere with elements of systematic analysis. The trivial and the important exist side by side, and the roles of private individual and professional become integrated. Maigret makes his own *personal interpretation* of a situation and thereby succeeds in finding the murderer. He is governed by the hermeneutic paradigm, but we could also say that he is inspired by a series of qualitative concepts and approaches. Tesch[52] lists a total of forty-six qualitative possibilities, Patton[53] lists ten theoretical traditions, and Helenius[54] makes a synthesis of seven traditions into the concept of hermeneutics. Without going into details of all these possibilities, I would like to relate hermeneutics to two other paradigmatic approaches: phenomenology and Taoism.

Phenomenology seems to be the more prevailing approach to qualitative research in the social sciences literature. According to Taylor and Bogdan, the "phenomenologist is committed to *understanding* social phenomena from the actor's own perspective. He or she examines how the world is experienced. The important reality is what people perceive it to be."[55] Odman clarifies the difference between phenomenology and hermeneutics in this way:

Whereas phenomenology is primarily oriented toward the immediate phenomena of human experience, such as thinking and feeling, hermeneutics is more context directed. In interpreting human "traces," hermeneutics often tries to go beyond the observable in order to "read between the lines." It can therefore be characterized as more transphenomenal.[56]

A simple example will illustrate the difference. Students and researchers conduct interviews with executives, customers, and others to get access to data about management issues. Those social scientists who are primarily controlled by the positivistic paradigm like to structure both questions and answers to simplify quantitative processing of data. They completely disregard non-verbal phenomena such as body language, physical environment, and unexpected events that may occur during an interview. Phenomenologists would register all cues in an effort to "understand" the respondent. Hermeneutic scientists would go a step further and "interpret" these immediate events also in the light of previous events, private experience, and whatever else they find pertinent to the situation under investigation.

Taoism is chosen here to represent a tradition with its origin in oriental religions and philosophies. It is unfair to try to explain Oriental thinking through a simple and short treatment, however. All the same, some brief comments provide us with a contrast to Western positivism.

We have already come across Taoism through the popular concepts yin and yang. The Taoist, according to Capra, is interested in intuitive wisdom rather than in rational knowledge and mistrusts conventional wisdom, reasoning, and the analytic method: "Nevertheless, the careful observation of nature, combined with a strong mystical intuition, led the Taoist sages to profound insights which are confirmed by modern scientific theories."[57] In this connection, I would like to mention the interest in getting insights and wisdom through inner-directed research as expressed in Eastern philosophies. As expressed in Buddhism: "Wisdom gained by understanding and development of the qualities of mind and heart is wisdom par excellence."[58] The Western scientific method is directed toward the external, and by empirical data, we mean observations in the environment, often limited to numbers.

The ancient techniques of meditation emanating from the Orient have been revived and have gained extensive acceptance in the West. One example is transcendental meditation, TM, a set of practical techniques to relax, balance, and expand one's mind and consciousness with, for example, increased creativity as a result. To an increasing extent, it is being applied both in scientific research and in business firms.[59] It is my firm belief that this way of approaching both research and the practice of management holds an enormous and yet untapped potential for gaining understanding and insights into management phenomena.

Thick books are available on these and other traditions, and the definitions are not as clear-cut and simple as stated above. For example, Howard[60] has written a book called *Three Faces of Hermeneutics*, and Palmer[61] discusses six "fairly distinct" variants of hermeneutics.

Out of all the alternatives to positivistic research, I have chosen to use the term *hermeneutics* for several reasons. I was first inspired to question the positivistic tradition by reading about hermeneutics; second, hermeneutics seems more inclusive than others; and third, it has its origin in the Western world, just as positivism has.

With this background, let us renew the acquaintance with detectives Holmes and Maigret. Both collect real-world data about a specific course of events. This data is then related to their preunderstanding, and certain conclusions are drawn. In other words, they start off by using an *inductive* method and subsequently adopt a *deductive* approach. As far is Holmes is concerned, this has been described in the following manner:

> It has many times been pointed out that Holmes' so-called deductions were actually inductions. Like the scientist trying to solve a mystery of nature, Holmes first gathered all the evidence he could that was relevant to his problem. At times he performed experiments to obtain fresh data. He then surveyed the total evidence in the light of his vast knowledge of crime and of sciences relevant to crime, to arrive at the most probable hypothesis. Deductions were made from the hypothesis; then the theory was further tested against new evidence, revised if need be, until finally the truth emerged with a probability close to certainty.[62]

Let us now discuss in a more systematic fashion the differences between a positivistic and a hermeneutic scientific paradigm and the requirements that have to be met for either paradigm to be useful in scientific work.

Even in the social sciences, positivism has been considered by many to be the "correct" scientific paradigm. Indeed, this is still the case. Rubenowitz characterizes positivism in the following terms:

The predominant research tradition in the social and behavioral sciences has been of a quantitative, empirical nature. This research tradition can be considered to be still prevalent. It is based on the statistical analysis of data collected by means of descriptive and comparative studies and experiments. This approach is usually termed *positivistic*. It assumes that only knowledge obtained by means of measurement and objective identification can be considered to possess truth. The view that this *logical empiricism* provides the only true basis for explanation and general theory has occasionally come into conflict with a *hermeneutic,* interpretative approach.[63]

Hermeneutics represents a reaction against the awkward rigidities of positivism in relation to certain types of problems in the social field. Instead of trying to explain causal relationships by means of objective "facts" and statistical analysis, hermeneutics uses a more personal interpretative process to "understand reality." Language takes on a central role, qualitative assessments partially replace quantitative data, and the general becomes of lesser interest than the specific.

Major differences between what might be roughly termed positivistic and hermeneutic research are presented in Table 5.2.[64] Some of these points have already been raised, and others will be discussed below.

The two paradigms, the positivistic and the hermeneutic, will be used as distinctly different vantage points, as two extremes. They will be referred to as the scientific paradigms.

The concept of firsthand preunderstanding was dealt with in Chapter 3. According to Andersson, in positivistic science, there is "no merit in having studied a problem area at first hand. On the contrary, it exposes the researcher to the risk of personal bias."[65] These insights gained from experience, which form a part of the researcher's preunderstanding, are considered to act as blocked preunderstanding.

The hermeneutic paradigm leads us to quite the opposite conclusions. According to this view,

TABLE 5.2 Comparison between the Positivistic and Hermeneutic Paradigms

Positivistic Paradigm	Hermeneutic Paradigm
Research concentrates on description and explanation.	Research concentrates on understanding and interpretation.
Well-defined, narrow studies.	Narrow as well as total studies (holistic view).
The vantage point is primarily deductive; thought is governed by explicitly stated theories and hypotheses.	The vantage point is primarily inductive; researchers' attention is less focused and is allowed to "float" more widely.
Research concentrates on generalization and abstraction.	Research concentrates on the specific and concrete ("local theory") but also attempts generalizations.
Researchers seek to maintain a clear distinction between facts and value judgments; search for objectivity.	Distinction between facts and value judgments is less clear; recognition of subjectivity.
Researchers strive to use a consistently rational, verbal, and logical approach to their object of research.	Preunderstanding that often cannot be articulated in words or is not entirely conscious—tacit knowledge—takes on an important role.
Statistical and mathematical techniques for quantitative processing of data are central.	Data are primarily nonquantitative.
Researchers are detached—i.e., they maintain a distance between themselves and the object of research; take on the role of external observer.	Both distance and involvement; researchers are actors who also want to experience what they are studying from the inside.
Distinction between science and personal experience.	Researchers accept influence from both science and personal experience; they use their personality as an instrument.
Researchers try to be emotionally neutral and make a clear distinction between reason and feeling.	Researchers allow both feelings and reason to govern their actions.
Researchers discover an object of research external to themselves rather than "creating" the actual object of study.	Researchers partially create what they study, for example, the meaning of a process or a document.

it is not possible to follow an interpretative approach at a distance. It requires a personal commitment on behalf of the researcher such that he invests his personality and experience into the field of research; a personal commitment is an actual requirement for understanding . . . hence personal experience of the area of study is considered to be a scientific merit. Indeed hermeneutics views it as a requirement rather than just a merit.[66]

According to this quotation, the positivistic researcher aims at being a spectator, whereas the hermeneutic researcher endeavors to be part of the action.

Both positivism and hermeneutics place demands on creativity and the ability to see reality in a new light. Analytical requirements, however, receive a higher priority in positivistic research than creativity and novel approaches. In hermeneutics, the researcher tries to sweep away "conventional wisdom" and see new things and *formulate problems*[67] out of allegedly familiar situations. The *ethnomethodologist* approach goes even further and says that "the meanings of actions are always ambiguous and problematic" and that there exist no taken-for-granted rules in social interaction.[68] If the academic researchers are asked to come up with a definition of their *problem*, the progressive business manager is more likely to define *challenges and opportunities*, a more productive way of identifying unknown phenomena. For example, the IBM employee[69] was asked to identify "windows of opportunity." The IBM culture included "occurrence management, which . . . requires concentrating on your organization's strength. If a product is selling well in Dallas but poorly in Seattle, you go to Dallas to find out what they're doing right, not to Seattle to find out what's wrong." In a dynamic business culture where innovation and entrepreneurship are highly regarded, it feels better to talk about opportunities than about problems. A problem is considered to be equivalent to difficulties and is associated with a static, bureaucratic environment that is incapable of risk taking and creativity.

There is an extensive catalog of methods available within the positivistic paradigm. The methods traditionally associated with the natural sciences and based on the *old mathematics* come into this category together with their adaptation to the problems of the social sciences. The *controlled experiment* is considered the most perfect method. When experiments are impossible on practical grounds, questionnaires, interviews, and observations may be used instead. However, the latter methods do not give the same control over the studied variables and their relationships. Whenever possible, one tries to use quantitative methods to test hypotheses. The researchers start with hypotheses that they try to verify or reject during the project.

Thus, the research process is described in positivistic textbooks as a series of logical, rational, step-by-step activities, following objective rules, and leading from the identification of a problem up to an end point of results. It is the same logical sequence that traditionally is supposed to guide the businessman's decision making. In decision making, however, the logical model has been challenged by alternatives, one of them being the *garbage can model* by Cohen et al.[70] In the latter model, decision making is seen as a garbage can in which members of an organization dump problems and solutions. The organization then consists of "a collection of choices looking for problems, issues and feelings looking for decision situations in which they might be aired, solutions looking for issues to which they might be the answer, and decision makers looking for work."[71] According to Martin,[72] the research process can also be described by means of the garbage can model.

If one is willing to accept the garbage can research model as more real than the rational model, the necessity of using judgment calls in scientific research comes up.[73] *Judgment call* is a term borrowed from baseball where it refers to a decision that has to be made but where the fixed, objective rules of the game are not sufficient. For example, "Was that pitch in the strike zone?" These judgment calls tend to accumulate in their effects, and the same happens in research "where there are many crucial decisions that must be made without the benefit of a hard and fast, 'objective' rule, or even an algorithm or general rule of thumb. And, as in baseball, the cumulative results of such judgment calls often determine the outcome of research."[74]

In the view of Andersson, there exists no catalog of available methods in the field of hermeneutics:

> Hermeneutics rejects the demands of positivism regarding the need for a lack of bias. On the contrary, it is claimed that *bias* is prevalent at all levels of the research process. The most striking example of this attitude is that hermeneutic studies rarely contain a technical chapter on methodology. However, if objectivity is considered to be a chimera, there is consequently no need for any methodological discussion. Hence the examination by positivists of what they consider to be "books on hermeneutical methodology" lead to misguided demands that hermeneutics can never meet. The formulation of a general set of rules for this interpretative approach would be to transform hermeneutics into positivism. Consequently there aren't any books on hermeneutical methodology. Nor indeed will there ever be any books on this subject.[75]

In my view, one need not go so far as to complete rejection of methodological literature in hermeneutics. Whereas positivistic research strives to establish unambiguous rules and criteria for mandatory application, hermeneutics by its nature should not do so. An account of optional strategies and guidelines can, however, assist in hermeneutic research, but it cannot prescribe mandatory procedures for an individual researcher in a specific case.

The demands placed on hermeneutic research are described by Molander in the following terms:

> The relationship between the researcher and the object of study is brought to a head. Is it possible to determine "objectively" which is the best interpretation? A result must be arrived at within the hermeneutic circle. The researcher and a person being studied can in principle sit down and compare interpretations and present facts within a context of meaningful actions. The ability to reach an agreement on the interpretation must be the result of an intersubjective process that ultimately depends on *insight*. If our interpretations do not coincide, something must be changed. . . . An inevitable consequence of this perspective is that the demands for neutrality and an unbiased solution will have to be dropped. . . .

Any thoughts of a "value-free" decision will disappear right away. The process of knowledge only allows participants. The behavioral and social sciences become in a radical sense "moral sciences." This places greater demands on the capacity for self-insight among researchers since our inability to understand stems from our understanding of ourselves. This may sound radical but Aristotle actually reached more or less the same conclusion.[76]

Odman[77] deals with some of the questions that confront the hermeneutic researchers who are seeking to establish credibility bases for their research. The first question concerns the manner in which the researchers present and justify to others the actions they have undertaken in a research or consultancy process. The researcher is involved in an "inner" process of interpretation that isn't particularly easy to follow for an outsider. A *communication* problem arises in which language plays a crucial role; the researcher strives to attain *clarity* and *simplicity*.

My impression is that substantial requirements are made of the writer while little is demanded of the reader. Careless reading is common among those who assess research or consultancy work. Reports also have the function of acting as a projective test for the readers; they project their own knowledge, preferences, sympathies, or aversion onto the author of the text, and thus, the readers should share a joint responsibility with the writer.[78] Written reports are also a highly inadequate means of conveying knowledge compared with the opportunities provided by personal contact. Noll[79] questions the ability to make any impact at all through writings. As a professor of law and rapidly approaching death due to cancer, devoting his remaining days to the essentials of life, he states that he has never seen a scientific publication that deals with the question of how the abundant literature affects thought and action.

The second question taken up by Odman refers to the *presentation of one's paradigm and preunderstanding*. This is a difficult task. It is often the case that one isn't aware of the paradigm that influences one's own thoughts and actions. One chooses instead—as in this book—to provide the reader with an account of one's own views, referring to examples and having recourse to a fairly rich verbal repertoire.

The third question refers to the opportunities open to the reader to *check* the way in which the interpretation has been formulated and the conclusions drawn. On this point, Odman's advice to researchers is to present the *documentary evidence*—notes, recordings, and so forth—and the *arguments* that support their conclusions.

The grounded theory of Glaser and Strauss[80] and their use of comparative analysis are well-developed examples of how aspects of both the positivistic and the hermeneutic paradigms have been applied while at the same time maintaining a set of rules for the assessment of the quality of research. For example, they have compiled a checklist of eight questions that can be asked to assess the ability of researchers to develop theories and models:[81]

1. Is the authors' main emphasis on the *verification* (testing, justification) or *generation* (discovery) of theory?
2. Are they more interested in *substantive* (limited and specific) or *formal* (more general) theory?
3. What is the *scope* of theory used in the report?
4. To what degree is the theory *grounded* on empirical, real-world data?
5. How *dense* in conceptual detail is the theory?
6. What *kinds of data* are used, and how are they related to the theory?
7. To what degree is the theory *integrated* or complete, thus allowing new data to fit naturally into the theory?
8. How much *clarity* do the authors reveal about the type of theory they use?

Grounded theory has created considerable interest in management research in Europe, particularly in Scandinavia[82] where Glaser and Strauss's work has become a standard reference in case study research. Often, however, only parts of their theory have been applied to research, and the fairly exacting rules laid down by the authors have sometimes been violated.[83]

Argyris and Schon[84] have developed a *theory of action* based on the learning capacity of companies and on intervention by researchers and consultants. They say that "theories created to understand and predict may be quite different from theories created to help people make events come about."[85] Consequently, theories concerned with action ought also to be *assessed from their ability to function in action.*

This section has examined differences between positivism and hermeneutics. The purpose of this discussion has been to show how two scientific paradigms create different starting points for research and how the quality assessment of research depends on these different points of departure.

Although I use the concepts positivism and hermeneutics, it should be borne in mind that these are not uniform and unambiguous. Nonetheless, it is reasonable to use them because they shed light on consequences of different scientific approaches. I do not consider these concepts as opposites excluding one another, which unfortunately is the way in which they are often presented. I view them rather as complements in the spirit of yin and yang. Consequently, there is nothing to stop a researcher from adopting a positivistic paradigm in a certain research situation and a hermeneutic in another, even in the same project.

Hence, the point is not so much one of choosing sides but rather the question per se, Which criteria can be used to evaluate research? I have previously devoted considerable attention to access and preunderstanding and suggested that it is in those case studies where the roles of researcher and consultant are effectively combined—action science—that the best opportunities for understanding a process of decision making, implementation, and change are created.

The most significant piece of advice to quality examiners is this: *Do not assess hermeneutic research from the vantage point of the positivistic paradigm!* Unfortunately, this is frequently done.

According to Shipman,[86] scientists can be distinguished from others on the following ground: *Their methods and the research procedures are made public.* This enables the consumer of the research[87] to find answers to *four key questions:*[88]

1. "If the investigation had been carried out by someone other than the author, using his methods, would the same results have been obtained?" This is the problem of replication usually referred to as *reliability*.
2. "Does the evidence really reflect the reality under examination?" This is the *validity* problem.
3. "What relevance do the results have beyond the actual research?" This is the degree to which the results can be *generalized*.
4. "Is there sufficient detail in the way the evidence was produced for the credibility of the research to be assessed?" If we follow the researcher's journey—from questions to methods of data gathering, interpretation, and answers—do we believe him or not? This is the problem of *credibility*.

In addition to the sources referred to in the above discussion, I have used two different types of source material to determine in a more detailed manner the criteria that ought to be used. On the one hand, I have studied research reports on change processes to identify the requirements that the authors have placed on their own research, and a few of these reports have been studied in considerable depth. The second type of source material consists of reports related to the assessment of case studies and doctoral dissertations.[89]

On the basis of this material and my own experience, I have identified a number of quality criteria for research, which are presented below. To be frank and probably provocative, the only common criterion that I found is not even mentioned in books on scientific methodology but seems to have implicit, universal acceptance: *A scientific report should be boring and difficult to read.* If it reads well, and even inspires a smile or a good laugh, the scientist will be suspected of being "unscientific" or of having written a popular textbook, the latter being scorned in many "scientific" circles. Peter Drucker, however, states that it "is only in the last twenty or thirty years that being incomprehensible has become a virtue in academia."[90]

The following explicitly expressed quality criteria for case study research have been identified:

1. Readers should be able to *follow the research process and draw their own conclusions:*

   A well-written, intelligible report

   A comprehensive account of the research process

   A statement of the problem, purpose, and research questions of the study

   A description of methods of data collection, coding, analysis, and interpretation procedures

   A well-documented and rich description of cases

   Motives for the selection of cases

   Limits of the research project

   Clear presentation of results and conclusions

   Information to the reader if taboo information has been discovered but is anonymized or disregarded

2. As far as realistically feasible, researchers should present their *paradigm and preunderstanding:*

   Personal and professional values and if these have changed in the course of the research

   Values of the system under analysis

   Theories and concepts that govern the project together with the reasons for the choice of these theories and concepts

   The researcher's prior experience and other pertinent information on the researcher

3. The research should possess *credibility:*

   Correct data, including correct rendering of statements and views of informants

   How analysis and interpretation are supported by data

   Demonstrated confidence in the theory, concepts, and conclusions used or generated in the research

   Honest presentation of alternative interpretations and contradictory data

   The avoidance of deliberate or unintentional deception

   The conclusions should accord with one another (internal logical consistency)

   The actors in the cases should be able to recognize what is presented in the report (external logical consistency)

   Presentation of all relevant data and information used in the case study

Selected methods and techniques should be appropriate to the problem, purpose and research questions

4. The researcher should have had adequate *access:*

Used methods and techniques that ensured adequate access to the processes under study

Account of any difficulties in deploying desired access methods

Account of any problems and limitations that arose through denied access

Account of any problems and limitations in access that arose through time and money constraints

How access limitations have possibly impaired the research

5. There should be an assessment on the *generality and validity* of the research:

To what areas the results apply

How closely the research represents the phenomenon that the researcher aimed to study

If other research confirms or disconfirms the findings

If results bear out or disagree with extant theories and concepts

6. The research should make a *contribution*:

Contribute to increased knowledge

Deal with relevant problems

Optimize the trade-off between methods, techniques, and results

Be of value to the scientific community, the client, and the public

Actively made available to the scientific community, the client, and the public

7. The research process should be *dynamic*:

The extent to which the researcher has continuously learned through personal reflection and dialogue with others

Demonstrated creativity and openness to new information and interpretations

The ability to switch between deep involvement and distance

A demonstrated awareness of changes of research design, methods application, and so on during the research process

8. The researcher should possess certain *personal qualities:*

Commitment to the task of research

Integrity and honesty, being able to voice his or her conviction

Flexibility and openness, being able to adjust to changed conditions and new—even disturbing—information

The criteria listed here can be used as a checklist, but they are not always applicable or of the same importance. Therefore, it should not be expected that a single case study scores top points on all of them. There is need for good judgment and common sense in the evaluation process.

I will return to a discussion and synthesis of these criteria at the end of this chapter and in Chapter 6.

Consultant Paradigms and Quality Criteria

Peter Drucker, one of the world's most read and listened to authorities on management, is not only a university professor and management consultant but also a journalist, novelist, and connoisseur of Japanese art. He claims that it was this last quality that made him one of three foreigners appointed by the Japanese as responsible for their economic recovery after World War II.[91] One reviewer says that Drucker "is a great success as a writer because he has brought to his task the creativity, the story telling skills, the concern for people of a great novelist."[92] His way of writing, however, is far from the traditional academic format. Although his first book, *The Practice of Management*,[93] contained references, the books that followed expressed opinion and gave examples but rarely referred to methodology or academic research carried out by others. Should this be considered scientific or not?

No single management book has received more exposure among business executives and academia alike than Peters and Waterman's *In Search of Excellence*.[94] Since its first publication in 1982, it has sold over 10 million copies and can still be found at airport newsstands. The book is of particular interest here as an epitome of differences in quality criteria for consultancy and academic research.

Both authors were McKinsey consultants with M.B.A.s; Peters is also a Ph.D. In an interview, Tom Peters has described the background of the book. They were due to meet the management of one of their clients but had fallen behind with their assignment (consultants occasionally run into such a predicament, and it is a challenge for their professional capability). They had no "hard facts" to present, no figures and charts. To save their skin, they decided to adopt a different and qualitative approach. They presented concepts that are essential in successful management and found that these gave birth to a heated discussion among the managers. So did their book.

The book is an account of the most successful companies in the United States—Caterpillar, Exxon, General Electric, Hewlett-Packard, Kodak, McDonald's, Wal-Mart, and Xerox, to mention a few. They all had a 20-year track record of sustained excellence, measured in terms of growth and financial performance. The book is narrative and absolutely crammed with anecdotes and normative statements. There are both personal and professional motives for writing such a book, and it is hard to tell the two apart. The book was written in the course of their consultancy work; being an author is a road to "name and fame" with the prospects of more and better paid assignments as well as future royalties. The strictly professional purpose of the book was to lay bare general strategies that lead to excellence, thus making the book educational and a guide for other companies.

A reviewer states that the greatest weakness of the book is that it is

> presented as a piece of serious research which clearly it is not. To go around asking people in reputedly successful business organizations why those organizations have been successful does not reach first base as research methodology. There is no easy way of testing the reliability and validity of the replies.[95]

Another reviewer concludes that from "a methodological point of view, that book is a disaster (no control group, measures not specified, and so forth)."[96]

I agree with the critics that the book cannot be classified as scientific, but I agree for other reasons. They have evaluated the book from the platform provided by the positivistic paradigm, but the authors are standing on the hermeneutic platform. The critics do not accept case study research based on informal interviews. They want tests of reliability and validity; one critic even says that there is no easy way of testing the reliability and validity of the replies. It is primarily in the research of trivia, however, that it is easy to carry out such tests. Positivistic researchers are "reliability freaks," but their methods of establishing reliability in the study of human behavior are more based on academic consensus—intersubjectivity—than on objectivity; validity can seldom be ascertained at all using so-called rigorous research designs. As Taylor and Bogdan point out, "qualitative researchers emphasize validity, quantitative researchers emphasize reliability" and "reliability has been overemphasized in social research."[97]

The conclusions of the book are reduced to nine strategies for success, all characterized by being basic and action oriented. These strategies offer no more than a subjective interpretation of the past, let alone an informed and in many ways systematic interpretation. It has been pointed out by critics that few of the companies in the study would qualify for inclusion today. Should we demand the nine criteria to have predictive value? Would that be a test of the generality and validity of the conclusions? No doubt, we would feel comfortable and secure if the answer was a distinct "Yes!" But the ability to make such predictions in social sciences is simply not there. Too many influencing factors, some clearly beyond the logical control of individual companies, determine the outcome. The merits of the conclusions are rather that they can be thought-provoking, draw attention to mismanagement or untapped potential, and assist in scenario writing.

Nevertheless, *In Search of Excellence* does not report research of acceptable academic standards because the reader cannot follow the journey of the researchers, neither in the inductive part nor in the logico-deductive part. The authors' "evidence" consists of lots of examples and amusing anecdotes; the text is crowded with quotations from business executives, and the format of presentation is journalistic. The authors' strengths are good access, preunderstanding, and theoretical sensitivity together with the fact that the first two parts of the book, which have attracted the least attention, include an account of the selection of the successful companies to be studied and a discussion of the methodological issues, as well as a creative analysis of the literature on organization theory.

It is obvious, however, that the two consultants' approach to the study has been successful. The reviewers use words such as *refreshing, appeal, readability,* and *stimulating* and phrases such as "easy and enjoyable" and "challenging and compulsory reading by all management."[98] How often does a "scientific" book based on "solid academic research" receive such an accolade? And how many sell ten million copies?

Consultants work with a variety of approaches related to their paradigm and preunderstanding. They can be arranged along an axis with consultants who have only a practical background at one end, and at the other end, those with only a research background. In between, there are various combinations of practician/researcher. The most common combinations would appear to be the following:

* *Consultants who have a university education combined with practical experience.* They have frequently worked in large companies where they became familiar with a particular "success method" in management. Their point of departure is a mixture of values drawn from the academic and work environments with which they are familiar.

* *Consultants with a university degree and recruited fresh from school.* Most of them have no practical experience, which by some consulting firms is considered an advantage; the recruits can more easily be socialized into a specific corporate culture and will more readily accept a specific mode of operation.

* *Researchers who have become consultants as a result of their research.* They either work as full-time consultants or combine academic research with part-time consultancy. This latter arrangement is usually combined with teaching at a university as well as appearances in executive training

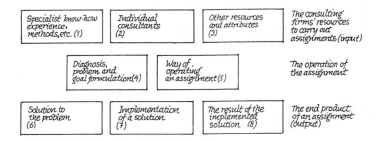

Figure 5.1. A Generic Model of Consulting Services
SOURCE: Gummesson, 1979.

programs, in-house seminars at companies, and conventions. The researcher is primarily influenced by the values prevalent in the academic world.

In an earlier research project,[99] I developed a model of the components of consultancy services and their quality appraisal. The model applies to consultancy services in general rather than just management consultancy. According to this model, a consultancy service comprises eight constituent parts (Figure 5.1). These will be discussed below in relation to the consultant's involvement with processes of change.

1. The *specialist know-how* provided by the consultants consists of their preunderstanding, both firsthand and secondhand. Their know-how can comprise methods derived from both the hermeneutic paradigm—for example, conducting qualitative interviews—and from the positivistic paradigm—for example, quantitative cost analysis. Both theoretical knowledge and techniques for the application of their knowledge are required.
2. *Individual consultants and their personal characteristics* represent part of the quality dimension. Personality, enthusiasm, motivation, social skills, and an ability to interact with the client's personnel have a decisive bearing on how their services are perceived by the clients.
3. *Other resources and attributes*—for example, access to other specialists through the consultant's own firm or through an external network of contacts, access to computer programs, and local offices.

4. *Diagnosis and problem and goal formulation* make up one of the most crucial aspects of consultancy: dealing with the right problem and setting realistic goals for an assignment. Here, the consultant is trying to establish the conditions vital to the future of the company and directing the assignment to these essentials.

5. *The way of operating the assignment.* The different roles were listed in Table 2.1, and each role is tied to a different modus operandi. As a change agent—using a combination of roles and methods best suited to achieve change in a specific situation—the consultant must often work closely with the client's personnel in the process of change over a long period of time.

6. *The solution to the defined problem.* This can be a recommendation about activities with direct short-term effects or with long-term effects. The example of the canceled advertising campaign from Chapter 4 has short-term effects; a change in organization structure that enables the new business concept to be implemented has more long-term effects.

7. *Implementation of the solution.* It is often desirable that the change agent take part in the implementation at least at the start—for example, when candidates are selected for executive positions in a new organizational structure.

8. *The result of the implemented solution* is the change that brings about, for example, improved productivity or adds to the competitive edge. The result can be measured in terms of changes in cost, revenue, and capital investment, expressed in various indicators of profitability. Other factors may also exert an influence on the outcome. Because the change agent works together with the client's personnel, it is not possible to make an objective assessment of the actual contribution made by the change agent; it is the product of an interactive relationship.

A consultancy service may comprise different combinations of these eight components. The actual number of components included in the combination indicate the *breadth* of the consultancy service. Account can also be taken of a *depth* dimension: the efficiency of each component. Taken together, these components represent the quality of the consultancy service.

The customer is usually primarily concerned with the final results and has only a limited interest in the methods employed.

Consequently, Components 6, 7, and 8 are of major importance. Hence, it is essential that the change agent should be at least partially involved at the implementation stage.

The components are also partially covered in academic research, but it is unusual for researchers to take part in the implementation of the solution (7) or be responsible for results (8). In positivistic research, the researcher as an individual (2) is allegedly "neutralized" by the use of quantitative measurements of reliability and validity and by strict demands on objectivity.

Within the hermeneutic paradigm, the individual is a component of the research process. Although consultants like to talk about objectivity, absence of bias, hard facts, and so forth, the consultant paradigm is influenced by hermeneutic value judgments. Geneen states that you cannot separate the "facts" from the person who reports them: "Facts from paper are not the same as facts from people. The reliability of the person giving you the facts is as important as the facts themselves. Keep in mind that facts are seldom facts but what people think are facts heavily tinged with assumptions."[100]

In evaluating fiction, John Gardner[101] finds the key in the complex qualities of the author's character and personality: wisdom, generosity, compassion, strength of will, and ability to perceive and understand the world around one. In a similar vein, the consultant's personality is part of the quality of a consultancy service. In the literature, almost all the good attributes that a human being can have are considered suitable requirements for a consultant. This has been condensed in the following formulas:[102]

Brains + either Appearance or Charisma = Success
Brains + Appearance + Charisma = Superstar

The social role play of the consultant is important to achieving results. One such instance is given by Dufty in *Sugar Blues,* an account of the health hazard of sugar consumption. A Dr. Wiley had been appointed consultant to President Roosevelt on food legislation. He advocated prohibition against the use of saccharin in food, but he did not understand the social context in which this piece of advice was given: "Dr. Wiley was no politician. All the others were. He was no intimate of the President's, as were the others. If he had ever had tea or coffee with the President he might have known what they knew. He walked into a trap." What Dr. Wiley did not know was that the President, being a potential diabetic, had been prescribed to use saccharin: "Wiley had contravened the advice of the President's own doctor. He stood convicted of lese majesté."[103]

The completely opposite situation occurred in Kosinski's novel *Being There* where a social hermit had by accident been taken to the President of the United States for an informal chat. In reply to a question from the President on the economic situation, which he was quite unable to answer, he took refuge in the one thing that he did know about, gardening: "In a garden, he said, growth has its seasons. There are spring and summer but there are also fall and winter. And then spring and summer again. As long as the roots are not severed, all is well and all will be well." The President was pleased: "What you've just said is one of the most refreshing and optimistic statements I've heard in a very, very long time."[104]

These accounts, one a factual anecdote, the other pure fiction, teach us the importance of social context. In the first case, Dr. Wiley knew what he was talking about, and his advice was sound. In the second case, the advice to the President was based on a metaphor that had nothing to do with the solution of the President's economic problem.

Block discusses three types of basic consultancy skills: technical skills, interpersonal skills, and consulting skills.[105] These are complemented by responsibility, feelings, and trust as well as an awareness of one's own requirements and how these affect consultancy work. More detailed lists of personality requirements have been suggested by Greiner and Metzger[106] and by Shay.[107] These are summarized in Tables 5.3 and 5.4.

On one occasion, I heard a consultant from a large firm of management consultants state that "when we enter a client firm, the results will soon show in its profit-and-loss statement." This could be deliberate bragging on the part of the consultant or just ignorance; it is rare that the role played by the consultant can be

TABLE 5.3 Personality Traits and Knowledge Required for
Business Consultancy

Diagnostic Ability	*Communication Skills*
Objectivity	Sensitive listening skills
Intense curiosity	Exceptional writing ability
Conceptual and analytical	Oral presentation skills
Inductive reasoning	Intervention skills
Solution Skills	*Personality Characteristics*
Imagination	Ethical standards
Courage	Empathy and trust
Teaching ability	Positive thinking
	Self-motivation
Knowledge	Team player
	Self-fulfillment
Management theory supported	Mobility
by scholarly research findings	Energy
Applied techniques	Self-awareness

quickly recorded in simple financial figures. Toffler takes a more relaxed and detached view on this point: "No company, let alone one as big as AT&T, changes because of a report. Only intellectual arrogance or self-puffery allows any consultant to claim the credit for basic restructuring of any large company."[108]

One instance in which the consultant's direct effects on the company can be assessed is the management-for-hire assignment. One consultant summarizes his view of the contributions made by the consultants in the following terms:

Since the completion of my final assignment as "company doctor," I have worked from 1968 onwards with about fifteen different loss-making companies. Although half of these companies have now completed at least three years of profitable operations following the completion of a structural overhaul, it is still too early to carry out a final evaluation of these changes. It is the long-term survival and development of the company which will provide final proof of

TABLE 5.4 Personality Traits Required for Business Consultancy

1. Good physical and mental health
2. Professional etiquette and courtesy
3. Stability of behavior and action
4. Self-confidence
5. Personal effectiveness (drives)
6. Integrity (the quality that engenders trust)
7. Independence
8. Intellectual competence
9. Good judgment (the faculty of sound appraisal with complete objectivity)
10. Strong analytical problem-solving ability
11. Creative imagination
12. Skill in interpersonal relations
    a. Orientation toward the people aspect of problems
    b. Receptivity to new information or points of view expressed by others
    c. Ability to gain the trust and respect of client personnel
    d. Ability to enlist client participation in the solution of problems
    e. Ability to effect a transfer of knowledge to client personnel
    f. Ability to apply the principles and techniques of planned change
13. Ability to communicate and persuade (with above-average facility)
    a. Oral
    b. Written
    c. Graphic
14. Psychological maturity

the validity of the hypothesis. This cannot be ascertained after a period of only three years.[109]

According to the industry joke, the type of consulting that gives advice but does not involve itself in the implementation of that advice is termed "the seagull model of consulting."[110] With reference to BCG, the Boston Consulting Group, a *Fortune* article described their mode of operation in the following terms: "You flew out from Boston, made a couple of circles around the client's head, dropped a strategy on him, and flew back."

From his strategy assignment for AT&T, Toffler concludes: "It is always easier to talk about change than to make it. It is easier to consult than to manage. In writing this report, I never tried to lose sight of these simple truths."[111]

In the study of change projects, one author[112] states that it is not possible to make a simple, objective assessment of the success of the projects. Each individual assessment will need to weigh up a number of different aspects of the project, such as improved productivity, increased job satisfaction, better job security, or other factors that the individual in question finds important.

Important aspects of the quality of consultancy are summarized in the following quotation. The figures relate to the components in Figure 5.1:

> The way of operating the assignment (5) can be more or less effective. Consultants with limited specialist knowledge (1) and who lack other resources (3) may nevertheless produce better solutions (6) than an exclusive specialist due to their personality (2) if they are dedicated and cooperate well with client personnel. A solution is usually worthless if it is not implemented (7). But the solution must be within reach for the company; the most sophisticated solution might not be implementable. Finally, it is the prediction of the ultimate result (8) of an implemented solution that would be most desirable for the client to evaluate when buying an assignment. Since this is not usually feasible—there are exceptions though—the client will instead have to rely on an assessment and joint evaluation of the various components of the planned assignment. The existence of a *trusting relationship* between consultant and client will be a major factor in this inevitably subjective process of weighing together different quality aspects of the solution. The interaction between consultants and client personnel is a crucial part of the implementation of assignments. Hence the quality of the results is also bound up with the clients' efficiency and their ability to cooperate. Important quality improvements may be attainable by means of *improvements in the clients' own ability to utilize the consultants' services.*[113]

Conclusions

Quality criteria and paradigms have been discussed in relation to academic research and consultancy assignments.

A conclusion concerning quality was that the scientist as well as the consultant has to aim at *customer-perceived quality* and that this, simply put, is the combined perception of two major dimensions of quality: an *intellectual* dimension and a *social* dimension. Although the ratio between these can vary, the customer segments—academia or the business community or both—will make a total evaluation in which these two qualities are somehow merged. This conclusion is supported by similar results from studies of how consumers and organizational buyers assess products and services.

It emerged from the discussion that a quality assessment involves a wide variety of requirements. The quality criteria emanate from basic sets of values and procedures—the scientific paradigm or consultant paradigm. Hence, the process of quality assessment requires that researchers/consultants possess an understanding of their own paradigms. Paradigms are subjective and not always easily described in explicit terms. They are often not so well understood by researchers/consultants themselves.

I have sought to clarify the discussion by comparing the positivistic and hermeneutic paradigms and by making certain suggestions regarding the possible contents of a scientific and a consultant paradigm. At the same time, I have stressed that there are variants within the positivistic and hermeneutic paradigms and also that the two basic paradigms need not be viewed as contradictory but rather as complementary to each other. Sjoberg expresses it in the following way: "The opposing views of different research traditions cannot simply be viewed in terms of a conflict between positivism and hermeneutics. The majority of different approaches combine an analytical stance . . . with a willingness to study mental phenomena."[114]

Broad-mindedness is rarely the hallmark of researchers who confess to a specific paradigm. In that respect, a paradigm is like a religious sect or a political party. Some are fundamentalists; others might be more willing to tolerate coexistence with others. Yet a strong commitment to a certain paradigm and to certain applications of this paradigm will tend to brand other approaches as marginal decorations. I believe that it is essential to become acquainted with several paradigms and to select among these paradigms when working as a researcher/consultant.

The representatives of the positivistic tradition usually consider themselves scientific, whereas they look on those belonging to the hermeneutic tradition with apprehension, even contempt. Mario Bunge is an ardent protector of traditional research methods, and a prosecutor of what he calls "charlatans in science." In a *Charter of Intellectual Academic Rights and Duties*, he presents ten "commandments" of science.[115] The intentions are commendable; aren't we all longing for simple guidelines that will lead us on the right path of science? His goal is to separate science from the "bunk" that has managed to infiltrate academe, disguised in false scientific clothing, "a postmodern Trojan horse" that has became the most lethal enemy of all, the enemy within.

His commandments all sound reasonable, but how will they be practiced? Bunge's Commandment 6 reads "Every academic has the right to discuss any unorthodox views that interest him, provided those views are clear enough to be discussed rationally." The immediate problem is who determines what is "clear enough" and what is "rational"; it is a matter of interpretation. If the ethics, good intentions, and wisdom of the scientist are lacking, no rules will reify the situation. That can only be done through subjective (individual) reflection and intersubjective (peer group) dialogue, both going far beyond the requisite "clear enough to be discussed rationally." And that is exactly what Bunge is doing too; he does not apply rational discussion. In his 15-page text, there are well over one hundred instances of abusive designations on research and researchers who deviate from his norm. These represent mysticism, freewheeling, deceit, anti-intellectualism, guts over brains, instinct over reason, contrived willful ignorance, gobbledygook and much, much more. Diverse personalities such as philosophers Herbert Marcuse and Michel Foucault and the Nobel Laureates in the Economic Sciences, Gary Becker and Milton Friedman, are bunched together as bad guys. (The fact that a person has received the 1 million U.S. dollar Nobel Prize is, of course, no objective or ultimate proof that the person is a role model for scientific research. Especially in such

a difficult-to-grasp domain as the economic sciences, the appointment of a "winner" is best characterized as Mission Impossible.
The selection committee has its own idiosyncrasies, limitations,
and social commitments, and the members subjectively choose
their criteria for evaluation of candidates.)

Representatives of the hermeneutic paradigm sometimes appear to experience a sense of inferiority and to try to be as positivistic as possible. They take on the burden of proof, a burden that
erroneously has been put on their shoulders. If positivists are of
the belief that their approach is both superior and of more general
application, then it is up to them to provide credibility for these
claims. It is my experience that they choose not to apply their own
scientific methods to this question. I have encountered this attitude among, for example, those who consider that marketing
theories developed in relation to consumer goods in the United
States apply to all types of marketing globally; this view is implic-
itly, and I fear unconsciously, put forward by U.S. marketing textbooks. In conjunction with the growing research interest in services marketing starting during the mid-1970s, the burden of proof
was placed on the exponents of services marketing. If, however,
the latter did not consider that consumer goods marketing was
applicable to their area, it was hardly incumbent on the representatives of services marketing to provide proof. On the contrary, the
burden of proof lay with those who claimed a general validity for
their statements.[116] The same is repeating itself in the 1990s when
those who foresee a paradigm shift in marketing—conventional
marketing management theory being jettisoned by a relationship
marketing paradigm—are met with resistance from those who
take it for granted that incremental development of existing theory is sufficient.[117]

There are grounds for suspicion regarding those researchers
and consultants who consider that they have found the ultimate
method; there is no such method in operation today. Measurements before and after change processes have taken place are
mostly difficult to carry out. How much is caused by external factors beyond the reach of individuals, companies, or governments?
What will the free trade within the EU (European Union) and

NAFTA (North American Free Trade Agreement), Hong Kong having left the British Commonwealth for China, deregulation, the merger of two major competitors, gene technology, and so forth, lead to? Success therefore must often be expressed in qualitative terms.

In Andersson's[118] view, it is not possible to adopt a "smorgasbord strategy" where one selects from both the hermeneutic and positivistic traditions. I have encountered this attitude among some researchers, although others seem to draw from both research traditions. Others contend that they can combine their different approaches by means of "relative procedures."[119] In my interpretation, this suggests that a number of different views can be deployed "in tandem" as long as one has clarified one's assumptions and the approaches have been used in the right context.

The research reports that have contributed to the quality criteria discussed earlier draw on both hermeneutic and positivistic traditions. The data collection methods as well as the methods of coding and analysis contain elements of both paradigms. Researchers have also discovered that even in operations research[120]—which is based on quantitative, analytical solutions to decision problems—a purely positivistic paradigm is inadequate, particularly when working as management consultants. They run into opposition as their clients find their problem definitions to be unrealistic and their solutions and terminology to be incomprehensible and far from implementable. As a result of these problems, there has been a growing interest in *process* or *actor qualities*[121]—that is, nonanalytical aspects concerning the capacity of models to operate in a social context.

My own view can be summarized as follows. The hermeneutic paradigm exercises a major influence of research concerning processes of change. Within case study research, however, a variety of positivistic methods and techniques using mathematics, statistics, and computer processing may also be applied. Examples are analyses of financial data, customer satisfaction surveys based on questionnaires, and structural equation modeling of the interaction between several variables as, for example, represented by the LISREL software package.[122] There is absolutely no reason for antagonism between that and the qualitative approaches; in fact, this antagonism is not dissimilar from racial wars in which the motives for hostilities are literally no more than skin-deep.

The academic and scientific approaches to business administration are largely an amalgamation of different paradigms. Research reports drawn up on more or less orthodox positivistic lines are the most common, as they represent the conventional knowledge transmitted in universities. On the other hand, a strict application of the hermeneutic approach is rare, mainly due to ignorance among academicians. The action-oriented researcher, however, needs to make use of both positivistic and hermeneutic knowledge.

Notes

1. Garvin, 1988, p. xi.
2. The paragraphs on the industrial approach to quality are based on Gummesson, 1987.
3. Ishikawa, 1985, p. 14.
4. Quality of software is specifically treated in Dunn and Ullman, 1982.
5. "Can We Trust Our Software?" 1990.
6. Gummesson, 1991, pp. 10-16.
7. ISO 9000, 1997.
8. For an overview of quality definitions and the development of quality control in manufacturing, see Garvin, 1988. For a more philosophical and literary approach to quality, see Pirsig, 1974.
9. Crosby, 1979. See also the comments on "conformance quality" in Buzzell and Gale, 1987, pp. 104, 118, 131.
10. Juran, 1982.
11. Gummesson, 1978, pp. 93-94
12. ISO 9000, 1997.
13. Jevons, 1986.
14. Ibid., p. 100.
15. Zeithaml et al., 1990.
16. Gummesson, 1979, 1993; Lehtinen, 1985; Gronroos, 1990.
17. Sjostrand, 1979, pp. 148-70.
18. Bernard, 1991.
19. Helenius, 1990, p. 21.
20. Mitroff and Kilmann, 1982, p. 20. For a full account of the study, see Mitroff, 1974.

21. Sjostrand, 1975, 1979; Lindahl and Lindwall, 1978; Hesslow, 1979. See also Naess, 1982, who discusses the conditions of science and the borders of non-science.

22. Sjostrand, 1975, p. 958.

23. Drucker, 1987, p. 227.

24. Fleck, [1935] 1979.

25. From a summary of a seminar held by Braben, in *The Strategic Planning Society News*, 1987, p. 3.

26. Behrman and Levin, 1984, pp. 141-42.

27. Payne and Lumsden, 1987, p. 54.

28. Washburn, 1984/85, p. 15.

29. Shipman, 1982, pp. 51-52; Broad and Wade, 1982, pp. 186-92; Sakharov, 1990.

30. For analyses of deception and ethical problems in scientific research, see Broad and Wade, 1982; Crossen, 1994; Howard, 1994; and specifically on gene manipulation, Shiva, 1997.

31. Ortmark, 1985.

32. Mitroff, 1974, pp. 251-71, also discusses science as a game but says that the issue is not whether science is a game as such; it is, rather, a metaphor that can help to focus on essential aspects of scientific practice.

33. Broad and Wade, 1982, p. 19.

34. Deceit in science is treated by Broad and Wade, 1982, M. Gardner, 1983, and Hansson, 1983, 1984. It is not clear from this literature where the borders are between deliberate deceit, misunderstandings, and different scientific paradigms.

35. Snow, [1934] 1958, p. 94.

36. Ibid., pp. 338-39.

37. Ibid., p. 341.

38. Severe criticism against Freud's case studies is found in Crews et al., 1997; in Freud's defense, see Forrester, 1997.

39. Overbye, 1990.

40. Descriptions of conflicts in academic research institutions can be found in Svanberg, 1970; Stolpe, 1970, pp. 130-56; and Stockfelt, 1982.

41. The scientific paradigm is discussed by Tornebohm, 1983, pp. 238-44.

42. Gummesson, 1977, pp. 149-50, and 1979.

43. Feyerabend, [1975] 1980, p. 295.

44. Carlzon, 1987.

45. These are authentic quotations, but I have chosen not to reveal the names of the consulting companies.

46. Doyle, [1915] 1960, p. 84.

47. Holberg, [1723] 1914, p. 134.

48. Asplund, 1970, pp. 12-25. See also the discussion on Holmes and Maigret as consultants and scientists by Granholm, 1975 and 1987.

49. Doyle, [1892] 1985c, pp. 2-3.

50. Ledgard and Singer, 1982.

51. Simenon, 1975, p. 96.

52. Tesch, 1990, p. 58.

53. Patton, 1990, p. 88.

54. Helenius, 1990, pp. 211-13.

55. Taylor and Bogdan, 1984, p. 2.
56. Odman, 1985, p. 2162.
57. Capra, 1984, p. 101.
58. Thera, n.d., p. 29.
59. Kory, 1976; Russell, 1976; Gustavsson, 1992.
60. Howard, 1982.
61. Palmer, 1969, pp. 33-45.
62. M. Gardner, 1983, p. 115.
63. Rubenowitz, 1980, p. 26.
64. The table is inspired by Andersson, 1981, p. 104, and Barmark, 1984, p. 90.
65. Andersson, 1981, p. 42.
66. Ibid., pp. 94-95.
67. Ibid., pp. 48-52; Arbnor et al., 1981.
68. Taylor and Bogdan, 1984, pp. 10-11, 108-09.
69. Rodgers, 1986, p. 122.
70. Cohen et al., 1972.
71. Ibid., p. 2.
72. Martin, 1982, pp. 17-39.
73. McGrath et al., 1982.
74. Ibid., p. 13.
75. Andersson, 1981, p. 82.
76. Molander, 1983, p. 237.
77. Odman, 1979, pp. 98-99.
78. Glaser and Strauss, 1967, p. 232.
79. Noll, 1984, pp. 110-13.
80. Glaser and Strauss, 1967; Glaser, 1978.
81. Ibid., p. 118.
82. Brunsson, 1982, pp. 103-04, and Holmquist et al., 1984, pp. 107-08.
83. Glaser has in a conversation with me (September 1984) expressed discontent over the fact that parts of "grounded theory" have been applied too loosely, which has affected the credibility of the theory. Since then, Glaser has become more understanding of researchers who limit themselves to selected grounded theory strategies as long as the researchers do not claim that grounded theory has been used in its original sense; see Glaser, 1995.
84. Argyris and Schon, 1974, 1978.
85. Ibid., 1978, p. 5.
86. Shipman, 1982, p. xiii.
87. Ibid., p. 15.
88. Ibid., pp. xi-xii.
89. Persson, 1980a, appendix 1, pp. 1-3; Persson, 1980b; Hagg and Hedlund, 1978, pp. 14-15; Lindgren, 1981, p. 8:2; Frenckner, 1981.
90. Drucker, 1987, p. 11.
91. Ibid., p. 222.
92. Mendoza, 1987, p. 62.
93. Drucker, 1955.
94. Peters and Waterman, 1982.
95. Sadler, 1983, pp. 108-09.
96. Lawler, 1985, p. 3.

97. Taylor and Bogdan, 1984, p. 7.
98. Sadler, 1983, p. 109.
99. Gummesson, 1977, pp. 136-50.
100. Geneen, 1984, p. 211.
101. J. Gardner, 1983, p. 9.
102. According to Jim Kennedy, in Kelley, 1981, p. 17.
103. Dufty, 1976, pp. 170-71.
104. Kosinski, 1983, p. 46.
105. Block, 1981, pp. 4-5, 11-14.
106. Greiner and Metzger, 1983, pp. 29-35.
107. Shay, 1974, pp. 41-42.
108. Toffler, 1985, p. 14.
109. af Trolle, 1975, p. 1052.
110. Kiechel, 1983, p. 36.
111. Toffler, 1985, p. 171.
112. Targama, 1981, pp. 43 and 50.
113. Gummesson, 1977, p. 150.
114. Sjoberg, 1982.
115. Bunge, 1996, pp. 110-11.
116. Gummesson, 1979, p. 30.
117. Gummesson, 1999.
118. Andersson, 1981, pp. 102-03.
119. Arbnor and Bjerke, 1997, pp. 438-41.
120. Naert and Leeflang, 1978, pp. 100-18, 321-53; Larréché, 1979, p. 185.
121. Gummesson, 1982, pp. 11-12 and 29-35.
122. For a presentation of LISREL, see the computer program by Jöreskog and Sörbom, 1995.

Six

A Management Action Science Paradigm

The following questions have been raised:

* Is it possible to improve academic research into processes of decision making, implementation, and change by combining it with management consultancy?

* Do academic researchers and management consultants share a common denominator?

These questions give rise to a single key question:

* Is action science possible?

This chapter tries to answer the last question by means of a synthesis of the earlier arguments, beginning with a summary of the arguments presented in earlier chapters, followed by a proposal on strategy for academic researchers/management consultants engaged in action science. Finally, my own assessment of the con-

TABLE 6.1   The Role of the Management Action Scientist

Question:

What is the role of the management action scientist?

Answer:

On the basis of their *paradigms* and *preunderstanding* and given *access to empirical, real-world data* through their *role as change agent,* management action scientists develop an *understanding* of the *specific decision, implementation, and change process* in the *cases* with which they are involved. They *generate a specific (local) theory* which is then *tested* and *modified* through *action.*

The interaction between the *role of academic researcher* and the *role of management consultant, within a single project* as well as *between projects,* can also help the scientist to generate a *more general theory,* which in turn becomes an instrument for *increased theoretical sensitivity* and an *ability to act* in a social context, a theory that is *never finalized* but is *continually being transcended.*

---

tribution of this book and the research project it is based on is presented.

The Role of the Management Action Scientist

On the basis of the arguments presented in the previous chapters, the role of the action scientist is summarized in Table 6.1. The words emphasized in Table 6.1 will be commented on below. These comments are a condensed version of earlier remarks.

Paradigm. The scientific and consultant paradigms represent an underlying influence on the work of the academic researcher and management consultant, respectively.

Preunderstanding. This concept was dealt with in Chapter 3 where it was stated that preunderstanding could be based on a combination of firsthand personal experience and the experience of others, which were then conveyed to the researcher secondhand (Figure 3.1). It was my contention that the researchers' own experiences were the most important; that certain types of knowledge had, however, to be communicated secondhand; and that the researchers' preunderstanding was too infrequently based on their own experiences.

Access. This was discussed in Chapter 2. Traditional forms of data collection—archival records, questionnaires, interviews, observations—were considered to provide only superficial access to processes of change. It was argued that *the role of change agent* would provide better access.

Empirical, real-world data. Management is an applied science (or maybe an art) that has to be connected to real-world data. Theories concerned with processes in organizations must be generated primarily on the basis of this real data (inductive method) and be assisted by logical deductions from established theory.

An *understanding* of a *specific decision, implementation, and change process* is created by an earlier preunderstanding, through the researcher's own experience as an active participant in processes as well as from access gained to other people's experiences by means of research (Figure 3.2). The researcher is concerned with one or several *cases.* The opportunity to carry out a large number of case studies of a process of change is limited by the fact that each individual case places considerable demands on the time and commitment of the action scientist.

One of the aims of research is to *generate theory* (in a wide sense, this includes hypotheses, concepts, categories, models, and so forth) suited to a *specific* and thereby *local* process of change. *The theory is tested in action*—that is, when the researcher participates in the process, intervenes and determines whether the action derived from theory works (e.g., improves profitability). The theory can also be *modified* in action.

In the long term, the researcher can develop a *more general theory.* This is based on the *interrelationship between the roles of researcher and consultant in a series of individual projects.* Action scientists may also conduct their research in terms of a combination of action and reflection within a single project. This leads to further reflection and the generation of theory that then interacts with a subsequent research project. The theory can then be developed from a specific, local theory (substantive theory) to a *more general theory* (generalized substantive theory and formal theory). This creates an opportunity for researchers to increase their *theoretical sensitivity* and *ability to act* when presented with new situations. Researchers/consultants should not try to mold reality to fit their theory but be able to accept new real-world data and treat the theory as a modifiable guide to action. The theory will *never take on a finalized form*. In social situations, it will probably not be possible to create a theory with a long life cycle. It will instead be *transcended*—that is, take on new and more adequate forms.[1]

In the light of this background summary, the following section outlines a researcher/consultant strategy for action science.

Researcher/Consultant Strategy

In many respects, the demands placed on consultancy work coincide with the demands placed on academic research. Greater emphasis is usually laid on the personal attributes required for consultancy—judgment, maturity, flexibility, and so forth—as well as an ability to take action within a specific time and financial framework. These differences are related to different paradigms and the values and traditions inherent in them. They are also related to the varying objectives of clients as well as to the specific objectives set by the researchers and the consultants themselves.

What can be done when the demands placed on research and consultancy work do not coincide? There are three possibilities:

* The methods adopted by the change agent are not accepted by the research community. This rejection of a possible means of access limits the opportunities available to researchers to work with management as an applied science.

* The change agent lives up to the demands required of a management consultant. These requirements then receive the approval of academic researchers because they

provide both an improved means of access to information and place a greater emphasis on the need for access. This is an oversimplified approach, however, and there is a considerable risk that the concept of science will become watered down.

✳ At the same time as the change agents meet the demands placed on the role of consultant, they also try to meet the requirements of the research community by carrying out certain additional work.

The last point offers the most fruitful approach. Academic researchers will become increasingly involved in management consultancy. Consultancy assignments generate research opportunities. The alternative is that the researcher explores different ways of obtaining empirical data for individual research projects that have already been formulated in theoretical and methodological terms. Both approaches are perfectly feasible.

In what sense then do conflicts arise between the demands of academic research and the requirements of management consultancy? The particular demands that may give rise to such a conflict are discussed in this section. They stand out most clearly when the management action science paradigm is applied. (The number of the paragraphs follows the list of quality criteria in Chapter 5.)

1. *The reporting of a project should be such as to allow the readers to draw their own conclusions.* The researcher's report should be sufficiently comprehensive to provide a coherent description of the research project and to allow the reader to assess its quality. The researcher is required to maintain documentary records that allow "outsiders" to follow the research process. In the role of consultant, the change agent is not required to do so except for his or her own need to support the change process; it is not certain that a final report is essential, and often, such reports are not written. Progress is reported through informal discussion, memos, and slide presentations. This continuous interaction with the consultant allows the client to monitor the progress of the project.

As mentioned in Chapter 4, I am skeptical regarding the opportunities open to the researcher to describe a change project so that the reader can follow it completely. This is because of access and preunderstanding; participating in a change process and gaining personal experience are essential parts of understanding. Tacit understanding cannot by definition be communicated in a written report because it has no language.

In their capacity as change agents, the researchers should be able to meet the demands for written documentation over and above their work as consultants. Researchers/consultants can find themselves in situations in which the demands of researcher and consultant roles come into conflict. For example, pressure of time may force them to devote all their energy to the execution of decisions rather than to the documentation of events. In this conflict, the consultant role of making things happen must take precedence over the recording and interpretive role of the researcher. However, the demands placed on the researcher may be at least partially met by a subsequent reconstruction of events.

The choice of scientific method and approach is of crucial importance to the researcher. Unless the client has bought a specific method, such as a questionnaire survey or a program for the preparation of ISO 9000 certification, the consultant has considerably greater freedom than the academic researcher. The consultant is focused on finding activities that lead to results, often simple and straightforward activities based on experience and hunch, even if these do not fulfill scientific standards. The type and scale of the consultancy assignment are to a certain extent predetermined, but the consultants should also question their clients' definition of the problem. They should restrict the assignment to what is manageable and meaningful in the light of the company's situation and objectives. Because consultants must take account of the need to reach conclusions and propose recommendations that are possible to implement, they are usually not in a position to adjust their analyses of the problem to fit a particular method and thereby impose a traditional research stamp on the project.

2. *Researchers, consultants, and their clients benefit from an awareness of the paradigms and preunderstanding that govern their way of*

working. Before a consultant is awarded a specific assignment, the client makes an assessment of the consultant's capabilities. The consultants' preunderstanding is of particular importance, such as previous experience and referrals from other clients, as well as their paradigm, including values, attitudes, and procedures. To avoid counterproductive future conflicts, consultants need to know about the paradigm of their prospective clients. We are, however, limited in our ability to explicitly identify deep-rooted and taken-for-granted values and modes of behavior. Researchers should to a much greater degree than is common today attempt to explain their preunderstanding and paradigm to others as well as to themselves.

3. *Showing credibility is a vital part of both the researcher and consultant roles.* The consultant is judged in terms of performance, be it tangible results or perceived confidence. The researcher's credibility is assessed by people who do not participate in the research process but read a report. The researcher/consultant has an opportunity to provide documentation over and above the material produced in conjunction with the assignment. Apart from relating to empirical data, consultants can justify their conclusions by statements such as "in my experience" and "we did that at Company A." Researchers' conclusions have to be accounted for more in detail and be related to theory, empirical data, and existing literature. The explanation of their preunderstanding and paradigm also adds to the reader's possibility of assessing the value of a report.

Consultants will have to choose methods appropriate to the specific problem and contribute to the development of the change process. Methodological studies are seldom of direct interest to clients unless the method is what they are looking for. Because there is usually a tight deadline, the empirical data is often less extensive than would be desirable. The consultant has to work under stricter requirements in terms of time available and an agreed budget, whereas research projects are notorious for late delivery. Consequently, intuition and judgment will be given a greater priority for consultants, and as a result, the motives for the consultants' conclusions cannot always be described. Nor will the change agents be able to hedge their recommendations in the same way as researchers can be guarded about their conclusions. Hence, the conclusions and recommendations must be viewed as a stage in a process in which other than explicit, analytical considerations are of importance. Researchers can attempt to describe and assess the importance of these shortcomings in their reports. Consultants are expected to be normative, to come up with recommendations or actions, whereas scholars/researchers often shun the normative.

4. *Considerable demands are placed on access, especially for the consultant.* Consultants have numerous opportunities to try out different forms of access without having to justify their choice of methods other than that they considered it appropriate to do A rather than B. The researcher is to a much greater extent required to adopt formal access methods and is more often assessed by the correct application of an "approved" technique than the actual access.

The methods for data collection used by consultants are frequently highly fragile from a scientific point of view. Creativity, intuition, experience, and bold action can be more important means of obtaining results than the deployment of formal method. The researcher could be experimenting with different research methods without directly having to produce usable results. The results in the form of implemented change seem to be of lesser importance to the academic researcher than the actual means by which these results are derived. Hence, the consultant becomes primarily concerned with pragmatic considerations, whereas the researcher is preoccupied with a scientific ritual.

5. *Clients are interested in the validity of the results in their specific cases but not as interested in the general validity.* However, there can be several similar cases in the company, and it is therefore desirable that the methods and results can also be applied in these cases. The researcher's findings should be of interest to a wider group of people than just the individual client. Companies are rarely interested in the fact that research findings may be borne out by other research or that they relate to theories and models in the literature. However, the interest in what other companies are

doing and whether comparable solutions have led to success is snowballing; companies are not as industry-myopic and parochial as before. TQM has brought in the notion of "benchmarking"—that is, comparing with the very best wherever it is to be found and aiming for "best-in-class," even "world class," performance.

6. *Academic research is intended to make a contribution to science; the consultancy assignment, to the client.* Researchers/consultants are therefore required to view their results in a larger context and to try to assess their value for others. Moreover, researchers must make their results available to other researchers, not just to their immediate client. This may come into conflict with the company's wish to keep the assignment confidential and with proprietary information. The conflict can be solved through anonymity and by conceptualizing substantive phenomena and events, lifting them to a more general level—the latter being a distinguishing hallmark of scholarly research and theory generation. From the client's point of view, it is of the utmost importance that relevant problems are examined. Considerable sums of money could be at stake of which the researcher/consultant fee forms only a minor part; it can be a question of survival or death for the organization.

7. *The demands for a dynamic approach to both the research process and consultancy work have increased.* It has long been noted that change occurs at a faster rate. Organizational changes are now continuous in large organizations. Lean production, just-in-time delivery, reduced time-to-market of new products and services, global competition—even "hypercompetition"[2]—and not least, new information technology speed up decisions and changes. A consequence is a need for more flexible and adaptable researchers and consultants. There is a risk that if the process is rapid and dramatic—such as when there is a threat of plant closure or a takeover—the researchers will be unable to devote all of their attention to participation in the process. This risk is due to the scientific demands for documentary records, strict adherence to an original research design, and reference to certain literature. There is also another dynamic aspect, particularly significant for scholars. True scholars grow and develop with their research, they challenge the

established "truths." They do not just repeat more of the same; they generate theory.

8. *The demands for personal qualities should apply to both consultants and researchers.* Tables 5.3 and 5.4 listed personal qualities required for consultants. They stressed not just intellectual properties; in fact, these did not top the lists. They were outranked by, for example, curiosity, intervention skills, physical health, and self-confidence. There are no corresponding lists for academic researchers, whose personalities seem to be nonexistent. According to the positivistic scientific paradigm, only the intellectual and analytical abilities—"being able to think rationally"—count. On the other hand, the hermeneutic paradigm contends that the researchers' entire personality is of importance: "The researcher is the research instrument." In essence, the same lists of personal qualities that apply to consultants apply to scholars, although the emphasis on qualities can vary.

If a gap exists between the demands confronting the researcher and the consultant, a *conflict of loyalties* may emerge in relation to carrying out research by means of the consultancy role:

* A researcher who concentrates on satisfying the requirements of the researcher role will be, first and foremost, an academic researcher, and considerations related to the consultancy role will be of secondary importance. From the client's point of view, there is a risk of becoming an inferior consultant.

* A researcher who concentrates on satisfying the requirements of the consultancy role may well come into conflict with the demands laid down for good research.

* Once the research role comes into conflict with the role of consultant, the latter must be given priority. If this does not take place, the change process will itself be affected by the academic research. This creates an unsatisfactory situation both for the client and for science.

The research strategy presented above relates primarily to an individual project. The proposal put forward by Sandberg and

Figure 6.1. Roles of Academic Researcher and of Management Consultant: Single-Project Strategy

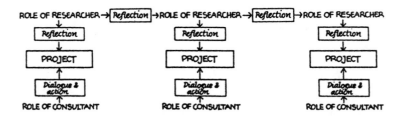

Figure 6.2. Roles of Academic Researcher and of Management Consultant: Program Strategy

Gustavsen[3] regarding entire research programs was discussed in Chapter 4. A program of several research projects and researchers provides a better opportunity to combine the roles of academic researcher and management consultant. In this light, the interrelationship between the researcher and consultant roles occurs *over time* as well as *between different researchers* within the framework of a larger program. This means that it would *not be necessary for the researcher to meet all the quality requirements in each individual project.* Researchers can instead view a single project as a springboard for subsequent projects to be conducted by themselves or by others.

Figure 6.1 illustrates the *single-project strategy,* and Figure 6.2 describes the *program strategy.* Today, it's more urgent than ever to work in larger programs with long-term goals and involving several researchers. Individual researchers can become isolated and lonely, when they are in need of both intellectual and emotional support from colleagues and others. It is easier to apply for grants if whole programs can be presented. The impact of research can be much greater if several studies are made within the same theme. This is not a recommendation that researchers should always work in programs. It might not fit their personality, and it might offer less freedom to develop a unique and creative research style. The wrong composition of a group of researchers can lead to forced compliance with mainstream science or a group's current fads or whims.

Summary of Contributions

One final question remains to be answered:

✳ What is the contribution of this book?

The purpose of the research presented in this book is twofold: (a) *to contribute to the methodology of research in management* and (b) *to act as a stimulus to a constructive discussion of the paradigms and methods adopted by academic researchers and management consultants.* The aim has also been to make the book readable for both researchers and consultants.

I have endeavored to integrate several different sources to create a greater unity. Consequently, literature dealing with scientific theory and methods has been integrated with literature concerned with management consultancy. In certain instances, I have made use of reports by investigative journalists, memoirs of executives and scientists, and also purely fictional material. Moreover, I have drawn on my general research experience and my previous research projects on consultancy services and action science. The large number of pure consultancy assignments with which I have been involved has also constituted an invaluable source of material. I believe that the integration of these different types of sources is unique.

I have also presented my thoughts in a context of management. This is unusual; textbooks on methodology and the theory of science are usually grounded in sociology, education, anthropology, or psychology.

In a book project like this one, for which I have not been dependent on a particular client or any other source of finance, I have been free to develop the text entirely according to my own preferences. The possibility of learning then becomes of central importance. At the same time, I want the book to be of use to others, and I do believe that I share the experience of certain fundamental problems presented here with a large number of academic researchers and management consultants.

There is no given method for the evaluation of quality of this type. This must accordingly be a question of my own personal assessment—the readers then being left to appraise the project in light of their own views.

The book has dealt with the following:

I started out from an inquiry into the differences between academic, scholarly research and management consultancy. My argument was that *the role of consultant created opportunities for in-depth research in business issues* and that these opportunities had received scant attention in the methodological literature as well as in university training and research. Management research could be improved if there was a greater awareness of the opportunities offered by the role of management consultant.

My interests soon broadened into *qualitative research in general* with specific focus on *case study research.* The reason was simple: Management consultants primarily work with qualitative methods in assignments—that is, in cases.

The book has been primarily concerned with *decision making, implementation, and change processes.* Progressively, however, this can be considered a fairly general approach because *the natural state of organizations today is change.*

To arrive at these conclusions, a number of different areas have come under intensive consideration.

Different types of consultancy assignments and the respective roles and principal characteristics of the academic researcher and the manage-

ment consultant were discussed in Chapter 2. This type of systematization ought in itself to be of value because consultants and researchers do not seem to have an overall grasp of these considerations. Although I have worked as a consultant for many years, this systematization was not altogether a simple matter. I have received a certain amount of help from the literature, but for the most part I have had to rely on my own observations.

Rather than the conventional focus on techniques for data collection, the book took a more generic approach and looked into *the needs and opportunities for access—that is, how to get close enough to reality.* On the basis of this discussion, a definition was proposed for the concept of *change agent.* The latter was shown to offer better opportunities for access to processes of change than was available from other methods or by means of other roles.

The introductory episodes in Chapter 2 illustrated how researchers and consultants could obtain superficial access without being aware of the limitations. Researchers mainly develop their *preunderstanding* and a specific knowledge of particular cases *secondhand, through intermediaries.* I have become increasingly convinced over the years that the *personal experiences* of the researcher/consultant must play a larger role in the improvement of preunderstanding and access. In connection with this, it was pointed out that the greatest difficulty facing the researcher/consultant is often not the intellectual knowledge of theories, models, and so forth but, rather, the *understanding of a social environment and institutional conditions.*

My conclusion is that both access and preunderstanding are treated too lightly by the research community. I have labeled them the researcher's Number 1 and Number 2 challenges.

To penetrate more deeply the complexity of change processes, one can work with only *a limited number of cases.* Consultants always work with *cases,* their assignments. Using *case studies as a research method* is gradually receiving scientific approval in the management field. One question that frequently emerges in relation to case study research is *validity* and the possibility of *generalizing* the results. I concluded that validity is high and that generalizations are possible. A more important conclusion, however, was the question as to whether it was desirable to generalize knowledge in a social context. It seems to be increasingly important to generate theories that act as a guide to action but that can be continually modified or completely revised. In a similar vein, TQM, as applied in business organizations, holds *continuing improvements* as a key strategy. This demands an openness and receptivity on the part of the researcher as well as a singular lack of authoritarian tendencies or susceptibility to fashionable trends. The theory will therefore become *local* rather than general. Consequently, it will be more important to show that it works in a specific context than that it possess a wide range of general and approximate application.

The role of historical analyses and *futures studies* in cases has been discussed. Researchers have spoken in favor of historical analysis and proposed general guidelines for its use. However, I find myself skeptical of these arguments, having experienced that preoccupation with the past is often a barrier to understanding what action to take in a new situation. Therefore, I rather follow the strategy of *carpe diem*—"seize the day"—because it is often not at all obvious where we are today. It is still less obvious where we will be tomorrow, and there is no way of predicting the future with any uncertainty when changes consist of discontinuity and quantum leaps. For example, take a look at what was said about the future of computer and telecom use five, even three, years ago and compare with the actual outcome! The focal point has to be on the present and the future, not the past. I have, however, been influenced by the history literature and find that a historical approach can help understanding corporate culture. The tools of historical analysis, however, are too blunt, and more practical methods are required.

The subject of *taboos and anonymity* was raised in relation to case studies. Considerations vital to a particular process are often swept under the carpet. I find that both researchers and consultants are too cowardly in attacking issues of a sensitive nature in favor of conventional explanations.

In summary, my conclusions in relation to case study research are that the concepts of validity and generalization, the value of historical analysis, and the existence of taboos are treated far too lightly by both researchers and consultants.

Attempts have also been made to review the *concept of quality* and identify *quality criteria* for both consultancy and scientific work—the researcher's Number 3 challenge. My conclusion is that it is difficult to make quality appraisals of the work of both researchers and consultants. To a large extent, it remains a *subjectively perceived quality,* and it requires considerable maturity to make the judgments.

Certain basic values and procedures, *paradigms,* underlie the behavior of both researchers and consultants and the way the quality of their work can be assessed. In this book, I have referred to *scientific* and *consultant paradigms.* Both can be associated with *positivistic* and *hermeneutic* paradigms. I have attempted to make the differences between positivistic and hermeneutic approaches clear and have also discussed the way the paradigms guide the researcher/consultant. Researchers all too often fail to analyze their paradigm and its effect on their work. Management consultants without any research background are generally unaware of paradigmatic considerations, and that must be considered as a substantial shortcoming.

A *management action science paradigm* including a researcher/consultant strategy for processes of change has been worked out as a synthesis. Research and consultancy are combined in the concept of management action science, a concept that has been further developed in this second edition of the book. However, *the requirements facing academic researchers and management consultants* have been shown to differ and can come into conflict with each other. This produces difficulties for the conduct of action science. A main contribution of this book has been to extend the general and primarily *societal concept of action science* and to propose a management action science concept. It has also been extended to include not only *real-time action science* but under certain provisions also *retrospective action science.*

It is not a matter of strictly applying a *positivistic or hermeneutic paradigm;* it is rather an attempt to combine the requirements of research and consultancy into action science within either a *single-project strategy* or a *program strategy*. The management action science paradigm has a different focus than does the original societal action science; it's about successful management instead of support to weaker groups, although the two sometimes concur.

To conclude, the book has sought to make a contribution to methodology and scientific approaches in studies of various management disciplines. The previous editions of the book have shown that there is a need for debate about the methodology used by business schools. In Chapter 1, I quoted the complaint, "My professor does not understand me. What shall I do?" It could equally well be extended to established researchers and faculty who depend on peer consensus and peer review; breaking the rules of an academic clique currently in power may be lethal to their careers. The root cause of the problem is unfamiliarity with the opportunities offered by qualitative methodology and case study research. I hope that this book can stimulate a broadened approach to management research, leading to more significant contributions from scholarly research as well as from management consultancy.

Notes

1. The terms *substantive theory, generalized substantive theory, formal theory, theoretical sensitivity,* and *transcendence,* are those used by Glaser and Strauss, 1967, and Glaser, 1978.

2. Hypercompetition is a designation for fast and ruthless competition, also known as marketing warfare; killing the competitor is the ultimate goal. See D'Aveni, 1994.

3. Sandberg, 1982, pp. 83-88; Gustavsen, 1982.

References

Abingdale, Frank W. (with Stan Redding). 1982. *Catch Me if You Can*. New York: Pocket Books.

Agar, Michael J. 1980. *The Professional Stranger*. New York: Academic Press.

Alkin, Marvin, Richard Daillak, and Peter White. 1979. *Using Evaluations: Does Evaluation Make a Difference?* Beverly Hills, CA: Sage.

Alloway, Robert M. 1977. *Research and Thesis Writing Using Comparative Cases*. Stockholm: Institute of International Business.

Alter, Jonathan. 1986. "Skipping through the News." *Newsweek*, Pacific Edition, June 9.

Alvesson, Mats, and Yvonne Due Billing. 1997. *Understanding Gender and Organization*. London: Sage.

Andersson, Sten. 1981. *Positivism kontra hermeneutik*. Uddevalla, Sweden: Korpen.

Araskog, Rand V. 1989. *The ITT Wars*. New York: Henry Holt.

Arbnor, Ingeman, and Lars Andersson. 1977. *Att förstå sociala system*. Lund, Sweden: Studentlitteratur.

Arbnor, Ingeman, and Björn Bjerke. 1997. *Methodology for Creating Business Knowledge*. London: Sage.

Arbnor, Ingeman, Sven-Erik Borglund, and Thomas Liljedahl. 1981. *Osynligt ockuperad*. Kristianstad, Sweden: Liber.

Archer, Jeffrey. 1984. *First among Equals*. New York: Pocket Books.

Åredal, Åke. 1986. "Procrustes: A Modern Management Pattern Found in a Classical Myth." *Journal of Management* 12(3):403-14.

Argyris, Chris. 1970. *Intervention Theory and Method*. Reading, MA: Addison-Wesley.

———. 1985. *Strategy, Change and Defensive Routines*. Marshfield, MA: Pitman.

————. 1990. *Overcoming Organizational Defenses.* Boston: Allyn & Bacon.

Argyris, Chris, Robert Putnam, and Diana McLain Smith. 1985. *Action Science.* San Francisco: Jossey-Bass.

Argyris, Chris, and Donald Schon. 1974. *Theory in Practice: Increasing Professional Effectiveness.* San Francisco: Jossey-Bass.

————. 1978. *Organizational Learning: A Theory of Action Perspective.* Reading, MA: Addison-Wesley.

Arndt, Johan. 1985. "On Making Marketing Science More Scientific: Role of Orientations, Paradigms, Metaphors, and Puzzle Solving." *Journal of Marketing* 43(Summer):2011-23.

Asplund, Gisele, and Göran Asplund. 1982. *An Integrated Development Strategy.* London: Wiley.

Asplund, Johan. 1970. *Om undran infor samhallet.* Kalmar, Sweden: Argus.

Bärmark, Jan. 1984. "Vetenskapens subjektiva sida." In *Forskning om forskning,* edited by Jan Bärmark. Lund, Sweden: Natur och Kultur.

Barnes, J. A. 1977. *The Ethics of Inquiry in Social Science.* New Delhi: Oxford University Press.

Batra, Ravi. [1978] 1990. *The Downfall of Capitalism & Communism: Can Capitalism Be Saved?* Dallas, TX: Venue.

Beckhard, Richard. 1969. *Organization Development: Strategies and Models.* Reading, MA: Addison-Wesley.

Beer, Michael. 1980. *Organization Change and Development: A System View.* Glenview, IL: Scott, Foresman.

Behrman, Jack N., and Richard I. Levin. 1984. "Are Business Schools Doing Their Job?" *Harvard Business Review* January-February: 140-47.

Bendrik, Sören. 1978. "Hårt vinklade foretagsstudier: Ny form av foretagsekonomisk 'forskning.' " *Arbetsgivaren* 40.

Bergström, Sören, and Sten Söderman. 1982. *Något om att identifisera och organisera kunskapsutveckling: Fallet forskare och konsulter som intellektuella praktiker.* Research Report R:5. Stockholm: University of Stockholm, Department of Business Administration.

Bergstrom, Villy. 1984. "Pamfletter och plattheter." *Dagens industri,* May 4.

Bernard, Andre (ed.). 1991. *Rotten Rejections: A Literary Companion.* New York: Viking Penguin.

Bernard, Russell H. 1995. *Research Methods in Anthropology.* Walnut Creek, CA: AltaMira.

Bernstein, Carl, and Robert Woodward. 1974. *All the President's Men.* New York: Simon & Schuster.

Biddle Barrows, Sydney (with William Novak). 1986. *Mayflower Madam.* London: Macdonald.

Bitner, Mary J., Jody D. Nyquist, and Bernard H. Booms. 1985. "The Critical Incident as a Technique for Analyzing the Service Encounter." In *Services Marketing in a Changing Environment,* edited by Thomas M. Block, Gregory D. Upah, and Valerie A. Zeithaml. Chicago: American Marketing Association.

Björklund, Ulf, and Ulf Hannerz. 1983. *Nyckelbegrepp i socialantropologin.* Stockholm: University of Stockholm, Socialantropologiska Institutionen.

Blanchard, Kenneth, and Spencer Johnson. 1984. *The One Minute Manager.* New York: Berkley.

Block, Peter. 1981. *Flawless Consulting.* Austin, TX: Learning Concepts.
Bohm, David. 1977. "Science as Perception-Communication." In *The Structure of Scientific Theories,* edited by F. Suppe. Urbana: University of Illinois Press.
———. 1980. *Wholeness and the Implicate Order.* London: Routledge & Kegan Paul.
Bolch, Judith, and Kay Miller. 1978. *Investigative and In-Depth Reporting.* New York: Hastings House.
de Bono, Edward. 1971. *The Use of Lateral Thinking.* London: Penguin.
Bonoma, Thomas V. 1985a. "Case Research in Marketing: Opportunities, Problems, and a Process." *Journal of Marketing Research* 22 (May):199-208.
———. 1985b. *The Marketing Edge.* New York: Free Press.
Braben, Donald. 1987. "Research: Don't Stifle the Heretics Pleads Dr. Donald Braben." *The Strategic Planning Society News* February.
Broad, William, and Nicholas Wade. 1982. *Betrayers of the Truth.* Oxford, UK: Oxford University Press.
Brown, C., P. Guillet de Monthoux, and A. McCullough. 1976. *The Access Casebook.* Stockholm: Teknisk Högskolelitteratur (THS).
Brunsson, Nils. 1982. *Företagsekonomi: Sanning eller moral?* Lund, Sweden: Studentlitteratur.
Bunge, Mario. 1996. "In Praise of Intolerance to Charlatanism in Academia." In *The Flight from Science and Reason,* edited by Paul R. Gross, Norman Levitt, and Martin W. Lewis, 98-115. New York: New York Academy of Sciences/Johns Hopkins University Press.
Burrell, Gibson. 1984. "Sex and Organization Analysis." *Organization Studies* No. 205/2.
Burrell, Gibson, and Gareth Morgan. 1985. *Sociological Paradigms and Organizational Analysis.* Aldershot, UK: Gower.
Buzzell, Robert D., and Bradley T. Gale. 1987. *The PIMS Principles.* New York: Free Press.
Calder, Bobby J. 1977. "Focus Group and the Nature of Qualitative Marketing Research." *Journal of Marketing Research* 14:353-64.
Capra, Fritjof. 1982. *The Turning Point.* London: Wildwood House.
———. 1984. *The Tao of Physics.* Toronto: Bantam.
———. 1988. *Uncommon Wisdom.* New York: Simon & Schuster.
———. 1997. *The Web of Life.* London: Flamingo/HarperCollins.
Carlson, Sune. 1983. *Studier utan slut.* Stockholm: SNS.
Carlzon, Jan. 1987. *Moments of Truth.* Cambridge, MA: Ballinger.
Clark, Peter A. 1972. *Action Research and Organizational Change.* London: Harper & Row.
Coffey, Amanda, and Paul Atkinson. 1996. *Making Sense of Qualitative Data.* Thousand Oaks, CA: Sage.
Coghlan, David, and J. McDonagh. 1997. "Doing Action Research in Your Own Organization." In *Business Research Methods: Strategies, Techniques and Sources,* edited by David Coghlan and Teresa Brannick, 139-61. Dublin: Oak Tree Press.
Cohen, D., J. G. March, and J. P. Olsen. 1972. "A Garbage Can Model of Organizational Choice." *Administrative Science Quarterly* 17:1-25.
Cravens, David. 1998. "Implementation Strategies in the Market-Driven Strategy Era." *Journal of the Academy of Marketing Science* 26(3):237-41.

Crews, Frederick et al. 1997. *The Memory Wars: Freud's Legacy in Dispute*. London: Granta.

Crosby, Philip B. 1979. *Quality Is Free*. New York: McGraw-Hill.

———. 1984. *Quality without Tears*. New York: Plume.

Crossen, Cynthia. 1994. *Tainted Truth: The Manipulation of Fact in America*. New York: Simon & Schuster.

Danielsson, Albert. 1977. *Företagsekonomi: En översikt*. Lund, Sweden: Studentlitteratur.

D'Aveni, Richard A. 1994. *Hypercompetition*. New York: Free Press.

Davies, Paul. 1984. *Andra världar*. Stockholm: Akademilitteratur.

———. 1987. *The Cosmic Blueprint*. London: Heinemann.

Deal, Terence E., and Allan A. Kennedy. 1983. *Foretagskultur*. Stockholm: Timo.

Dichter, Ernest. 1979. *Getting Motivated by Ernest Dichter*. Elmsford, NY: Pergamon.

Downie, Leonard, Jr. 1978. *The New Muckrakers*. New York: New American Library.

Doyle, Arthur Conan. [1891] 1985a. "The Blue Carbuncle." In *Sherlock Holmes: Selected Stories*. London: Chancellor.

———. [1891] 1985b. "A Scandal in Bohemia." In *Sherlock Holmes: Selected Stories*. London: Chancellor.

———. [1892] 1985c. "Silver Blaze." In *Sherlock Holmes: Selected Stories*. London: Chancellor.

———. [1915] 1960. *The Valley of Fear*. London: John Murray.

Drucker, Peter. 1955. *The Practice of Management*. London: Heinemann.

———. 1987. *The Frontiers of Management*. London: Heinemann.

———. 1989. *The New Realities*. London: Heinemann.

Dufty, William. 1976. *Sugar Blues*. New York: Warner.

Dunn, Robert, and Richard Ullman. 1982. *Quality Assurance for Computer Software*. New York: McGraw-Hill.

Easterby-Smith, Mark, Richard Thorpe, and Andy Low. 1991. *Management Research: An Introduction*. London, Sage.

Eberwein, Willhelm, and Tholen, Jochen. 1997. *Market or Mafia*. Aldershot, UK: Ashgate.

Edström, A., R.-A. Larsson, B. Sandberg, and H. Wirdenius. 1984, February. *Förnyelse av ledningsfilosofi, ledarskap och organisation*. Working Paper. Stockholm: F Aradet.

Edvinsson, Leif, and Michael S. Malone. 1997. *Intellectual Capital*. New York: Harper Collins.

Eisenhardt, K. 1989. "Building Theories from Case Study Research." *Academy of Management Review*, 14(4):532-50.

Elden, Max, and Rupert F. Chisholm. 1993. "Emerging Varieties and Action Research: Introduction to the Special Issue." *Human Relations*, 46(2):121-42.

El-Sayed, Refaat, and Carl Hamilton. 1989. *Refaat El-Sayeds memoarer: Makten och ärligheten*. Stockholm: Norstedts.

Elson, John. 1990. "Sorting through the Runes." *Time*, April 23.

Elton, G. R. [1967] 1989. *The Practice of History*. London: Fontana.

Encyclopedia Britannica. 1965. Chicago: William Benton.

Ernst, Bruno. 1992. *The Eye Beguiled*. Cologne, Germany: Benedikt Taschen Verlag.

Evans-Pritchard, E. E. 1937. *Witchcraft, Oracles and Magic among the Azende*. New York: Oxford University Press.

Falcone, Giovanni, and Marcelle Padovani. 1991. *Cosa Nostra: Domarens kamp mot maffian.* Stockholm: Forum.

Feldt, Kjell-Olof. 1991. *Alla dessa dagar.* Stockholm: Norstedts.

Feyerabend, Paul. [1975] 1980. *Against Method.* London: Verso.

Fiorentini, Gianluca, and Sam Peltzman, eds. 1995. *The Economics of Organized Crime.* Cambridge, UK: Cambridge University Press.

Fleck, Ludwik. [1935] 1979. *Genesis and Development of a Scientific Fact.* Chicago: University of Chicago Press.

"Focus on Participatory Research." 1988. *Convergence* 21(2-3).

Fordyce, Jack K., and R. Weil. 1971. *Managing with People.* Reading, MA: Addison-Wesley.

Forrester, John. 1997. *Dispatches from the Freud Wars.* Boston, MA: Harvard University Press.

French, Wendell L., and Cecil H. Bell, Jr. 1978. *Organization Development.* Englewood Cliffs, NJ: Prentice Hall.

French, Wendell L., Cecil H. Bell, Jr., and Robert A. Zawacki. 1978. *Organization Development: Theory, Practice and Research.* Dallas, TX: Business Publications.

Frenckner, Paulsson. 1981. *Motiverat vägval vid avhandlingar i företagsekonomi.* Working Paper. Stockholm: University of Stockholm, Department of Business Administration.

Fukuyama, Francis. 1995. *Trust.* New York: Free Press.

Gardner, John. 1983. *The Art of Fiction.* New York: Random House.

Gardner, Martin. 1983. *Science: Good, Bad and Bogus.* Oxford, UK: Oxford University Press.

Garthon, Per. 1983. *Riksdagen innifrån.* Stockholm: Prisma.

Garvin, David A. 1988. *Managing Quality.* New York: Free Press.

Gates, Bill. 1995. *The Road Ahead.* New York: Viking.

Geneen, Harold S. (with Alvin Moscow). 1984. *Managing.* Worcester, UK: Granada.

Glaser, Barney G. 1978. *Theoretical Sensitivity.* Mill Valley, CA: Sociology Press.

———. 1992. *Basics of Grounded Theory Analysis.* Mill Valley, CA: Sociology Press.

———. 1995. *Grounded Theory: 1984-1994* (Volume 2). Mill Valley, CA: Sociology Press.

Glaser, Barney G., and Anselm L. Strauss. 1967. *The Discovery of Grounded Theory.* New York: Aldine.

Goldman, Marshall I. 1988. "Gorbachev, Turnaround CEO." *Harvard Business Review* May-June:107-13.

Granholm, Arne. 1975. "Kommissarie Maigret: En av skönlitteraturens mest systematiska skildringar av en utredares vardag." *Jury* 1.

———. 1987. "Sherlock Holmes: Konsulten och foretagaren." *Jury* 2.

Greenbaum, Thomas L. 1998. *The Handbook for Focus Group Research.* Thousand Oaks, CA: Sage.

Greene, Graham. 1984. *Getting to Know the General.* New York: Washington Square.

Greiner, Larry E., and Robert O. Metzger. 1983. *Consulting to Management.* Englewood Cliffs, NJ: Prentice Hall.

Grönroos, Christian. 1990. *Service Management and Marketing.* Lexington, MA: Lexington Books.

Guillet de Monthoux, Pierre. 1978. *Handling och existens: Anarkoexistensiell analys av projekt, företag och organisation.* Stockholm: Liber.

230 QUALITATIVE METHODS IN MANAGEMENT RESEARCH

Gummesson, Evert. 1977. *Marknadsföring och inköp av konsulttjänster.* Stockholm: University of Stockholm / Marketing Technology Center (MTC) / Akademilitteratur.

———. 1978. "Toward a Theory of Professional Service Marketing." *Industrial Marketing Management* 7(2):89-95.

———. 1979. "The Marketing of Professional Service: An Organizational Dilemma." *European Journal of Marketing* 13(5).

———. 1982. *Att anvanda företags- och marknadsstrategiska beslutsmodeller.* Stockholm: Marketing Technology Center (MTC).

———. 1987. *Quality: The Ericsson Approach.* Stockholm: Ericsson.

———. 1990. *Yuppiesnusk eller ledarskapets fornyelse.* Stockholm: SNS.

———. 1991. "Service Quality: A Holistic View." In *Service Quality: Multidisciplinary and Multinational Perspectives,* edited by Stephen Brown et al. Lexington, MA: Lexington / Macmillan.

———. 1993. *Quality Management in Service Organizations.* New York: St. John's University and the International Service Quality Association.

———. 1998. "Implementation Requires a Relationship Marketing Paradigm." *Journal of the Academy of Marketing Science* 26(3):242-49.

———. 1999. *Total Relationship Marketing.* Oxford, UK: Butterworth-Heinemann.

Gustafsson, Lars. 1977. *Den lilla världen.* Stockholm: Alba.

Gustavsen, Björn. 1982. "Utviklingstrekk och problemstillinger i den handlingsrettede arbetslivsforskning i de nordiske lande." *Sociologisk Forskning* 2-3.

Gustavsen, Björn, and Øyvind Palshaugen. 1984. "Knowledge and Action Research in Social Research." Unpublished paper. Oslo: Arbeidsforskningsinstituttene.

Gustavsen, Björn, and Bjørg Aase Sorensen. 1982. "Aksjonsforskning." In *Kvalitativa metoder i samfunnsforskning,* edited by Harriet Holter and Ragnvald Kalleberg. Drammen, Norway: Universitetsforlaget.

Gustavsson, Bengt. 1992. *The Transcendent Organization.* Stockholm: Stockholm University.

Habermas, Jurgen. [1968] 1987. *Knowledge and Human Interest.* Cambridge, UK: Polity.

Hägg, Ingemund. 1982. "Validering och generalisering—problem i företagsekonomisk forskning." In *Företagsekonomi: Sanning eller moral?* edited by Nils Brunsson. Lund, Sweden: Studentlitteratur.

Hagg, Ingemund, and Gunnar Hedlund. 1978. *Case Studies in Social Science Research.* Working Paper No. 2078-16. Brussels: European Institute for Advanced Studies in Management.

Hailey, Arthur. 1965. *Hotel.* London: Pan.

———. 1968. *Airport.* London: Pan.

———. 1984. *Strong Medicine.* London: Pan.

Hall, Edward T. [1959] 1973. *The Silent Language.* Garden City, NY: Anchor / Doubleday.

Hall, Edward T., and Mildred Reed Hall. 1977. "The Sounds of Silence." In *Conformity and Conflict,* edited by J. P. Spardley and D. W. McCurdy. Boston, MA: Little, Brown.

Hansson, Sven Ove. 1983. *Vetenskap och ovetenskap.* Kristianstad, Sweden: Tiden.

———. 1984. "Bekrfätar fysiken mystiken?" *Forskning och Framsteg* 5.

Helenius, Ralf. 1990. *Första och bättre veta*. Stockholm: Carlssons.

Henderson, Bruce D. 1984/85. "Credo." *Journal of Management Consulting* 2(1):11-14.

Heran, Jeff, Deborah I. Sheppard, Peta Tancred-Sheriff, and Gibson Burrell, eds. 1989. *The Sexuality of Organization*. Newbury Park, CA: Sage.

Hesslow, Germund. 1979. *Medicinsk veterskapsteori*. Lund, Sweden: Studentlitteratur.

Hildebrandt, Steen. 1980. "The Changing Role of the Analyst in Effective Implementation of Operations Research and Management Science." *European Journal of Operational Research* 5:359-65.

Hofstede, Geert. 1980. *Culture's Consequences*. Beverly Hills, CA: Sage.

Holberg, Ludvig. [1723] 1914. "Erasmus Montanus." In *Comedies by Holberg*. New York: American-Scandinavian Foundation.

Holm-Lofgren, Barbro. 1980. *Ansvar, avund och arbetsglädje*. Stockholm: Askild & Karnekull.

Holmquist, Carin, Rolf A. Lundin, and Elisabeth Sundin. 1984. *Forhandla mer, räkna mindre*. Stockholm: Liber.

Howard, Philip. 1994. *The Death of Common Sense: How Law Is Suffocating America*. New York: Random House.

Howard, Roy J. 1982. *Three Faces of Hermeneutics*. Berkeley: University of California Press.

Hult, Margareta, and Sven-Ake Lennung. 1978a. "Aktionsforskning—vad är det?" *Ehrvervsokonomisk Tidskrift* 42.

———. 1978b. "What Is Action Research?" *Pedagogical Bulletin*. University of Lund, No. 205.

Hunt, Shelby B. 1983. *Marketing Theory: The Philosophy of Marketing Science*. Homewood, IL: Irwin.

Hygstedt, Bjorn. 1990. "Han graver fram de obehagliga svaren." *Svenska Dagbladet*, June 10.

Iacocca, Lee (with William Novak). 1984. *Iacocca: An Autobiography*. New York: Bantam.

Imai, Masaaki. 1986. *Kaizen*. New York: McGraw-Hill.

Ingvar, David H. 1984. "Ledarskap och neurobiologi." *Skandinaviska Enskilda Bankens Kvartalsskrift* 3:72-78.

———. 1985. "Memory of the Future: An Essay on the Temporal Organization of Conscious Awareness." *Human Neurobiology* 4:127-36.

Ingvar, David H., and C. G. Sandberg. 1985. *Det medvetna företaget*. Stockholm: Timbro.

Ishikawa, Kaoru. 1985. *What Is Total Quality Control? The Japanese Way*. Englewood Cliffs, NJ: Prentice Hall.

ISO 9000. 1997. *International Standards for Quality Management*. Geneva: International Standards Organization.

Issal, Raimo. 1984. *Överleva med bidrag*. Malmö, Sweden: Acta Wexionensia.

Jackson, Philip W. 1968. *Life in the Classroom*. New York: Holt, Rinehart & Winston.

Jeffmar, Marianne. 1984. "Konsulten: En analytiker." *Svenska Dagbladet*, October 26.

Jevons, Marshall. 1986. *The Fatal Equilibrium*. New York: Ballantine.

Jick, Todd D. 1983. "Mixing Qualitative and Quantitative Methods: Triangulation in Action." In *Qualitative Methodology*, edited by John Van Maanen. Beverly Hills, CA: Sage.

Johannisson, Bengt. 1980. *Den organisatoriska smältdegeln*. Stockholm: Liber.

Johnsen, Erik, ed. 1980. *Konsulentrollen*. Copenhagen: Civilokonomernes Forlag.

Johnson, Paul. 1987. "The Heartless Lovers of Humankind." *Wall Street Journal*, January 9.

———. 1989. *Intellectuals*. New York: Harper & Row.

Jöreskog, K. G., and D. Sörbom. 1995. *LISREL* (computer program). Chicago, IL: Scientific Software International.

Juran, J. M. 1982. *Upper Management and Quality*. New York: Juran Institute.

Kaldor, N. 1960a. *Essays on Economic Stability and Growth*. London: Duckworth.

———. 1960b. *Essays on Value and Distribution*. London: Duckworth.

Kalleberg, Ragnvald. 1972. "En introduktion till Frankfurtskolans vetenskapsteori." In *Positivism, marxism och kritisk teori*, edited by I. Johansson, R. Kalleberg, and S.-E. Liedman. Stockholm: Pan/Norstedts.

Kanter, Rosabeth Moss. 1983. *The Change Masters*. New York: Simon & Schuster.

Kantrow, Alan E., ed. 1986. "Why History Matters to Managers." *Harvard Business Review* January-February:81-88.

Kaplan, Robert S., and David P. Norton. 1996. *The Balanced Scorecard*. Boston, MA: Harvard Business School Press.

Kapstein, Jonathan. 1987. "Scandal in Sweden: How the Fermenta Dream Turned Sour." *Business Week*, May 18, pp. 30-34.

Kelley, Robert E. 1981. *Consulting*. New York: Scribner.

———. 1985. *The Gold Collar Worker*. Reading, MA: Addison-Wesley.

Kerlinger, Fred N. 1976. *Foundations of Behavioral Research*. London: Holt, Rhinehart & Winston.

Kidder, Tracy J. 1981. *The Soul of a New Machine*. Boston, MA: Little, Brown.

Kiechel, Walter, III. 1983. "Corporate Strategists under Fire." *Fortune*, December 27, pp. 34-39.

Kihlmann, Ralph H., M. J. Saxton, and P. Serpa, eds. 1985. *Gaining Control of Corporate Culture*. San Francisco: Jossey-Bass.

Kirk, Jerome, and Marc L. Miller. 1986. *Reliability and Validity in Qualitative Research*. Beverly Hills, CA: Sage.

Kjellen, Bengt, and Sten Söderman. 1980. *Praktikfallsmetodik*. Malmo, Sweden: SIAR/Liber.

Kolb, David, and Alan L. Frohman. 1970. "An Organization Development Approach to Consulting." *Sloan Management Review* Fall.

Koopmans, Tjalling C. 1947. "Measurement without Theory." *Review of Economic Statistics* 29(3):161-72.

Kory, Robert B. 1976. *The Transcendental Meditation Program for Business People*. New York: American Management Association.

Kosinski, Jerzy. 1983. *Being There*. London: Black Swan.

Kotter, John P. 1978. *Organizational Dynamics: Diagnosis and Intervention*. Reading, MA: Addison-Wesley.

Krueger, Richard A. 1994. *Focus Groups: A Practical Guide for Applied Research*. Thousand Oaks, CA: Sage.

Kubr, M., ed. 1983. *Management Consulting.* Geneva, Switzerland: International Labour Office.

Kuhn, Thomas S. 1962. *The Structure of Scientific Revolutions.* Chicago: University of Chicago Press.

———. 1970. *The Structure of Scientific Revolutions.* 2d ed. Chicago: University of Chicago Press.

———. 1979. "Foreword." In *Genesis and Development of a Scientific Fact,* edited by Ludwik Fleck. Chicago: University of Chicago Press, pp. vii-xi.

Kulka, Richard A. 1982. "Idiosyncracy and Circumstance: Choices and Constraints in the Research Process." In *Judgment Calls in Research,* edited by Joseph E. McGrath, Joanne Martin, and Richard A. Kulka. Beverly Hills, CA: Sage.

Lacey, Robert. 1986. *Ford.* London: Heinemann.

Larréché, Jean-Claude. 1979. *Integrative Complexity and Use of Marketing Models.* TIMS Studies in Management Sciences, No. 2013.

Lawler, Edward E., III. 1985. "Challenging Traditional Research Assumptions." In *Doing Research That Is Useful for Theory and Practice,* edited by Edward B. Lawler, III et al., 1-17. San Francisco: Jossey-Bass.

Lawler, Edward E., III et al., eds. 1985. *Doing Research That Is Useful for Theory and Practice.* San Francisco: Jossey-Bass.

Ledgard, Henry, and Andrew Singer. 1982. *Elementary Basic.* New York: Random House.

Lehtinen, Jarmo R. 1985. "Improving Service Quality by Analyzing the Service Production Process." In *Service Marketing: Nordic School Perspectives.* Research Report R, edited by C. Grönroos and E. Gummesson, p. 2. Stockholm: University of Stockholm, Department of Business Administration.

Lewin, Kurt. 1946. "Action Research and Minority Problems." *Journal of Social Issues* 2:34-36.

Liles, Shelley. 1989. "Being a Consultant Pays Off." *USA Today,* July 21, p. 8B.

Lindahl, Olov, and Lars Lindwall. 1978. *Vetenskap och beprövad erfarenhat.* Stockholm: Natur och Kultur.

Lindberg, Börje. 1982. *Konsult.* Stockholm: Börje Lindberg.

Lindgren, Ulf. 1981. *Praktikfallsforskning: En metodologisk betraktelse.* Stockholm: Stockholm School of Economics, Institute of International Business.

Lindholm, Stig. 1980. *Vetenskap, verklighet och paradigm.* Uppsala, Sweden: AWE/Gebers.

Lindstrmö, Johan. 1973. *Dialog och försåtelse.* Gothenburg, Sweden: University of Gothenburg.

Long Range Planning. 1983. "Collected Commentaries of the Reviewers." December: 108-09.

Mao Tse-Tung. [1937] 1969. "Om Praktiken." *Skrifter i urval.* Uddevalla, Sweden: n.p.

Marketing News. 1986. "Hypothesis-Free Research Needed to Avoid Marketing to Stereotypes." Chicago: American Marketing Association June 6, pp. 6, 8.

Martin, Joanne. 1982. "A Garbage Can Model of the Research Process." In *Judgment Calls in Research,* edited by, Joseph E. McGrath, Joanne Martin, and Richard A. Kulka. Beverly Hills, CA: Sage.

Masterman, Margret. 1970. "The Nature of a Paradigm." In *Criticism and the Growth of Knowledge*, edited by Imre Lakatos and Alan Musgrave, 59-89. Cambridge, UK: Cambridge University Press.

Mattsson, Lars-Gunnar. 1982. "Om utveckling av marknadsföring och distributionsekonomi i Sverige." In *Företagsekonomi: Sanning eller moral?* edited by Nils Brunsson. Lund, Sweden: Studentlitteratur.

McCormack, Mark H. 1984. "Reading People." In *What They Don't Teach You at Harvard Business School*. London: Collins.

McGivern, C. K., and S. Fineman. 1983. "Research and Consultancy: Towards a Conceptual Synthesis." *Journal of Management Studies* 20(4).

McGrath, Joseph E., Joanne Martin, and Richard A. Kulka, eds. 1982. *Judgment Calls in Research*. Beverly Hills, CA: Sage.

McKenna, Regis. 1985. *The Regis Touch*. Reading, MA: Addison-Wesley.

McLuhan, Marshall. 1966. *Understanding Media: The Extension of Man*. New York: McGraw-Hill.

Mendoza, Gaby. 1987. "The Secret of Peter Drucker's Success as a Writer." *World Executive's Digest* May.

Meurling, John, and Richard Jeans. 1985. *A Switch in Time*. Chicago: Telephony.

———. 1994. *The Mobile Phone Book*. London: Communications Week International.

Mintzberg, Henry. 1994. *The Rise and Fall of Strategic Planning*. New York: Free Press.

Mitroff, Ian I. 1974. *The Subjective Side of Science*. Amsterdam, The Netherlands: Elsevier.

Mitroff, Ian I., and Ralph H. Kilmann. 1982. *Methodological Approaches to Social Sciences*. San Francisco: Jossey-Bass.

Molander, Bengt. 1983. *Vetenskapsfilosofi*. Stockholm: Norstedts.

Morgan, Gareth. 1997. *Images of Organization*. Thousand Oaks, CA: Sage.

Myrdal, Gunnar. 1970. *Objectivity in Social Research*. London: Duckworth.

Nachmias, David, and Chava Nachmias. 1987. *Research Methods in the Social Sciences*. New York: St. Martin's.

Nader, Ralph. 1965. *Unsafe at Any Speed*. New York: Grossman.

Naert, Philippe A., and Peter H. Leeflang. 1978. *Building Implementable Marketing Models*. Leiden/Boston: Martinus Nijhoff.

Naess, Arne. 1982. *Anklagelser mot vetenskapen*. Gothenburg, Sweden: AWE/Gebers.

Nagel, Thomas. 1986. *The View from Nowhere*. Oxford, UK: Oxford University Press.

Nash, Jeffrey E. 1977. "Decoding the Runner's Wardrobe." In *Conformity and Conflict*, edited by J. P. Spradley and D. W. McCurdy. Boston: Little, Brown.

New Encyclopedia Britannica. Vol. 11, p. 20917. 1986. Chicago: Encyclopedia Britannica.

"Can We Trust Our Software?" 1990. *Newsweek*, January 29, pp. 42-44.

Nilson, Ulf. 1989. "Poor Marx." *Scanorama*, February.

Noll, Peter. 1984. *Diktate über Sterben und Tot*. Zurich, Switzerland: Pendo-Verlag.

Normann, Richard. 1970. *A Personal Quest for Methodology*. Stockholm: Scandinavian Institutes for Administrative Research.

Nyquist, Jody D., Mary J. Bitner, and Bernard H. Booms. 1985. "Identifying Communication Difficulties in the Service Encounter: A Critical Incident

Approach." In *The Service Encounter*, edited by John A. Czepiel, Michael R. Solomon, and Carol F. Surprenant. Lexington, MA: Lexington Books.

Ödman, Per-Johan. 1979. *Tolkning, försåtelse, vetande*. Halmstad, Sweden: AWE/Gebers.

———. 1985. "Hermeneutics." In *The International Encyclopedia of Education*, edited by Torsten Husen and Neville T. Postlethwaite, 2162-69. Oxford, UK: Pergamon.

Ohmae, Kenichi. 1995. *The End of the Nation State*. New York: Free Press.

Orme-Johnson, David. 1988. "The Cosmic Psyche." *Modern Science and Vedic Science* 2(2).

Ortmark, Åke. 1985. *Maktens människor*. Malmo, Sweden: Wahlstrmö & Widstrand.

Ouchi, William G. 1981.*Theory Z*. New York: Avon.

Overbye, Dennis. 1990. "Einstein in Love." *Time*, April 30, p. 56.

Packard, Vance. [1957] 1971. *The Hidden Persuaders*. Harmondsworth, UK: Penguin.

———. 1961. *The Waste Makers*. London: John Farquarson.

Palmer, Richard E. 1969. *Hermeneutics*. Evanston, IL: Northwestern University Press.

Patton, Michael Quinn. 1980. *Qualititative Evaluation Methods*. Beverly Hills, CA: Sage.

———. 1990. *Qualitative Evaluations and Research Methods*. 2d ed. Newbury Park, CA: Sage.

Payne, Adrian, and Cedric Lumsden. 1987. "Strategy Consulting: A Shooting Star." *Long Range Planning* 20(3):53-64.

Persson, Lars. 1980a. *En syn på företagsekonomisk forskning*. Working Paper W 1980:1. Stockholm: University of Stockholm, Department of Business Administration.

———. 1980b. *PM med synspunkter inför seminarium 1980-10-17 kring B's disputation*. Stockholm: University of Stockholm, Department of Business Administration.

Peters, Thomas J. 1988. *Thriving on Chaos*. London: Macmillan.

Peters, Thomas J., and Robert J. Waterman, Jr. 1982. *In Search of Excellence*. New York: Harper & Row.

Piercy, Nigel F. 1998. "Marketing Implementation: The Implications of Marketing Paradigm Weakness for the Strategy Execution Process." *Journal of the Academy of Marketing Science* 26(3):222-36.

Pirsig, Robert M. 1974. *Zen and the Art of Motorcycle Maintenance*. New York: William Morrow.

"Playboy Interview: Fidel Castro." *Playboy*, August 1985.

Polanyi, Michael. 1962. *Personal Knowledge*. London: Routledge & Kegan Paul.

Popper, Karl R. 1979/1959. *The Logic of Scientific Discovery*. London: Hutchinson.

Postman, Neil. 1985. *Amusing Ourselves to Death*. New York: Penguin.

Prigogene, Ilya, and Isabelle Stengers. 1985. *Order out of Chaos*. London: Fontana/Flamingo.

Quinn, James Brian. 1992. *The Intelligent Enterprise*. New York: Free Press.

Reutersvräd, Oscar. 1984. *Omöjliga figurer*. Lund, Sweden: Doxa.

Rodgers, F. G. "Buck." 1986. (with Robert L. Shook). In *The IBM Way*. New York: Harper & Row.

Rubenowitz, Sigvard. 1980. *Utrednings- och forskningsmetodik.* Gothenburg, Sweden: Scandinavian University Books.

Rudberg, Hans. 1979. *Ett haveri.* Lund, Sweden: Raben & Sjögren.

Russell, Bertrand. [1912] 1948. *The Problems of Philosophy.* London: Oxford University Press.

Russell, Peter. 1976. *The TM Technique.* London: Routledge & Kegan Paul.

Rylander, Leif. 1995. *Tillväxtföretag i startfas.* Stockholm: Stockholm University.

Sadler, Philip. 1983. "Collected Commentaries of the Reviewers." *Long Range Planning* December:108-09.

Sakharov, Andre, ed. 1990. *Memoirs.* New York: Knopf.

Sampson, Anthony. 1973. *The Sovereign State: The Secret History of ITT.* London: Hodder & Stoughton.

———. 1984. *Empires of the Sky.* Sevenoaks, UK: Hodder & Stoughton.

———. [1977] 1985. *The Arms Bazaar.* London: Coronet.

———. 1990. *The Midas Touch.* New York: Dutton.

Sandberg, Åke. 1982. "Från aktionsforskning till praxisforskning." *Sociologisk Forskning* 2-3.

Schein, Edgar H. 1969. *Process Consultation: Its Role in Organization Development.* Reading, MA: Addison-Wesley.

———. 1995. "Process Consultation, Action Research and Clinical Inquiry: Are They the Same?" *Journal of Managerial Psychology* 10(6):14-19.

Schmid, Herman. 1982. "Tillampad forskning som praktik." *Sociologisk Forskning* 2-3.

Schon, Donald A. 1983. *The Reflective Practitioner.* New York: Basic Books.

Sculley, John (with John A. Byrne). 1987. *Odyssey: Pepsi to Apple.* London: Collins.

Sen, Amartya. 1980. "Description as Choice." *Oxford Economic Papers* 3:353-69.

Seymour, Daniel T. 1988. *Marketing Research: Qualitative Methods for the Marketing Professional.* Chicago, IL: Probus.

Shay, P. W. 1974. *The Common Body of Knowledge for Management Consultants.* New York: Association of Consulting Management Engineers.

Shelton, Judy. 1990. *Coming Soviet Crash: Gorbachev's Desperate Search for Credit in the Western Financial Market.* New York: Macmillan.

Shipman, Marten. 1982. *The Limitations of Social Research.* London: Longman.

Shiva, Vandana. 1997. *Biopiracy: The Plunder of Nature and Knowledge.* Boston, MA: South End.

Silverman, David, ed. 1997. *Qualitative Research.* London: Sage.

Simenon, George. 1975. *Maigret and the Loner.* New York: Harcourt Brace Jovanovich.

Sjöberg, Lennart. 1982. "Vetenskapsteori och samhälle." *Svenska Dagbladet,* March 31.

Sjöstrand, Torgny. 1975. "Vetenskapssamhället och utvecklingen." *Läkartidningen* 72(10).

———. 1979. *Medicinsk vetenskap.* Stockholm: Natur och Kultur.

Sloan, Alfred P. [1963] 1986. *My Years with General Motors.* London: Penguin.

Smith, George David, and Laurence E. Steadman. 1981. "Present Value of Corporate History." *Harvard Business Review* November-December.

Snow, C. P. [1934] 1958. *The Search.* London: Macmillan.

Stacey, Ralph D. 1996. *Strategic Management and Organisational Dynamics* (2d ed.). London: Pitman.

Statskontoret. 1980. *Ny organisation? Metoder och arbetsformer vid organisations-utredningar.* Stockholm: Liber.

Stockdale, Margaret S., ed. 1996. *Sexual Harassment in the Workplace.* Thousand Oaks, CA: Sage.

Stockfelt, Torbjörn. 1982. *Professorn.* Taby, Stockholm: MaxiMedia.

Stolpe, Sven. 1970. *Låt mig berätta.* Stockholm: Askild & Karnekull.

Strauss, Anselm L., and Barney G. Glaser. 1970. *Anguish: A Case History of a Dying Trajectory.* San Francisco: University of California Medical Center.

Sundqvist, Sven-Ivan. 1987. *Refaat & Fermenta.* Stockholm: Forfattarforlaget.

Svanberg, Victor. 1970. *Leva för att leva.* Stockholm: Askild & Karnekull.

Sveiby, Karl Erik. 1994. *Towards a Knowledge Perspective on Organisation.* Stockholm: Stockholm University.

———. 1997. *The New Organizational Wealth.* San Francisco: Berret-Koehler.

Sveiby, Karl-Erik, and Anders Risling. 1986. *Kunskapsföretaget.* Malmo, Sweden: Liber.

Tandon, Rajesh. 1988. "Social Transformation and Participatory Research." *Convergence* 12(2-3).

Targama, Axel. 1981. *Att genomföra administrativa förändringar.* Stockholm: Sveriges Mekanförbund.

Taylor, Frederick W. 1911. *Principles of Scientific Management.* New York: n.p.

Taylor, Steven J., and Robert Bogdan. 1984. *Introduction to Qualitative Research Methods.* New York: John Wiley.

Tesch, Renata. 1990. *Qualitative Research: Analysis Types and Software Tools.* New York: Falmer.

Thera, Piyadassi. n.d. *Buddhism: A Living Message.* Bangkok, Thailand: n.p.

Tilles, Seymour. 1961. "Understanding the Consultant's Role." *Harvard Business Review* November-December:87-99.

Tisdall, Patricia. 1982. *Agents of Change.* London: Heinemann/Institute of Management Consultants.

Toffler, Alvin. 1981. *The Third Wave.* London: Pan Books.

———. 1985. *The Adaptive Corporation.* London: Pan Books.

Törnebohm, Håkan. 1976. *En systematik över paradigm.* Gothenburg, Sweden: University of Gothenburg.

———. 1983. *Studier av kunskapsutveckling.* Karlshamn, Sweden: Doxa.

Townsend, Patrick L., with Joan E. Gebhardt. 1990. *Commit to Quality.* New York: John Wiley.

af Trolle, Ulf. 1975. "At vara 'företagsdoktor.' " *Affarsvärlden* No. 2025-26.

———. 1979. *Effektivt styrelsearbete.* Kristianstad, Sweden: Affarsfrölaget.

Uttal, B. 1983. "The Corporate Culture Vultures." *Fortune* October 17, pp. 66-72.

Valdelin, Jan. 1974. *Produktutveckling och marknadsföring.* Stockholm: EFI.

Van Maanen, John. 1982. "Fieldwork on the Beat." In *Varieties of Qualitative Research,* edited by John Van Maanen, James M. Dabbs, Jr., and Robert R. Faulkner. Beverly Hills, CA: Sage.

———. 1985. "Epilogue: Qualitative Methods Reclaimed." In *Qualitative Methodology,* edited by John Van Maanen. Beverly Hills, CA: Sage.

Wallander, Jan. 1994. *Budgeten: Ett onödigt ont?* Stockholm: SNS.

Wallraff, Gunter. 1985 *Ganz Unten*. Cologne, Germany: Verlag Kiepenheuer & Witsch.

Warneryd, Karl-Erik. 1985. "Management Research and Methodology." *Scandinavian Journal of Management Studies* 2(1):3-17.

Washburn, Stewart A. ed. 1984/85. "Management Consultants and : Seven Views of the Relationship." *Journal of Management Consulting* 2(1):15-25.

Webb, Eugene J., Donald T. Campbell, Richard D. Schwartz, and Lee Sechrest. 1966. *Unobtrusive Measures*. Chicago: Rand McNally.

Webb, Eugene, and Karl E. Weick. 1983. "Unobtrusive Measures." In *Qualitative Methodology*, edited by John Van Maanen. Beverly Hills, CA: Sage.

Weber, Max. 1968. *Economy and Society*. New York: Bedminster.

Whitley, Richard D. 1984. "The Scientific Status of Management Research as a Practically Oriented Social Science." *Journal of Management Studies* 21(4):369-90.

Williams, Paul N. 1978. *Investigative Reporting and Editing*. Englewood Cliffs, NJ: Prentice Hall.

von Wright, Georg Henrik. 1986. *Vetenskapen och förnuftet*. Stockholm: Bonniers.

Yin, Robart K. 1994. *Case Study Research*. Thousand Oaks, CA: Sage.

Zeithaml, V. A., A. Parasuraman, and L. L. Berry. 1990. *Delivering Quality Service*. New York: Free Press.

Zohar, Danah, and Ian Marshall. 1993. *The Quantum Society*. London: Bloomsbury.

Zukav, Gary. 1979. *The Dancing Wu-Li Masters: An Overview of the New Physics*. New York: William Morrow.

Index

About the Author

Evert Gummesson graduated from the Stockholm School of Economics and received his Ph.D. from Stockholm University, where he is Professor of Service Management and Marketing, and Research Director of its School of Business. The university has 34,000 students; its business school has 3,500 undergraduate and masters students, and more then 100 Ph.D. candidates. Dr. Gummesson is also a fellow of the Swedish School of Economics and Business Administration, Helsinki, and the University of Tampere, both in Finland.

He has taken a particular interest in the theory of science and how research methodology is practiced by academic researchers and consultants. His focal interest is on qualitative methods and how these can be applied in case study research.

His research is directed to relationship marketing and quality management with a particular emphasis on the service sector. In 1977, he published the first book on services marketing in Scandinavia, and he has been featured in the *Journal of Retailing* as one of the international pioneers of services marketing. His latest book—*Total Relationship Marketing*—has become a bestseller and was appointed *Best Marketing Book of the Year* by the Swedish Marketing Federation. He has authored and coauthored more than twenty books and numerous articles in refereed journals, such as *European Journal of Marketing, Journal of the Academy of Marketing*

250 QUALITATIVE METHODS IN MANAGEMENT RESEARCH

Science, Journal of Marketing Management, Long Range Planning and *Service Industry Management.*

Dr. Gummesson is a cofounder of the Service Research Center (CTF), University of Karlstad, Sweden, and the series of international Quality in Services conferences, QUIS. He was a founding director of ISQA, The International Service Quality Association, New York, and is an elected fellow of the World Academy of Productivity Science.

He frequently gives seminars and presentations at universities, conferences, and major corporations around the world. He is a member of editorial boards for professional journals and publishers.

Dr. Gummesson has 25 years of experience in business, among other positions as product and marketing manager at the Reader's Digest Swedish subsidiary. From 1968 to 1982, he was employed by PA Consulting Group, one of the largest consultancies in Europe, where he became senior management consultant and a director in the Scandinavian Division. Among his clients have been Ericsson, IBM, Mastercard, the Swedish Cooperative Union, Swedish Railroads, Swedish Telecom, and the United Nations.